Martin Zähringer, Simon Probst, Matthias Grotkopp (eds.)
Climatic Subjects

I0616414

Martin Zähringer is a literary critic and climate cultures journalist based in Berlin. He writes documentaries and radio features with an international approach, often on climate crisis relations. He is one of the founders and art director of the CLImATE CULTURES network berlin e.V., which tries to connect people from different professional branches and with interests in science, arts, journalism, literature, politics and activism – gathering global impressions of climate cultures bottom up and connecting them.

Simon Probst (Dr. phil.), born in 1993, is a postdoctoral scholar at Universität Vechta, where he works in the DFG-project "Natural-cultural Memory in the Anthropocene. Archives, Media and Literatures of Earth History" (2024-2026), which addresses cultural dimensions of planetary crises from the perspective of interdisciplinary memory studies. At the intersection of literature and knowledge, his work brings together cultural and literary theory with different fields of scientific knowledge such as climatology, earth system science, or ecosemiotics, developing planetary and ecological perspectives on German literature from the 18th to the 21st century.

Matthias Grotkopp is an assistant professor for digital film studies at the Seminar for Film Studies at Freie Universität Berlin. His research interests include the audiovisuality of the climate crisis and ecological disaster, genre theory and the relation of politics and poetics, the films of the so-called Berlin School as well as digital methods of film analysis.

Martin Zähringer, Simon Probst, Matthias Grotkopp (eds.)

Climatic Subjects

Cultural Interventions, Writing Climate, and a Burning Planet

[transcript]

This publication was financed in part by the open access fund for books of Freie Universität Berlin.

This publication was supported by the open access fund NiedersachsenOPEN, funded by zukunft.niedersachsen.

Bibliographic information published by the Deutsche Nationalbibliothek

The Deutsche Nationalbibliothek lists this publication in the Deutsche Nationalbibliografie; detailed bibliographic data are available online at https://dnb.dnb.de

2026 © Martin Zähringer, Simon Probst, Matthias Grotkopp (eds.)

transcript Verlag | Hermannstraße 26 | D-33602 Bielefeld | live@transcript-verlag.de

Cover design: Matthias Grotkopp
Cover illustration: © Alexander Nikolsky
https://doi.org/10.14361/9783839409503
Print-ISBN: 978-3-8376-7786-7 | PDF-ISBN: 978-3-8394-0950-3
ISSN of series: 2702-8968 | eISSN of series: 2702-8976

Contents

Concepts and Worldviews

Signs and Matters

Visions and Relations

Introduction

Martin Zähringer, Simon Probst and Matthias Grotkopp

Since 2020, a multidisciplinary network has been evolving in Berlin that seeks to address the critical issues of environment, nature and climate change through a multifaceted cultural lens. The network's main idea is to reach out to a diversity of actors contributing to and reflecting on various climate cultures of our planet and to continuously connect their activities in relation to the global climate, biodiversity and pollution crisis—which in its intimate conjunction with a global rise in authoritarianism constitutes a good reason to speak of a verityble polycrisis. As a result, the Climate Cultures network Berlin has evolved as a provisionally connected group of scientists, artists, writers, and journalists. Bringing them together, showed an interesting effect: the more you curate meetings, conferences, or festivals across disciplines and genres, the more you encounter surprising aspects and perspectives, ideas and visions, that challenge how the climate crisis is dominantly perceived, thought, and felt. For this book, we as editors followed the network's trans- and multidisciplinary principle and curated positions on the climate crisis across the fields of activism, journalism, literature, science, and photography. We hope that from this assemblage of written accounts, similar to our gatherings on the Climate Cultures festivals, unexpected insights on the climate crisis will emerge. The book owes its existence largely to the dedicated work of all its contributors. Thank you, Climatic Subjects!

Martin Zähringer: CCnetwork Berlin has been active since 2020 and I was initially involved as a literary critic. I had been working on ecology, alternative worldviews and climate change in literature for some time and published my first article on climate fiction in a German-language newspaper in 2018. As I had been involved in criticism of international literature for 20 years, climate fiction naturally caught my eye. But the chance to make something of it came from three translations of American novels that were published in 2018 and my editor Angela Schader from the NZZ, who was always open to new topics, commissioned me to write a longer article. After that, I was on the trail and in 2020, together with literary critic Sieglinde Geisel and my partner Jane Tversted, I drew up the plan for a Climate Fiction Festival. All three of us had no experience in organizing a festival, but the Literaturhaus Berlin was immediately interested in the project and the Berlin Senate generously funded it. And so, I wrote the program for a festival with European climate fiction, which, despite the seriousness of the topic, was incredibly rewarding. Unfortunately, there was a Covid lockdown at the end of 2020, so we held the entire festival over three days as a livestream event: The Goethe Institute filmed the panels in London and Copenhagen, pro helvetia helped with a panel in Zurich and the others were filmed at the Literaturhaus Berlin, always with masks on. Today I can only marvel that everyone took part.

The basic idea at the time was to bring science and art, literature and climate activism into conversation, for example at the Berlin panel no. 9 "Tipping Points" with climate researcher John Schellnhuber, author Ilija Trojanow from Vienna and CliFi author Maggie Gee from London. Somewhere in the depths of the Internet on YouTube, these three days can still be seen. But then I thought: Well, somehow there has to be something more to it, more action and more theory, more culture and context. So, I designed the next program for the Planet Writes Back festival! That ran the following year, when we were all still on the road with Covid masks. Simon was there too.

Simon Probst: The first time, Martin and I met, was in November 2021 when 'the planet wrote back.' Just a week ago, I had defended my PhD thesis *Instauration of the Earth* and was still enjoying the afterglow of making it through this time of endless writing, doubts, breakthroughs, and throwbacks. In my thesis, I had addressed the relations between literature, narrative, and Earth, aiming at a theoretical understanding that embeds human meaning-making in its material, planetary contexts. Though the end of the PhD for many in my field is a moment to move on and turn towards new topics (to do so seems an academic obligation), I had the feeling not of closure but of just beginning. So, I was looking for alliances and sites to continue this work of 'landing literature on Earth,' to speak in the tongue of Bruno Latour. Naturally, I was curious, when a fellow PhD student, Florian Auerochs, who did research on the poetics of petroculture, invited me to a panel he had curated for the Climate Cultures festival, a reading with Lukas Bärfuss and Katharina Hagena. The event "Planet writes back!" was held in the Red Salon (Roter Salon) at the Volksbühne Rosa-Luxemburg-Platz, just a few minutes by bike from where I lived in Wedding. I went to as many readings, screenings, and discussions as possible. The atmosphere was lively, intimate, and, as I remember it, quite conspiratorial. There seemed to be a shared feeling that this was not a well-rehearsed scene in the play of contemporary culture but, maybe, an opening towards a new stance of understanding, of connecting planetary dots, of reflecting cultural attitudes and practices in the horizon of the climate crisis. A gathering of climatic subjects, one might say. It was in the backyard of the Red Salon, that I approached Martin. In the neon lights of the theatre's signs, we got to talk and share ideas. In the following months, we, together with Jane, often met for walks on this warming planet. The year after, in 2022, I joined the network and curated a panel on Afrofuturism for the festival "counter!views," which was held under the motto "Pass the mic!" and intended to amplify climate voices from the Global South. What, back in 2022, felt like a new beginning of connecting climate cultures, was till now the last climate culture festival that got the funding to be realized.

Since then, there have been many throwbacks, cuts in public funding, a decreasing interest in the climate question, an overload of public attention with war, the rise of authoritarianism and sham debates about migration. But, as many other initiatives, the Climate Cultures network continues its work. For me personally and as a scholar of the Environmental Humanities, the intuition remains, that despite the urgencies we are now faced with, there is a need for thoughts and visions that reach into the future at least a little further. Climate culture for me is one such vision to transform our understanding of culture in a way, as to see it not only as an expression of human exceptionalism (though art is pretty exceptional!), but as way of connecting us to the broader world that we inhabit, to think and feel the planetary relations we are entangled within. Thinking and feeling with climate means to understand culture as something that does not happen anywhere or nowhere, but down here on Earth.

Matthias Grotkopp: How do we connect? How do we move forward (or backward, or sideways)? These are questions that are both of metaphorical, conceptual dimensions but also very concrete and material. I met Martin on a bridge in Berlin, which is doubly symbolic. The bridge was blocked by a protest against government subsidies for fossil fuels. That spot was chosen because it is a site of an ongoing expansion of Berlin's inner-city motorway, at the mind-blowing costs of 246.000 €.[1] Per meter. So not only did we come together at a conceptual point, where the fossil subjectivities of the past and the climatic subjectivities of the future meet, but also at the point, where the forces of the fossil lifestyle and its corporate interests block the transition to a just and sustainable future.

I had known about the Climate Cultures Festival and we were in contact per email for a short while, when I was planning a research project on the audiovisuality of the climate crisis and was looking for potential partners outside academia. As I did not pursue that any further, I had the mixed feeling of joy and regret, when Martin and Jane approached me at the demonstration, looking for interview partners for a radio feature. I was not on the street, in the disobedient part of the protest, but

---

1   "A100-Ausbau soll mit 1,8 Milliarden Euro nochmal deutlich teurer werden", September 18, 2024 (https://www.rbb24.de/panorama/beitrag/2024/09/berlin-a100-kosten-verlaengerung-ausbau-milliarden-stadtautobahn.html).

on the side-walk, because I was asked to hold a talk on the necessity of a complete reversal of the energy and transport system of the West in general and Germany quite in particular: Getting the cars from the street, by getting the people out of the cars, which means to get the cars out of the people.

As a scholar from the humanities, I have become painfully aware of the fact that, on the one hand, changing the resource intensity of the Western lifestyle would not just need cleaner technologies but a change in attitudes and understanding, but that, on the other hand, the material conditions of our everyday life shape these attitudes in such a profound way, that the interventions by activists, artists or scientists do not have the large-scale impact they wish for. When we are surrounded by images and narratives of living the good life as consumers, car-drivers and home-owners with pools and clean lawns, it is a difficult battle to keep telling people that it is exactly this 'good life' that destroys the liveability of the planet.

It took me a while from holding my first seminar on ecological disasters in films at the beginning of my PhD, still believing that the right films and the right scientific reports will lead the powerful people in politics and economy to change course, to becoming engaged at Scientist Rebellion and demanding an end to the business-as-usual of society and academia. This was a step both for me as an individual, who prefers the public privacy of the cinema seat to the mass gathering, and as a researcher who was educated according to an ethos that you study media, culture and society but that you refrain from drawing direct, real-life applications yourself: this is left to other fields or systems of society. But as we are seeing with the ecological polycrisis, the communication between the social systems of science, politics and economy is dysfunctional. Playing by these rules serves the current system of extraction and exploitation that tries to forever externalise its ecological costs. The activist academic is performing the tightrope act of speaking for the moral imperatives that follow from scientific insights while at the same time always fighting the accusation that a bias for certain moral obligations influences the objectivity and the constitutive incompleteness of the scientific process. Writing about film and the climate crisis for me thus became entangled with permanently thinking about and justifying our need to transform what we think of as science and academia in this situation: Why do we do research and who is it that we are researching with and for? Bringing research down to Earth as well.

MZ: I considered Matthias as a scientific activist of highest interest also for our journalistic perspectives esp. in the context of a new epistemological approach towards climate culture journalism. Unfortunately, the mainstream German media and editors do not see the point until now. Anyway, for me, Matthias with his connection to Scientist Rebellion was what I understood as a climatic subject until this point: A professional of any branch or field – from a young student (see Fridays4Future) to a senior academic, from a visual artist to a fiction writer, from a factory worker to a bus driver, from a journalist to a schoolteacher –, who is spending another large part of his time besides his or her profession to fight for climate justice, energy transformation and system change. In this sense, I considered the climatic subject as a citizen of climate cultures. As we found out with this book, the 'subject' of climatic subject is much more, it's complicated with many possible approaches which could challenge the most prolific creative thinking of our time, and it is very exciting.

Climatic Subjects Writing Climate

It is the question of the climatic subject that brought the three of us together as editors of this book. In composing it, we felt that the book should reflect the connections between scholars, artists, journalists, and activists that are so essential for addressing the climate crisis. The book thus collects not only academic articles, but also interviews, short stories, poems, and political essays. The term of the climatic subject, we soon realized, can be used in very different modes and scales and the contributions in the volume all try to find a different application for this conceptual tool. Some are employing the concept as an analytical lens to describe different ways to engage with the climate between the vast pluralities of culturally, politically, economically positioned subjectivities (section 1). Others test its suitability as a diagnostic tool, to make pathologies of our current state of things readable as signs showing that the established modes of subjectivation are under climatic stress (section 2). But then, the climatic subject can also work as a normative idea, as a connector for visions of new subjectivities still to be fully developed and embodied in cultural practices (section 3). Where do we find the examples, the stories, the relationships of future climatic subjects?

Between these diverse approaches, we sometimes find the 'climatic subject' as an entity, as a historical force or field of political power struggles–like the 'bourgeois', the 'proletarian', or the 'colonised subject'. But we also find the 'climatic subject' as a question, a displacement of the coordinates of subjectivation that is both the cause and the result of registering the 'climatic subject' as it interrupts the routines and facades of normalcy in the societies of the industrialised West. This is not an accident or oversight, because we were certain from the beginning, that these singular terms were in need of pluralization and that we were looking for climatized subjectivities on different spatial and temporal scales, in all kinds of aggregation states – solid, liquid and gaseous – and in different assemblages of bodies, media and elements. As the contributions to this volume represent a journey through these emergent manifestations of climatic subjectivities, there are many different possibilities to narrate and assemble their connections. For this introduction, we have chosen one possible path through them, which voluntarily does not match the sequence in the book (another path). And we are sure that our readers will find different ones.

Our 'climatic subject' – optimistically understood as a citizen of a new climate culture – is expressed in an exemplary way by **Mike Hulme**, a well-known figure in the field of climate change science. In his article for this book, he describes himself as a person who has lived his entire life with an awareness of climate and weather and who went through a characteristic development: From child weather observer to scientific author for the IPPC, from founding director of the Tyndall Center for Climate Change research to professor of human geography at Cambridge. However, we very definitely also find the climatic subject in that world of climate knowledge which Mike Hulme calls 'more-than-science-based': it consists of local knowledge, civil resistance, the creative arts and religious traditions. This is where science must be localized and where it must stay dedicated to this world. The flipside of this climate awareness in our political economy is foregrounded by **Imre Szeman and Mark Simpson** from the perspective of the Energy Humanities' study of Petrocultures. They argue that "energy subjectivity is not a flexible or voluntary position but an ontological condition sedimented through centuries of fossil-fuelled modernity." A very short resume of their conclusion could be that this fossil subject already is a climatic subject that just doesn't realize it. It is no wonder that Szeman and Simpson start with a quotation by the philosopher Adorno as their article is a profound dialectical investigation of climatic subjectivity. **Simon Probst** also addresses the tension between climatic subjects and societies that are based on energy infrastructures of fossil fuel. He discusses how the decision of Germany's Federal Constitutional Court in 2021 to condemn insufficient climate policies as a violation of freedom, which was celebrated as one of the most important achievements in the history of the German climate movement, can at the same time be read as a concession to an understanding of freedom that is tied to the modern illusion of autonomy based on fossil fuels. In this decision, climate action and freedom figure as antagonists. His chapter searches for a relational understanding of freedom where climate action is no restriction but an integral part of cultural freedom.

Thinking the climatic subject as relational, its scalar and ontological diversity comes to full play in **Blanche Verlie**'s sixfold typology of climatic subjects, reaching from individual human beings to atmospheric phenomena and the Earth's global climate. And even such typology, as Verlie reflects herself, only allows a small glimpse into the beings and relations that come into view when we think climate as an entity and process that is lived and living, emerging from the "interactions and relationships between all bodies". For Verlie, the climate is living and the atmosphere is intermeshed with humans, glaciers, lichens, snails, clouds and many other beings that make climates and live within them in "mutual ongoing processes of becoming". The concept of living climates poses the ethical question: "In what climates do we want to live? And thus, how do we need to live – who do we need to be – in order to help create and live with those climates?" In her sketches of speculative ethnography in South-East Asia, **Kathrin Eitel** shows that this emphasis on relationship means that we also have to overcome hierarchies of individualism and collectivity, plants and humans, technology and waste to see new connections – and different ruptures. Only by navigating disaster, techno-fossil leftovers and the obstinate life of more-than-human beings together can we hope to turn the ecological crisis into a mode of becoming "elsewise." In one of the three interviews which **Angelina Davydova** brought into this book we find an exemplification of such "elsewise" movements in the art of dancing. **Vera Shchelkina** describes how she always searched for a better connection to the non-human parts of this world and how she, as a choreographer, works in touch with climatic subjects like animals but also cells or microbes. What happens when a dancer stops to control the body? Becoming embryo or bacillus? What are the obstacles to becoming "elsewise"? This is highlighted in **Juliane Schumachers** essay on the power of middle-class ideology and the way its promises of individual freedom and progress are endangered by the climate crisis. She argues that it is precisely the loss of theses promises that overshadows the affective reaction of the urban, educated middle-class to the realization of the dangers of catastrophic climate change. Juliane's contributions calls for new narrations of our critical situation and the losses it entails.

An often overlooked, or rather overheard, dimension of planetary loss is that of sound and sonic ecologies. **Michaela Vieser and Isaac Yuen** explore different sonic subjectivities – from the inner pulses of rivers and oceans to the melting of ice – and how they are endangered in exactly the same moment, when they, through new technologies and instrumentations, become audible to humans for the first time. In their contribution, Vieser and Yuen journey through new soundscapes of the Anthropocene and remember lost sonic spaces, obliterated by human ignorance and noise. Davydovas second interview, with the photographer **Alexander Nikolsky**, adds the contribution of visual culture to the question of how the arts gain the power of insight. In the context of the polycrisis, there is an ongoing aesthetical investigation of how visual perception and activist engagement interact. What can photographs say when climate change is a shapeless hyperobject? How do they make landscapes speak to us? How can the literary imagination present us with the perspectives of more-than-human agency? Focusing on one element, an intimate encounter with the ice of a glacier is narrated in **Catherine Bush's** short story "Glacial", imagining the ice not as abstract or dead matter, but as a subject with whom one might even have a conversation. In this short story, the climatic subject is challenged by the encounter with a glacier who demands that the subject takes off all of its skin. The subject follows this glacial demand and immerses itself into snow, rocks, earth, and melt-water. The story narrates a subjectivity that is becoming more and more porous to the elemental world around it. Staying in the realm of elemental subjectivity, but expanding the idea beyond Earth, **Miriam Ysa Calista** in her poem "fiery" thinks and feels with the sun. Her speculative poetry blinks into the sun's inner life and follows the solar subjectivities and relations radiating from it. With this poetic imagination we could speculatively ask what happens when the sun, our ultimate climatic agent as abundant energy source for a future climate culture, turns into a climatic subject itself and makes its heat felt in our reading bodies?

The elemental dimension of climatic subjectivity is not universal. Elements are mediated differently by bodies, and also by those bodies' intersectional position in relation to political, economic, technological and symbolic power. **Lebogang Neidhardt-Mokoena** in her contribution analyses how images in climate change journalism portray people differently in terms of agency and vulnerability, depending on where they are from. Drawing on research about the news coverage of flooding in both Germany and South Africa in 2021 and 2022, she criticizes how postcolonial and racial biases influence the making of climatic subjects in the media. Based on this analysis, Neidhardt-Mokoena envisions an ethics of journalistic care inspired by concepts of African relationality and acknowledges "cultural and social differences as well as "pluralities of knowing and being" in encountering climate change. **Matthias Grotkopp** also starts from looking at the biases and problems in audiovisual forms of climate communication. Drawing a lesson from the disappointments in many Western media products, he proposes to let other voices and perspectives, namely Indigenous people, scholars and artists, intervene in the discourse, in our senses and our sense-making. One substantial contributor to the climate crisis that is usually underexposed in this context is the cultural realm of the Soviet Union and post-soviet Russia. In the third interview with Angelina Davydova, **Ilya Kalinin** describes the long history of oil in Soviet and Russian film, starting with the ideological basics when oil was the natural partner of the proletarian revolution up to a contemporary imaginary of oil as the embodiment of limitless greed and finally opening to ideas to overcome petroculture towards a climatic 'community' of humans and all energy materials themselves.

But petro-cultures do not dissolve on their own. The interview with the Ugandan climate activists **Evelyn Acham, Aidah Nakku and Nicholas Omonuk Okoit** shows two different kinds of being a climatic subject in interaction: One subjectvity that always already was climatic by being grounded in lived relations to land, water, and other beings and a subject that is striving to become climatic by fighting for a liveable climate for one's people on the stage of global politics because these lived relations are vanishing. This climatic subject asks for justice and solidarity and keeps reminding us in the West that, as much as we might feel to be in opposition, the damage to the climate is done in the name of our comfort and prosperity.

Seeking out information on the climate crisis within the media environments of Western consumer culture and online public sphere is therefore filled with contradictions: The fictional diary of digital weather and digital news by writer **Zara Zerbe** shows how, being on social media platforms, one encounters a whiplash of devastating news and equally devastating silence and ignorance. The observation of the everyday, the weather we get as opposed to the climate we expect, rubs against the rise of authoritarianism in global and national politics and the disappearing coverage of the climate crisis – and in this friction the climatic subject is gradually worn down. **Martin Zähringer** also locates a speculative human individual in the clutches of social media and tests the climatic subject through the process of writing. He shows what happens when catastrophic floods are flooding the laboratory of his text and faces the global political disasters of our new world disorder. The question for him as a writer and climate cultures activist is, how a new climate writing could respond to this crisis. How might writing contribute to the emergence of new climate cultures?

At the horizon of this book lies the urgent transformation of the social systems and political economies that dominate the globe. And it is our belief that these systems will only be changed when the available practical, technological and socio-cultural solutions as well as the shifts in the conditions of political and economic power are moved by different imaginaries, different narratives and different concepts of each being's and each action's entanglement. This change must start and indeed is starting worldwide, has been starting for a very long time in many different places, with many voices in literature and the arts, in natural and social science, in philosophy and cultural phenomenology. With our collection we hope to speak to the diversity of these modes of being, declaring, analyzing, conjuring the kind of climatic subject that we have always been and that we need to fully realize (again). Of course, the book offers only a small glimpse into the possibilities of approaching the climatic subject – and so we are curious to see what new climatic subjectivities readers will explore and look forward to future encounters.

Burning coal mine, Urals, Russia, 2021

© Alexander Nikolsky

"There is probably also the Anti-Climatic Subject"
Interview with Simon Probst

Jane Tversted and Martin Zähringer

Simon Probst: With your Climate Fiction festival in 2020, you have made an important contribution to making literature dealing with the climate crisis visible in German-speaking countries. When did you first encounter climate change in literature?

Martin Zähringer: That was the article I wrote for the Neue Zürcher Zeitung in 2018 entitled "Irgendwann schlägt die Natur zurück"[1] [At some point, nature strikes back]. It was about climate fiction, when such topics in a broader sense were still en vogue or were becoming so for a short time in the NZZ. I had been working on Nature Writing and Ecocriticism for a while before that. More in English, internationally. I then saw that Nature Writing was slowly becoming popular in Germany too. Especially through the publishing house Matthes & Seitz, where classics such as Henry Thoreau, John Muir or the French 'pope of insects' Fabré were translated. Then this Nature Writing wave started here. I observed this for a while and I also dealt with it as a critic, especially when Nature Writing was accompanied by a clear criticism of the destruction of nature.

SP: Did you observe such criticism of the destruction of nature in single works or as a general tendency?

MZ: For example, in Annie Proulx's novel *From Hard Wood*[2], where she describes 300 years of overexploitation of the American forests in an epic novel of over 800 pages, at the age of 80, admirable. But one day, in the spring 2017 program, I saw two titles translated from the American. And that was Climate Fiction: *American War* by Omar El Akkad at S. Fischer, and *Gold Ruhm Zitrus* by Claire Watkins at Ullstein. These are big publishers and that's when I realized that there was something new. I reviewed

---

1   Zähringer, Martin (2018): "Irgendwann schlägt die Natur zurück". In: NZZ, 3 March, 2018, (https://www.nzz.ch/feuilleton/irgendwann-schlaegt-die-natur-zurueck-ld.1355040).

2   Zähringer, Martin (2017): "Vom Sysiphos zum Waldherrn", 9 July 2017 (https://www.deutschl andfunk.de/annie-proulx-aus-hartem-holz-vom-sysiphos-zum-waldherrn-100.html).

both titles on Deutschlandfunk together with Kim Stanley Robinson's *Green Earth*. At the time, I was also following the story of Dan Bloom. Dan Bloom is a journalist, who lives in Taiwan, propagates Climate Fiction or CliFi, and says, from now on he only deals with climate fiction. And since then, I've been specializing a bit in climate fiction, but not as extreme as Dan Bloom.

Jane Tversted: In spring 2018, we convinced the editor Leslie Rosin from WDR, who sadly passed away recently, that a radio feature about this literature would be worthwhile. And then we travelled to America and basically tried to get out of the confines of literature and literary criticism and connect literature with reality. That was the USA trip project, a road trip to meet writers who deal with the climate.

SP: Which authors did you visit on your literary road trip?

JT: First, we visited Amy Brady in New York, who was propagating and critically reflecting on climate fiction or CliFi in the USA at the time. At the time, she wrote a column called Burning Worlds[3] for the Chicago Review of Books. And I think she interviewed an author once a month. It was always about climate fiction and, remarkably, it was often young debutantes who started their careers with this topic. But of course, Amy Brady also interviewed Kim Stanley Robinson, who is a really big name in the USA as a science fiction author. That was very attractive for us, because he had just published his novel *New York 2140*, in which the first climate catastrophe had already happened, and the lower part of New York is 15 meters under water. The inhabitants try to come to terms with the situation, and it works quite well with clever collective concepts, until the real estate sharks of New York, who have also survived, start up again.

MZ: Absolutely fantastic book, and we went on a boat trip around Manhattan with Amy Brady to see the locations of *New York 2140* from the outside. That was also a nice adventure, if we talk about the "Sitz im Leben" ['seat in life'] of literature, because Kim Stanley Robinson may write science fiction, but he loves facts, writes extremely realistically and has researched his New York setting meticulously. From New York, we drove to New Jersey and visited Patricia Smith, a black American poet. She comes from the Chicago Poetry Slam scene, now lives in New Jersey and has written Blood Dazzler – Poems about Hurricane Katrina (2008), an entire volume of poetry about the Louisiana flood disaster in 2004, I think she calls her approach factual poetry. It's about survival in the disaster, disenfranchised people, animals, plants. And about

---

3   "Burning Worlds", 24 February 2021 (https://chireviewofbooks.com/category/burning-world s/).

the failure of the state. I can only wonder why this book has still not been translated into German.

JT: We then went to Louisiana where we met the author C. Morgan Babst, who is rather privileged herself, white, wealthy, lives with a Wall Street man in a huge Louisiana mansion and has written a great novel about Katrina. She drove us around the area and showed us all the locations from her novel The Floating Worlds, so we were back at the real sites of the disaster. When we went there more than 10 years after there were still ruined houses and destroyed landscapes. This disaster literature about Katrina is very clearly tied to the landscape. During our research, we also got to know other people, American environmental activists. We drove through the bayous with the former literature professor John Hazlett. He runs kayak tours there for those who are interested in these precarious environments. The bayous are primeval swamps that are threatened by rising sea water, the salt water is killing the ancient trees. So, we simply drove through a quiet landscape and experienced how the American environmentalists are campaigning for this. It was exciting, getting quite close to a large alligator in a light kayak and all that. You're on the literary trail, but there are these excursions into other discourses.

MZ: These other discourses, especially those discovered by chance, are naturally included in a radio feature because this genre is much about linking symbolic worlds, language and the reality of places. When making features, we learned how dynamic such research can become through these links: You travel to an author who deals with climate issues on location and suddenly you realize that there is a very deep discourse on flood literature in Louisiana. Especially in African American literature and Blues music, because these are the communities that are most affected by disasters. But there are also other works of fiction and poetry about the historical floodings in New Orleans. That was a result of the on-site research that we hadn't expected beforehand. Perhaps you can listen to our Long Night of Climate in Literature again on Deutschlandfunk,[4] three hours long, where we also present the flood literature of the American South, and many other things between CliFi and Climate Writing.

SP: With Kim Stanley Robinson in California, you focused on literature. You said he was always sitting and writing in his garden, which is also, where you met him. How do the surprising and worldy connections that interest you so much come about in such a rather enclosed situation?

---

4   "Lange Nacht vom Klima in der Literatur", 27 May 2023 (https://www.deutschlandfunkku ltur.de/lange-nacht-vom-klima-in-der-literatur-dlf-kultur-f3ce6034-100.html); "Der Planet schlägt zurück", 7 March 2020 (https://assets.deutschlandfunk.de/FILE_cea9083ecae5e9294 1ae57d8217ec8cd/original.pdf).

MZ: Through the motifs, for example. The floods were a leitmotif for our research. Kim Stanley Robinson's New York novel *New York 2140* shows a flooded world, a dystopia but at the same time a utopia, because the story signals at the end that there are already ways to think out of the depression of the catastrophe. These are clearly thought-through anti-capitalist concepts of a better economy and life. And if you look at the way he lives… He writes in the garden in front of his house. Such a small, fenced-in area. Beautiful flowers. He sits outside with his laptop and writes his thousands of pages, with an inconspicuous Buddha figure on the table.

SP: There seems to bes an interesting contrast between the authors writing about Katrina in Louisiana and Kim Stanley Robinson. On the one hand, you have an author who writes planetary literature and imagines the future with a global scope, and on the other, authors who write about concrete disasters on the ground and in the present.

JT: Yes, but the contrast is not so clear. Patricia Smith never lived in Louisiana, she has relatives there, but grew up in Chicago. Kim Stanley Robinson became famous with his three books about Mars, he certainly never lived there either.

MZ: Kim Stanley in the garden with science. He has a deep relationship with science, he is always concerned with science, or to put it more openly, with ways of knowing. He takes this into literature. Of course, it's interesting who he discusses with. Before the New York book, it was a group of economists in Santa Cruz who developed a new political economy theory.

JT: In principle, he has embedded a research project in every novel. In *New York 2140*, he goes through this macroeconomic theory of how to defeat the power of finance capital. *Green Earth* is about the art of good governance, geoengineering and about literature. It's set in Washington, and a guiding principle is that the hero is engaged with Nature Writing all the time. What else do we have?

MZ: Robinson's scientists are actually activists. In *Green Earth*, they are concerned with convincing the American government that it needs to make climate policy. They include Tibetan monks from the island kingdom of Khembalung, which is quite interesting. They are busy developing new concepts for a state in a climate catastrophe. It's a bit like a thesis novel, but with very good descriptions and dialogue, a CO_2 atom that talks and a rather sarcastic narrator character. A very good montage novel, but not yet translated.[5]

---

5   "Out Now: GREEN EARTH", 9 November 2015 (https://www.kimstanleyrobinson.info/conten t/out-now-green-earth).

SP: Kim Stanley Robinson – Science Fiction or Climate Fiction?

JT: He said that whenever Science Fiction becomes interesting, like now with the predictions in relation to climate change, someone comes along and wants to name it something else as if Science Fiction was not good enough. Robinson didn't like that; he was very frank about it. We had come all this way to talk to him about Climate Fiction. But he is a committed Science Fiction author, a highly educated Science Fiction author right from the start and we had a great interview anyway. He did his doctorate under Frederick Jameson, who plays a major role in the Marxist postmodern debate.

MZ: He said he learned how to think from Jameson and how to write from Ursula LeGuin. I didn't know her until then either, another lucky strike in our research. He later described himself also as a Climate Fiction author, if I remember correctly, for example in the interview for the Climate Cultures Festival "Planet Writes Back!"[6]

SP: A lot has happened in the literary world in the meantime. Climate fiction started out as a niche label. It is now a term that describes not only science fiction, but all forms of fictional works that deal with the climate. You undertook this journey in the initial phase of your engagement with the topic. You got to know different landscapes, met different authors who deal with climate and the climate crisis. How did this trip shape your work and your approach to the topic when you returned to Germany?

MZ: First of all, I noticed a gap between Nature Writing as a newer paradigm on the market in Germany and what is going on in the larger Anglophone world. I wouldn't say that Nature Writing is behind the times, but in principle I had the impression that it is a backward-looking project and Climate Fiction is a forward-looking project, a future-oriented project.

JT: The climate road trip through the States[7] was a key moment. We are freelance journalists and always have to look for new tasks. Two new tasks emerged from this trip. One task was to do something about Germany: Does Climate Fiction exist in Germany? When we first started, we thought it didn't exist; Climate Fiction wasn't an established term. Then we got to know the literary and cultural scientist Gabriele Dürbeck, who is well-known in the field of Ecocritcism. We conducted an interview

---

6   "Climate Cultures Festival. Planet Writes Back! Panel 12", November 2021 (https://www.plan et-festival.de/panels/en.panel_12.html).

7   "Climate Fiction", 30 November 2018 (https://www.hoerspielundfeature.de/ueber-den-klim awandel-in-der-literatur-climate-fiction-100.html).

with her and used it for a feature on Deutschlandfunk. Interestingly, it wasn't in the literature department there, but in the feature series Zeitfragen a format about issues of the day; the literary editors didn't want to do it. We found out why: In the interview Gabriele talked about heteronomy. She said that Climate Fiction always points somewhere else, i.e. out of the literary bubble, heteronomous literature, that was the term she used.[8]

MZ: This creates a tension when you commit to the ideal of autonomous literature. The problem is no longer the climate crisis, but the real problem is heteronomy, if you want to discuss, promote and debate this type of literature seriously, permanently and competently. But that remains a productive challenge for us.

JT: That was the moment when things got exciting for us. When we realized that there was a real challenge. There is a literature that we want to make visible, that already exists, but which is not perceived, especially in the official establishment, in the feuilleton pages, in the perception of what is available in German-language literature. So, we asked ourselves the question: How can we make this visible?

SP: How did you start to make climate fiction visible in Germany? How was the response to the project?

MZ: You could perhaps divide our work into a time before and a time after the Climate Fiction Festival. Before the Climate Fiction Festival 2020, we were out and about more as cultural journalists and literary critics, seeing what was possible. We did this feature and I had articles in the Neue Zürcher Zeitung, where the editor Angela Schader was very open to ecological topics at the time.

JT: We then realized, aha, science remains interesting for us. And then we attended the conference on Narratives of Scale organized by Gabriele Dürbeck and Philip Hüpkes.[9] There we got to know Axel Goodbody personally. Axel Goodbody is the British Germanist who was the first to map German climate fiction. He wrote the first academic article on authors he counts as climate fiction, from Günter Grass to the present day. It was exciting that he didn't use this distinction between E and U, but it was simply Günter Grass with his social novel *Die Rättin (The Rat)* and then someone like Sven Böttcher with his thriller *Die Prophezeiung (The Prophecy)*.

---

8   "Sind wir noch zu retten?", 5 March 2019 (https://www.deutschlandfunkkultur.de/klimawan del-im-deutschen-roman-sind-wir-noch-zu-retten-100.html).

9   Probst, Simon (2020): "Tagungsbericht: Narratives of Scale in the Anthropocene. Imagining Human Responsibility in an Age of Scalar Complexity", In: H-Soz-Kult, 13 January 2020 (https://www.hsozkult.de/conferencereport/id/fdkn-127156).

MZ: While participating in a workshop by the broadcaster Deutschlandfunk Kultur, we sat down in the canteen and Sieglinde Geisel, a literary critic, was sitting there and we got talking. The idea arose relatively spontaneously that we could do something bigger on Climate Fiction. This then became the Climate Fiction Festival, the festival idea. We've come a few steps further since then, but back then it was just about showing that there is such a thing as Climate Fiction in Germany, in other words something different from Nature Writing. Now we were doing a Climate Fiction literature festival, and during the conception we realized that only German literature wouldn't work, there's not enough for a multi-day programme. And anyway, CliFi is literature about a global problem, we're starting out as a European project. These were various European authors, some of whom have been doing this for a very long time. Maggie Gee from England has been active with CliFi for 30 years. The idea was also that if Science Fiction or Climate Fiction is based on science, then science must play a role. So, we were not just doing a pure literature festival, we were also inviting scientists, climate scientists and activists.

JT: The Climate Fiction Festival[10] was our first festival ever. We had never done anything like it before. We found a good team, but it was still quite complicated to do a festival because it was Covid time, lockdown 2020 right when we wanted to do it. But I think the festival got a lot more attention because of Covid, because it was digital and there was nothing else going on.

SP: In other words, you just went ahead with the festival as planned, only online.

JT: Exactly. As a livestream, three days. That's what happened when the program says there will be a panel with Danish authors from 11 am to 1 pm: The Danish authors weren't sitting with us in Berlin, but in Copenhagen, at the Literaturhaus. The Goethe-Institut then organized the broadcast or recording there. Some of it wasn't broadcasted live, it was edited beforehand and so on. Now panels were held in Zurich, London and Copenhagen, filmed and then streamed as planned in the live schedule. And the others live in Berlin, all with masks. Unfortunately, it was very impersonal.

MZ: It didn't go so well because there was nothing going on due to Covid, but I think we really conjured up something completely new on the literary market. But I was very sad because I was so looking forward to talking to all these people who were coming and seeing how they exchanged ideas. I was very curious to find out what happens when a climate scientist communicates with a fiction writer, even behind

---

10   "Climate Fiction Festival", December 2020 (https://www.climate-fiction-festival.de/en.home
      .html).

the scenes. Of course, that didn't happen, but we managed to do it later, still under Covid conditions at the next festival in 2021.

SP: Was Covid also a topic at the festival? Over time, there have been many links between the climate discourse and talking about the pandemic.

Impressions from the Climate Cultures Festival

© Jan Michalko

MZ: In 2020, that wasn't an issue at all. There was no reflection on it. We were just stressed about it. It was the beginning of the Covid 19 pandemic. We were fully committed to pulling off our first big project and really only had stress, because one person took it very seriously, the other less so. At this festival, we only focused on the climate, the pandemic was not reflected. That came much later anyway. But it was still a pretty good thing of all those involved that they took part under the conditions. For us, that was proof of how important everyone took this festival. "Planet Writes Back!"[11] was the second Climate Cultures Festival in 2021, we had a large international program, Canada, Greenland, China, the US, Scandinavia, and it was quite complicated to get all these people or most of them to Berlin. But traveling was no longer prohibited, the Covid regulations in public life were clear, we could do it without endangering anyone.

SP: You didn't stop with the festival, and despite the hurdles of the pandemic, you were determined to continue and decided not to simply continue doing Climate Fiction festivals, but to reorganize the festival for the second edition. What were your thoughts on how to continue the festival after you had done it the first time?

MZ: It was through working with people like Axel Goodbody that I got aware of Mike Hulme, the cultural geographer from the UK. Mike has been running the project Climates and Cultures for some time, which brings together many different approaches and people who are researching climate change in various fields. It has now grown into a six-volume work. Only one volume deals specifically with literature and art, but still. You can see that literature is part of a complex climate discourse. That was interesting for us. Above all, this idea that we can't just think about things from a Western perspective, that the climate crisis is not just our concern. In principle, we are the perpetrators, due to our industrial history and in the North-South relationship, we are absolutely the perpetrators. But it affects everyone. And we are not even in a position here to talk in consensus about climate change, the climate crisis, the climate catastrophe and the extent to which we can manage this socially here in Germany, in Europe or in the USA.

SP: What kind of concepts did you set up to get a broader approach to the question of global climate crisis?

MZ: Mainly a set of questions. What does the global situation look like? What kind of bottom-up discourse, ideas and insights are there on the subject? What problems are there? How can aspects of symbolic cultural productivity lead to a better understanding of abstract aspects in real climate change? How can we translate all these different local activities, if you see them as expressions of one global language in the polycrisis? Is this possible? How to combine classical sociological analysis with political ecology? And with political economy? And so on. The idea was to explore this

---

11   "Climate Cultures Festival", November 2020, (https://www.planet-festival.de/en.home.htm l).

broad field and make it visible through the lenses of all these different actors from many fields and genres and traditions of knowledge.

So that was my wish, in the direction of a global overview. Of course, that was totally presumptuous, a festival series and somehow around the globe. Like the Berlin International Literature Festival or the Frankfurt Book Fair with these different country focuses. Of course, it's difficult for an association like ours to set up a global project. But in the beginning, it seemed like it could work, we got public funding for three climate cultures projects, three well-curated festivals in a row and got them up and running with a lot of response in the media.

SP: What do you think was convincing for the funding decisions?

MZ: Perhaps our transdisciplinary concepts in order to show how far science has come, where the social sciences are, where cultural studies are in African countries, in India and so on. What does the literature look like there? And what happens when you bring together an Indigenous activist from Greenland with a photographer from New York and an author from Canada? What do they have to say to each other? This curatorial idea of going on a global search for ways of describing the given. That was my dream.

JT: I don't know if I had a dream with it. In principle, it was about talking about the climate and the climate crisis in a different way. After all, we are journalists. And you often have a technical and economic approach to the climate. Either you have a catastrophe that has just happened, then you go there and report on it. Or you somehow have technical questions, innovations, renewable energies, you can solve this and that problem, or something like that. We just wanted to do it differently. How can you approach the climate issue culturally? For example, via the new paradigm of Energy Humanities or the dialogue with Indigenous forms of knowledge.

MZ: At the beginning, we asked ourselves what theoretical concepts there were. Iman Tafari-Ama and Esther Figueroa from Jamaica explained to us in our third festival "Counter!views"[12] the Plantationocene, the enslaved economy as an origin of the Anthropocene, if you look at it again as the Capitalocene: the capitalist transformation of landscapes into plantations in the Caribbean leads via the triangular trade to the global capitalist mode of disposal over nature and landscape and labour, a cause of the climate crisis. This was surprising, and I believe that if an event should have a political relevance and a productive dynamic, then there has to be surprise in

---

12   "Climate Cultures Festival. Counter!Views", August 2022 (https://www.climate-cultures-festi val.de/en.program.html).

it. You put together a program, but you don't know exactly what people are going to do, our guest curators have a free hand.

SP: As I understand it, it is important to you to break down hegemonic perspectives on the climate. You approach climate culture from different local, national, regional perspectives, different knowledge practices. What would interest me, is this broadening of the view and the transition from Climate Fiction to Climate Cultures as an umbrella term for your work. How do you understand the term Climate Cultures? In addition to what you have just said, what practical implications does this have for your work, both as journalists, as cultural workers, and festival organizers?

MZ: Difficult, so I like to hold back a bit with definitions. I've now seen that in this current book project *Climatic Subjects*, some contributors are very interested in definitions and of course I find that exciting. I like clear definitions, but I myself hold back on them in this really big issue of Climate Cultures. Of course, I have already written a lot of proposal prose, which is relatively concrete, but I am not so interested in a fixed definition, more in the practical expansion of an unknown field.

Jane Tversted and Martin Zähringer

© Jan Michalko

JT: Right from the start, we took a more practical approach and didn't have a ready-made theory. At some point, there was a phase in which we organized our work more theoretically, because when you're doing a festival, you also have to communicate what we're doing here. Firstly, we are interested in climate from the perspective of culture, i.e. from the perspective of high culture, the arts and so on, but also from the perspective of everyday culture. We are also interested in critical cultural debate. Thirdly, we asked about perspectives for a new culture, i.e. how a new Climate Culture could be created.

MZ: I could probably come up with 200 pages of application prose right now. But from a practical experience, I would say that Climate Culture is the opposite of Petroculture. We have gathered enough information about what Petroculture is at our festivals, and in this book, very important thinkers in research on Petrocultures have their say. I am very pleased that Imre Szeman and Mark Simpson are involved and also that there is this global network on Energy Studies. Petroculture is the state we are in now and we can no longer afford it. It has to change to something else. And my idea is for transdisciplinary and multi-perspective discussions in cultural practice to determine what a Climate Culture could be. So not this classic cultural-geographical term, adaptations to the climate. We are looking for ways into a material Climate Culture via symbolic cultural practices, new ways of living, which of course consists of many facets, Climate Cultures with plural s, but that is more of a global project of transformation. I would call it Climate Culture.

JT: But we already had the idea of inviting artists, thinkers and activists from different climate zones and to compare cultural articulations and manifestations from these different zones. What makes them unique? How is climate articulated? Is there a special connection between climate and culture?

MZ: There is a relationship between the two concepts: climate cultures and climate zones. But the grand utopia as an alternative can already be called 'Climate Culture'. Of course, we would be presumptuous if we Westerners were to come back and say that we are now creating what 'the' Climate Culture is for everyone. That won't be the case, but I could imagine, if you can talk about it, that capitalism with its extractivist forms of economy and the way in which it is currently maltreating the planet is already a totality, and if you want to get out of this totality, then you'll end up somewhere in another totality. Right?

SP: This reminds me to one of the first CliFi authors in Germany, Dirk C. Fleck, who wrote the dystopian novel "Go! The Eco-Dictatorship" in 1993.

MZ: Oh yes, a journalist who also writes novels, what I like very much. He was at our Climate Fiction Festival in 2020. After the "Eco-Dictatorship" he wrote some impressive utopian novels, where Indigenous knowledge plays a bigger role for new ways of living, thinking, and managing the crisis. Of course, I don't want an eco-dictatorship.

SP: What kind of Climate Culture are you looking for?

MZ: We must continue to negotiate and research this issue and it was interesting at the beginning to say: let's look at the different approaches to the problem of climate change. How does Earth System Theory work? What do different climates look like on Earth? How is climate researched scientifically? And then you suddenly realize that what science is doing is nothing very new, Europeans have been in Greenland, for example, for a long time, carrying out ice drilling, research trips and measurements of all kinds. But for a long time, they didn't take into account that there are people there who have a culture, adapted to the climate of course, in this respect also a living Climate Culture. A different Climate Culture than in the Sahara under certain aspects and so you have a cultural-geographical way of differentiating. Well, in the Sahara they tell different stories, but then you realize that somehow, they have similar, sustainable forms of economy. When Nomadism plays a major role, you find another way of seeing and knowing, and this is where alternatives come into play in the climate crisis. If they have lived successfully for so long in this harsh climate, in the Sahara or in the ice, then there must be something to this nomadic way of life.

SP: In other words, if I understand correctly, climate culture is also a normative term for you, i.e. a term that is about living with the climate in a sustainable way. An alternative understanding would be, that it's about certain ways in which cultures are influenced by the climate and, conversely, influence the climate. Then you could say that capitalism is also a certain form of Climate Culture. Or would you rather rule that out?

JT: Climate Culture is not just a utopian concept. It certainly isn't for me. I don't know about Martin, but I would say that capitalism is the wrong Climate Culture. It is a destructive Climate Culture, one with fatal consequences for the Earth.

MZ: In the tradition of Imre Szeman and Mark Simpson, this wrong culture means Petroculture or Petrocultures. I was very pleased that they began their article for this book with a quote from Adorno's Minima Moralia, that I remember being a quite popular saying among Spontis (leftist activists in the 1970s and 80s, often acting in a creative and spontaneous way): There is no true life in a false one, which today means that there is no sustainable life in Petroculture. Then there is of course the question of an alternative, which I call Climate Culture. I am not a powerful person, I don't define, therefore I have little influence and can't determine things, but I can however think about ways in which we can understand Climate Culture. When it comes to determining what is climate reality on the Earth, it's about the whole spectrum on this planet, letting people from all these different lifestyles and cultures speak for themselves. Talk bottom up about the crisis that affects us all. That is the crux of the matter. And then it becomes political.

SP: So, this brings me to a crucial question for this book: Who is the political subject bringing Climate Culture alive? What is the climatic subject?

MZ: Ah yes, the climatic subject. Exactly what I understood for a while as that which establishes and activates itself autonomously, self-determinedly and creatively on the way to Climate Culture, collectively, individually, cross-species, ecologically, politically networked. And of course, now we got an absolutely inspiring volume of thoughts and ideas about the climatic subject or subjectivity in this book, thanks to our engaged and insightful contributors. But on the other side we can see that there is probably also the anti-climatic subject in the real life, which has been in full swing since January 2025 with the new Government in the United States, they want to flood us away with a huge jet of oil. The MAGA project is known to have a quasi-scientific script, it comes from the Heritage Foundation think tank and is called "Project 2025", it is already in action plan in the first 100 days of the MAGA president. And the German fascist party is now copying this and talking about a "Project 2029" regarding the next federal election. And I think that we are no longer on a path of self-empowerment, where we are slowly developing our future prospects, but we are in a confrontation with an anti-climatic petro-power subject and in this struggle the climatic subject is probably a dialectical one. For me, that is one result at the moment, the analysis is still ongoing. I wrote more about especially the American nightmare in my contribution for this book as a Climate Culture journalist, "Writing Climate or Flooding the Text."

SP: If you say, as you once did at a festival, that we are climatic subjects, what does that mean for our identity?

MZ: The idea came about at the time due to the fact that all the people on the panels already had their main profession, geologist or musician, writer, artist. But they were all intensively involved with climate change and also committed to it. So, I thought that the climatic subject today could be the one who invests part of their energy in the issue of climate change, in the fight for climate protection and climate justice and so on, and combines this with their original professional activity, with political and activist work.

JT: I don't know exactly. I think back then, when the term "climatic subject" came up, it was actually more about showing or perhaps postulating that the problem simply cannot be ignored. That dealing with climate change is also a kind of civil or human duty.

MZ: I don't really believe in this civil duty when I look around me in this country.

JT: But somehow, as something that is unavoidable, it is so explosive and urgent that it is simply unavoidable to get involved and deal with the climate crisis.

MZ: But now you get the impression that it is avoidable; the climate didn't play a role in the last federal election.

JT: No, and not really in culture either. Or perhaps more subliminally, but that is also perhaps the sensible way to deal with climate, this subliminal thing that you always have 'climate and …'. I think we've had that before, that it has to be linked to something practical somehow. You can't do much with 'the climate', you can quickly suppress it.

SP: So, are you interested in how climate change is finding its way into all areas of life and politics?

JT: Yes, it definitely makes sense to look at the specific changes in detail. That's what we're working on journalistically at the moment. We've just been looking at sustainable architecture. Climate issues have become an integral part of urban development. Another issue that concerns us is the conflict between the Sami and energy companies that are building wind turbines and thus endangering the traditional Sami way of life. This is a form of green colonialism. These are just two examples. Our current radio project is about the German neofascist movement against wind energy. The climate issue is seeping in everywhere.

MZ: Yes, it seeps in. But the question is where it leaks out. Mostly, the editorial offices treat it like one topic among others or distribute it to some abstract climate competence centres. They strictly avoid talking about anything like a Climate Culture. There is no will to bring the topics together and present them as an unavoidable and important task of culture. They are always individual topics. Unfortunately, this is also how we must work as cultural journalists, as freelancers. But we do work in that sense, at least I do, half of my topics, including in literature, have to deal with the climate issue. And a radio feature about the Sami in Norway, reindeer herders who are fighting against wind turbines because they are disrupting their traditional way of life, that is of course a Climate Culture topic for me. So, for me, it's clearly Climate

Culture. I can't sell it labelled as that, but it's the horizon. Right from the start, our aim was to make people's perspectives audible. In other words, not to report on what the new climate policy plans are, where the Green New Deal stands, what the carbon footprint here and there looks like. These are all questions that politicians need to clarify with the economists. We promote and demand a social conversation about the possibilities and the struggles, a Climate Culture bottom up. In other words, we will continue, even if Trump's America follows the principle of 'flooding the zone with shit'. We continue to contribute the perspectives of Climate Culture.

SP: That would be a good keyword for a question about the outlook: Where do you go from here?

MZ: The project we are currently working on is the Warsaw-Berlin Climate Culture Bridge. We want to bring together writers from Poland and Germany. The idea is to bring something climatic to this exchange. Germany and Poland are still primarily associated with the Second World War and post-war history. Every second person who deals with Poland naturally deals with Warsaw, the Warsaw Uprising, the Ghetto Uprising – that is absolutely essential. We want to try to bring a further dimension to this cultural exchange via the climate issue. After all, we have the same problems in the present and in the future, the climate catastrophe. Or do we not? So that's what we need to find out.

JT: We are planning a project on energy fights. In it, we will address Indigenous energy struggles but also go beyond them. The explosive nature of energy struggles can be seen in the verdict against Greenpeace in America. It was about the Dakota Access Pipeline and Greenpeace was ordered to pay a fine of around 660 million dollars. It's a farce and a deliberate manoeuvre to weaken civil society and any kind of climate action. This shows the political explosiveness of energy battles. The political pressure is enormous and the anti-climatic subject has become really powerful. The project on energy struggles brings us very close to these new histories of power formation and subjectivity.

One issue that also concerns us, are the different levels of problems. The interview with the Agape Earth Coalition in this book shows that political action in Uganda, for example, faces completely different problems than FridaysForFuture in Berlin's middle class. If you are an activist in Uganda, you can expect to be interrogated by a secret police officer at the airport when you come back from an assignment abroad. If you're out of luck, you could disappear for a few weeks. No one knows where you are.

MZ: We are currently facing the problem of precarity in our work. We have no assets. And so, we always have to look for funding. You spend some months writing a perfect application and don't know who will end up sitting on which jury. Of course, as a freelancer, you don't get paid for submitting applications for a festival. That works well for a while because curating and planning can be fulfilling, but at some point, your personal resources are exhausted and you also have to constantly look for new jobs in journalism. If we don't find new opportunities, collaborations with others in the run-up to this project, then we will have to downsize a bit. For the energy fight project, we will collaborate with the Petrocultures Conference 2026,[13] which will be hosted by the TU Dresden and is organized by Moritz Ingwersen. In cultural journalism, we are toying with the idea of making a cultural history of energy. Four or five podcasts about wind, sun, oil, coal, gas, i.e. the various energy sources and systems as a climate-cultural task.

JT: And now at the end we want to say "Thank you!" to all the fantastic people who were at the Climate Cultures festivals and showed great interest and brought insightful and engaged knowledge and powerful impacts. And also to the contributors to this book, thank you very much. Connecting Climate Cultures!

---

13   "Petrocultures Research Group" (https://www.petrocultures.com/).

Canyon in the melting Aktru glacier, Altai, Russia, 2023

© Alexander Nikolsky

Digital Weather
A Journal on Climate (and) Crisis

Zara Zerbe

1.

18th December 2023

"Have you heard? There's going to be a white Christmas after all!" My desk neighbour at work is the first person to address this topic today.

"It's a good thing I cancelled my Airbnb for Christmas, the weather in Sweden is supposed to be really bad over the holidays. Snow guarantee in Värmland my ass. I might as well stay at home."

"Are you sure? I thought it was just going to be a bit colder."

"Yes, Weather Forecastle posted that on Instagram."

If they say so?

In the evening, I have my writer friend group over for a Christmas cookies baking session. Apparently, I'm the only one not yet following Weather Forecastle on instagram. "White Christmas!", they confirm unanimously. "There's a low-pressure area coming from the North Sea."

I run the palm of my hand over the kettle to check if the mulled wine is already at drinking temperature, while my friends shape vanilla shortcrust pastry into little crescents. My scalp itches as if I'm still wearing the hat that it was too warm for earlier on the dog walk. Christmas Eve is six days away. There's hardly anything left of the snow we had at the end of November. Only a few pitiful remnants have not yet melted because they have fused with grit and road dirt to form dark matter. Could this be used to protect permafrost soils from thawing off?

This is the time of the year when I start getting nervous about winter not following the winter protocol, which is: November is grey and rainy, December, January and February are basically the same, but more frosty; no snow before mid-December (at least, it rarely snows in the German Baltic Sea coastal area, where I live). At the same time, I am aware of winter protocol being another thing that is swept away by the climate crisis. Sometimes I do really envy climate researchers: Their job is to point out how bad climate change has already gotten based on the scientific facts they gathered, and maybe, someday, people in power positions would actually listen to them and adjust their policymaking to the result of their research. I am just a writer who is also terminally online. My job is transforming daily observations into stories; and for now, I am stuck in observing the weather offline and online. Sometimes I think that contemplating the state of my surroundings while walking my dog – like early snow, unusual temperatures, cracks in dried-out soil – kind of feels the same like always sticking to the weather- and climate-related news in my social media feeds. For now, I cannot say if this is a good or a bad thing.

19th December 2023

A volcanic eruption on the Icelandic peninsula of Reykjanes, some 2,000 kilometres from my bed, where I scroll through my Instagram feed as a matter of routine before getting up. A fissure has opened in the ground near Grindavik, and lava is now pouring out of it. The whole village had to be evacuated. So close to Christmas I feel sorry for the people of Grindavik and hope that none of the 13 Jólasveinar are affected. At least it's a natural disaster that doesn't reflect the climate crisis. Or is it? At the breakfast table I google "connection between volcanic eruption and climate crisis."

Of course there is a link. Changes in the Earth's pressure due to melting glaciers, whose weight should be pushing the Earth's surface towards the centre. When that pressure is removed, tensions are created that can be released in the form of increased volcanic activity. Heavy rainfall can also favour volcanic eruptions if it leads to instability on volcanic slopes. Disillusioned, I put down my smartphone and watch thick raindrops trickling down the window pane.

21st December 2023

The official start of winter season. Also: the shortest day of the year (or: the longest night, although I'm not sure whether the night from the 20th to the 21st or from the 21st to the 22nd is the longest. Or are they both the same length?) It rains like there's no tomorrow. My dog scorns my pathetic suggestion to go for a walk.

24th December 2023

Merry Christmas Flooding! I am spending the holidays with my sister and her family. On the afternoon before Christmas Eve, we go for a walk. "Let's go to the river", my sister decides. "It's twice as wide as usual because of all the rain." Actually, we don't get very far: the river has already expanded to the road we planned to walk. I take a few photos of construction beacons sticking out of the dark grey water like out-of-place Christmas decorations. A few metres away, an elderly man is taking the same pictures with a DSLR and a huge telephoto lens. He looks like he is working for the local newspaper. I plan to look for an article about the Christmas Flooding after the Holidays, but I already know that I'll forget about it unless it happens to wash up on my timeline.

28th December 2023

The time between the years takes the form of flooded landscapes. "Are your Lower Saxony families doing well?", one of my writer friends wants to know. "Yes, why?", I ask in return. "Well, because of the floods."

As I type "floods in Lower Saxony" in the search bar of Google, I realise that I should've known. It's only been a few days since my holiday visit to Lower Saxony, there are still Christmas cookies in the jar and the river around the corner from my sister's house is far from having receded into its original bed. But at least where she lives, the situation is safe. Maybe a few cellars are flooded, which in this case mainly affects the mansion district. At least there seems to be something like poetic climate justice in my sister's hometown.

30th December 2023

People have been shooting off firecrackers since 28th December. Is it just me, or do they start earlier every year? It's not really an original thought, since complaining about New Year's Eve fireworks has become an important moment of social media bonding over the last few years.

My dog is scared of fireworks, so I walk him far outside city limits when it gets closer to New Year's Eve. Today, I plan to take him to my favourite beach, which is actually more of a coastal cliff at the Baltic Sea, a few kilometres up north. During summertime, I use to visit this place every other day, whenever I feel the need to clear my head (and stay away from the internet). In November, a storm tide has severely damaged those cliffs. "completely swept away", some people claimed. I haven't been there since, and all I've seen on Instagram is a photo of the destroyed wooden staircase, which will probably no longer be used to get down from the cliff to the beach.

I want that staircase to just stay on Instagram.

I don't want the photographs of the cliffs I've taken over the past two or three summers on this stretch of coast to be the only thing I have left. Even though I've been mentally preparing myself for years to realise that this place may soon cease to exist. There are new landslides whenever I come here, variations of fresh boulder clay and old landslides long overgrown with spontaneous vegetation. Every time I discover new cracks in the dusty earth at the top of the cliff that do not bode well. How is it even possible to still find peace of mind in this particular place? I guess the

Baltic Sea is washing away every thought, positive or negative, as long as you don't look into the abyss.

Although I have been determined to face the situation at my favourite beach when I got in the car, I lose my courage along the way and drive to a stretch of coast a little further up north. A dog owner friend of mine told me there were beautiful cliffs too, with a comfortable hiking path on the top.

Walking from the parking lot towards the shoreline, it takes me a while to find anything resembling a cliff. Also, I am unable to identify a hiking path. A field of clay stretches out in front of me. Maybe I have to walk through it and it will get better after a few metres? I decide to take a few steps. The dog, who does not like muddy ground, follows me with some uncertainty. When I take one step that is maybe a bit incautious, I slip and fall. Within seconds my clothes are soaked in cold mud, a really uncomfortable feeling. Are there any witnesses? I want to go home badly, but I need to properly walk the dog first. So I pick myself up and take the other direction, hoping for a proper trail.

Down by the beach, I have a chat with another dog owner living in the village. "The cliffs have been completely washed away by the last storm tide. There's nothing left. Only sludge", the old man tells me. "You can hardly take a decent walk around here anymore."

"Well, I've noticed", I say, telling him about my accident.

"It's barely visible", he says, understating the case with great courtesy. My left trouser leg and the left half of my coat are covered in mud. I have to keep moving to avoid becoming a statue.

At home I read that the authorities in the flooded areas of Lower Saxony are urging people not to use fireworks on New Year's Eve this year because the emergency services and hospitals are already overstretched with flooding injuries. The comment sections are as expected: "Well, I'll buy lots of fireworks this year. The wokies can't stop me!"

2ⁿᵈ January 2024

We start the year with heavy rain that never seems to stop. Is this the rainy version of Snowpiercer? Someone on Instagram said it was Waterworld. I can't judge as I haven't seen the film. But the Wikipedia summary convinces me once again that webbed feet and gills would be a really useful mutation.

10ᵗʰ January 2024

Awfully cold. Probably froze my toes off cycling home from work (it's a ten-minute ride). Today the investigative journalism newsroom *correctiv.org* published a report about right-wing activists, politicians (AfD and also "Werteunion", the republicans of the CDU) and some businessmen seriously discussing deporting anyone who is not "German" enough once they take over the government. The report is all over my Instagram stories, everyone is sharing the article and writing about how urgently we need to stop the Nazis and abolish the AfD, but I fear this is again mostly happening within the realm of my so-called bubble. It is quite exhausting to worry about climate crisis and fascists who are of course in complete denial about climate change at the same time. Sometimes I think that climate crisis/human extinction would at least end fascism, but as a reader and writer, I resent climate crisis stories automatically leading to apocalyptic human extinction scenarios. As much as it is important to raise awareness for fascism being a major threat to the wellbeing of the planet and the people living on it, I am longing for narratives pointing towards an exit to this horror show. Where is this exit now?

11th January 2024

Still cold.

14th January 2024

Still cold. Nevertheless, 8,000 people took to the streets in my city to protest against right-wing extremism. Maybe we're not completely doomed.

20th January 2024

My oldest relative (a great-aunt, my grandmothers second-oldest sister) turned 100 (in words: one hundred) yesterday. Something that also happened yesterday: in Hamburg, 130,000 people marched against Nazis in Hamburg, but the demonstration was cancelled due to overcrowding (said the police). I searched my feeds for weather updates, and all I could find were aerial shots of the rally in Hamburg. The comment section under the coverage of the protests are grim, dark places.

On the 8th of May 1945, when the German Instrument of Surrender was signed, my now 100-year-old great-aunt was 21. I wonder how it feels to have a bunch of right-wing horror clowns reenact the Wannsee Conference so close to your 100th birthday (it would be bad enough if it was actually just reenactment). Well, that and all the minor and major dam bursts that have occurred since 2015, or indeed since 2006, when, in the course of the Football World Cup in Germany, national colours and "relaxed" patriotism became socially acceptable for the first time since the end of World War II.

23rd January 2024

Storm tide in Hamburg. I have no idea how to feel about it.

1st February 2024

Cold, crisp air and a blizzard forecast for Norway. A friend of a friend is stuck in Oslo because the ferries are restricted for good reason. My weather app says it's -29°C in Svalbard. Didn't I save an article explaining that, paradoxically, Scandinavia is getting colder because of global warming? I searched in vain. Maybe the internet actually does forget some information at some point?

6th February 2024

Windy, wet and cold. Or rather, what do you mean by windy? It's so windy that it takes me almost twice as long to get to work (16 minutes instead of 10). It's strange, actually, that this storm isn't newsworthy at all. Isn't it? I scroll through my timelines looking for the name of the current storm, but I can't find it. Apparently, the algorithm thinks I'm no longer interested in the weather (let alone the climate), but these are the posts I keep getting stuck on. I imagine what I do (hyperfocussing on local and global weather and climate news) is something more urgent than ordinary, procrastinatory scrolling, advanced scrolling or just meteorological scrolling. According to the German Weather Service (DWD), the wind and rain outside is just "distinctive weather." The only name that I can dig up is Nadine, but the report about this particular stormfront is already three days old. I reluctantly resign myself to the fact that it's just anonymous squalls making my leaky windows whistle.

8th February 2024

The first thing I see on Instagram today is a picture of a withered sunflower. "For the first time: global warming averages over 1.5°C in twelve consecutive months," reads the Tagesschau headline, imposed over the tips of its withered sepals. We are now apparently at 1,52°C plus. I think of the graphs of different climate change scenarios that I have already seen on various info-tiles on social media, vividly depicting different manifestations of the potential horror for ordinary people. It has long been considered unlikely that the 1.5°C target can be met at all. Nevertheless, in 2018 the Intergovernmental Panel on Climate Change (IPCC) published a special report comparing the 1.5°C target with a 2°C target and also produced a separate summary for policymakers.[1] This special report is summarised in the Wikipedia article on the 1.5°C target under the heading: "Advantages over a 2 degree target." With a 1.5°C target, fewer species would go extinct, there would be "less pronounced increases in average temperatures, heat extremes, droughts, heavy precipitation and precipitation deficits"[2] and less adaptation would be required, although this would reach its limits even at 1.5°C. In summary, 1.5°C means slightly fewer disasters than an average warming of 2°C. What catastrophes fit into the 0.02°C that we are now, 6 years after the IPCC Special Report, already above 1.5°C?

The month that has just passed has also set a record: Not only is January getting longer and longer, but for the eighth year in a row it has the distinction of being the "warmest January since records began." One small consolation is that we've still got a few weeks of winter ahead of us, and at least until then the temperature records won't be illustrated with stock photos of happy people in the swimming pool.

2.

15th November 2024

No weather talks due to current events. Technically, October was too warm and too dry, but nobody in my social media feeds has made an issue of that. Instead: rays of sunshine on copper-coloured foliage (this is the only bit of nature writing you are going to read in this piece), the celebration of a golden autumn that came to an abrupt end in November. The only copper colour I see now is the complexion of the newly elected or re-elected US president. We are collectively freezing, our bodies still struggling with the sudden transition from the most beautiful to the worst autumn month. Online, I see sprinkles of a press release claiming that 2024 is likely to be the first year in history to exceed the 1.5°C limit, but this unsettling bit of information soon disappears behind fired finance ministers (rightly so) and the announcement of early Bundestag elections (oh dear).

---

1   IPCC (2018): Summary for Policymakers. In: Global Warming of 1.5°C. An IPCC Special Report on the impacts of global warming of 1.5°C above pre-industrial levels and related global greenhouse gas emission pathways, in the context of strengthening the global response to the threat of climate change, sustainable development, and efforts to eradicate poverty [Masson-Delmotte, V., P. Zhai, H.-O. Pörtner, D. Roberts, J. Skea, P.R. Shukla, A. Pirani, W. Moufouma-Okia, C. Péan, R. Pidcock, S. Connors, J.B.R. Matthews, Y. Chen, X. Zhou, M.I. Gomis, E. Lonnoy, T. Maycock, M. Tignor, and T. Waterfield (eds.)]. Cambridge, UK and New York, NY :Cambridge University Press, pp. 3–24, doi:10.1017/9781009157940.001.

2   "1,5-Grad-Ziel" (https://de.wikipedia.org/wiki/1,5-Grad-Ziel).

22nd November 2024

We are living in the worst possible weather condition. In the morning, the world outside is covered by a soft blanket of snow. Very pretty, but isn't it a bit early for snow? It's not even December yet. As the day progresses, showers of snow and drizzle keep on chasing each other. I am trapped in this ongoing cycle every time I leave the house. As I dry my jacket, I come to the conclusion that we're actually going through a very classic November: It's cold, grey, wet and stuffed with bad news, like every year.

3rd December 2024

Climate hardships: I feel like I am supposed to be wearing a cozy woolen hat by this time of the year, but it's actually way too warm outside. Nevertheless, I put one on every time I leave the house. After all, there are Christmas decorations in the streets and I now open a little door on the Advent calendar every day. However, I can't even think about white Christmas as long as a former Finance Minister, who has recently and rightfully been fired from his job, is allowed to spread misinformation about the climate crisis on TV. He claims that CO_2 neutrality would bankrupt us, that we would perish in a noble, emissions-neutral way; we would be climate-neutral, but no longer competitive. A famous Climate activist debunked this fake news on Instagram today and conclusively and firmly demonstrates the opposite: That it no longer corresponds to any market logic at all to NOT want to take any more measures against climate change. I'm annoyed that market logic has to be used to argue about climate protection at all, but neoliberal morons also need to be met where they stand (although the former Finance Minister won't get into anything other than a Porsche anyway).

4th December 2024

Drizzling rain and discomforting 6°C. From time to time, I am counting the number of swipes it takes for a climate-related post to appear in my Instagram feed. Today: I scrolled through 20 feed metres and found nothing, as well as in my stories. The news that November 2024 was the warmest November since the beginning of weather records is not expected until mid-December. Between the re-election of Donald Trump in the USA, the German government coalition crumbling apart, Ukraine, Gaza, Georgia, the brief interlude of martial law in South Korea and all the other current crises, there are no capacities left for dealing with climate issues. Instead, I find myself and my novel in a radio programme in which the climate crisis is labeled as a 'trending topic' in contemporary literature. Meanwhile, the slender-billed curlew (*Numenius tenuirostris*) is the first European bird species to be declared extinct (it has not been spotted since 1995).

10th December 2024

Climate crisis may not be an issue in my Instagram feed at the moment – meanwhile Bluesky, the current alternative for Twitter, turns out to be a reliable source for climate content.

1.6°C temperature deviation in 2024 – that's probably what it's going to come down to.
It's getting worse and worse.
I promise.
It's physics and it applies to everyone.
Without exception.
#climate catastrophe

a meteorologist writes in the caption of a video, giving more details in the introductory words to the weather report. 1.6°C – Tagesschau has recently proclaimed 1,5°C on Instagram, and even that is devastating. Although the air outside smells of night frost and black ice, there isn't even hoarfrost in the morning. December is just as slushy kale green as November, a real disappointment.

12th December 2024

Just sweating today; hate everything about it.

16th December 2024

My dog now has a better winter coat than I do, but I am not sure if there is going to be any use of it. It is stormy outside, but with a lukewarm 11°C. At least it's partly typical seasonal weather, as autumn is officially still lasting a few days. But there is not much going out this week anyway. All plans have been cancelled by a positive covid test – not mine, but my partner's – and so I am missing out a lot of cozy Christmas events. At the same time, the current Chancellor is losing his vote of confidence, which feels like the end of any climate politics that could have made a positive impact.

27th December 2024

Every time I look out of the window, I try to remember if we ever had such a slushy green-brown December as this one. I've done all my Christmas walks sweating,

7–10°C, why did I even buy a winter jacket? Then I think back 15 years ago, when we drove my grandma home after Christmas Eve celebrations, I didn't zip up my jacket because it hadn't been that cold even then. At least no Christmas flooding this year.

29th December 2024

Off to Denmark. This year, we spend New Year's Eve on Sjælands Odde peninsula, which forms a northern tip of the island of Zealand and lies between Kattegat and Storebælt. Yesterday we arrived in fog and darkness. Today I can hear the sound of the sea as I open the front door, even though it's 1.5 kilometres to the beach. It's 7°C and windy; towards the early afternoon the sky clears and I see the sun for perhaps the first time in almost two weeks. On the beach, I run slaloms around generously scattered piles of seaweed. The Baltic Sea has thrown the seaweed almost up to the dunes. I notice finding less rubbish here than on the beaches around Kiel. After my walk on the seaside, I do some research up on how the Kattegat area is faring in the climate crisis. Here, too, the sea level threatens to rise by 40 cm by the end of the century – how could it be otherwise? The tip of the peninsula I am on was once a real island that was connected to the mainland by land uplift. I wonder if the rising sea levels will restore this state of affairs to some extent. My research takes me to the Helmholtz Centres' annual review. There I learn that in 2024 a potentially serious factor for the sharp rise in global warming was discovered: The planet's reflectivity is decreasing because we lack certain clouds. So now we also lack planetary albedo.[3]

31st December 2024

The last day of the year starts with drizzle and a woman with an umbrella scaring my dog. At 1.30 pm I realise that the sun will be setting in just over two hours, so we are heading to the beach again. The dog, usually a bit afraid of storm and crashing waves, dares to put his paws into the sea. The rain radar is still displaying a dark yellow wind level; it will change from orange to red in the course of the late afternoon and hopefully stop the children in the neighbourhood from setting off firecrackers. We walk a few miles between the dunes sheltering us from the wind, and I think about the jump in average annual temperatures from 2023 to 2024. From 10.6°C to 10.9°C. That's the first jump of three decimal places since we passed the 10°C mark. How do I know that? Not from Instagram, where the algorithm has been swallowing up all climate news for some time. Thanks to some active climate scientists, Bluesky is both a reliable news source on this topic and a reason to scream. After all, it is not algorithm-driven; perhaps the last synchronised place in the reality of social media.

---

3   "Was uns in diesem Jahr bewegt hat", 19 December 2024 (https://www.helmholtz.de/newsr oom/artikel/was-uns-in-diesem-jahr-bewegt-hat/).

3ʳᵈ January 2025

After a rainy and stormy New Year, it has now been cold and sunny for two days and the air is crystal clear. The dog refuses to set foot on the beach because of the ongoing storm. Understandable: fine grains of sand are blown across the ground at his eye level. Occasionally they also hit me in the face, so we dodge onto a path in the dunes. While my dog is protected from the storm by heavy chunks of dune grass, I find myself with a frozen face halfway through the walk. Over the last few days, I've noticed that most people here wear snowsuits (my legs, which are icy despite my thick jeans, are envious). I had always considered those to be for children and skiers, but well. The icy wind and my own, frozen legs prove them right. On the way back, I meet an older gentleman in a signal yellow and black snowsuit. He starts talking to me in Danish and I have the nerve to tell him that unfortunately I don't understand him. However, he turns out to be fluent in German and knows a bit about the political events in my home country. "Do you know B-S-Dabbelju?" he asks. Oh dear. He asks about my opinion on this party. Their party leader is quite insufferable, I answer, and that I wouldn't vote for her. He is bewildered. "But they're the only party that would do something against the war! Otherwise, you are going to be dependent on American gas!"

I point out to him that we were previously dependent on Russia's gas and fossil fuels because political decision-makers in Germany have been opposed to all kinds of renewable energies for years. "True", he admits. I tell him that I'm always jealous of the electric cars and solar panels on almost every roof in Denmark and Sweden. Well, I couldn't afford a car either way and I don't have a property with solar panels on the roof, but I'm envious of everyone who lives in a society that takes such things for granted. The ski suit grandad nods. He tries to make friends with my dog, who doesn't like him because he's a big, loud old man (funnily enough, this is an absolute red flag for my dog). Eventually, we part ways and I am relieved; I have not been prepared for this kind of small talk in this otherwise very introvert-friendly place. Or maybe this has been a real-life comment section.

8ᵗʰ January 2025

Can a body be expected to cope with temperature fluctuations of more than 3°C? Since we got back from Denmark last Saturday, I've had all kinds of rainfall and endured temperatures between -1°C and 11°C. The higher plus degrees were actually the worst, just as disconcerting as the current news situation. Tesla Guy openly supports the AfD, announces a live talk with their lead candidate on X. Meta Guy announces that he will end fact checks on his social media platforms 'to give freedom of opinion more space again'. He is clearly pandering to the newly elected POTUS, as fact-checks are particularly harmful to right-wingers. In Austria, a fascist is likely to become president.

A few days ago, I read a study by a climate researcher on Bluesky, the last tolerable refuge in social media. She compared the reach etc of her posts on climate topics on Bluesky and Threads: While the topics on Bluesky are doing well, their reach on the meta-platform Threads has been visibly curtailed since the US elections in November. This definitely fits with my impression that this is absolutely no longer an issue on Instagram. I usually try not to be too pessimistic, but here's what it looks like right now: Multi-billionaires are ruining all platforms and hollowing out democracy to such an extent that I now DO want a one-way Mars mission: either for them or for everyone else who can't help it. At the moment, I also don't see anyone in politics not adopting right-wing narratives. With regard to the early elections due in six weeks, this really fuels my anxiety.

10th January 2025

Wildfires in Los Angeles. The EU Copernicus programme's climate change service confirms that 2024 was the warmest year ever measured and therefore exceeded the 1.5°C limit (both read on Instagram). The former Finance Minister is in favour of closing the Federal Environment Agency (he already said so on 16th December, but I can hear it again on the radio this morning). 'Climate change will manifest as a series of disasters viewed through phones with footage that gets closer and closer to where you live until you're the one filming it,' I read on Instagram in front of a wall of flames, the author of this quote is unknown. The year is only 10 days old and already promises to be an absolute disaster. Yesterday, a right-wing conservative Nestlé mascot posted that AfD voters could get all their needs met by the CDU and apparently deleted the post after half an hour of criticism. I can hardly decide whether I wish the election campaign was finally over or whether I dread the time after the federal elections even more.

21st January 2025

Freezing to death on Inauguration Day and the morning after. The streets are covered in so-called black ice and I wonder if this weather phenomenon would be an appropriate metaphor for the world of today. I continue pondering this idea when I see the picture of Tesla Guy making a Hitler salute, which has been shared thousands of times. "Is it really a Hitler salute? It's a suspected Hitler salute! Or maybe just a Roman salute! He can't help it, he's autistic!", German media unleashed. In addition to an absolute low point for democracy and the climate, we have also reached a low point for journalism, that much is certain.

When there is black ice on the streets, official warnings are being issued because it is actually very dangerous but doesn't immediately catch your eye when you look out of the window. At the same time, fascists are very visibly being fascists in these days. How can the obvious be denied to such an extent? Imagine seeing someone slip on black ice and still pretend it doesn't exist or use all our random fact knowledge to explain the accident with the most far-fetched reason possible. I don't know. I sure won't be writing anything explaining the current political situation with the metaphorical help of weather phenomenons.

At least, I finally managed to install a website blocker that prevents me from accessing social media during my self-imposed writing hours. My smartphone is currently hidden in the bedroom, and it will stay there until all this is over (but I guess this is not happening).

Concepts and Worldviews

Freedom without Affluence?
Energy Subjects and New Climate Subjectivities

Imre Szeman and Mark Simpson

> The forms of humanity's own global
> societal constitutions threaten its life, if
> a self-conscious global subject does not
> develop and intervene. The possibility of
> progress, of averting the most extreme,
> total disaster, has migrated to this global
> subject alone. Everything else involving
> progress must crystallize around it.
> *Theodor W. Adorno*

Explaining the characteristics and contradictions of modern subjectivity has pre-occupied philosophy, sociology, and critical theory from the 18th century to the present. One might suppose that those studying the impact of fossil fuels on modernity have sought to participate and extend this discussion by showing how the ever-increasing availability of energy has reshaped modern subjectivity and led to a 21st century subject ontologically distinct from the one existing at the start of the fossil fuel era. But even though invocations of and allusions to an energy subject recur in recent studies of energy, in both the energy humanities and other fields, they tend to remain only gestural: shorthand placeholders for a more sustained account of the modern subject in terms of energy or resource use, one that goes beyond historical investigations of the life and times of energy modernity or of the capacities fuel has engendered socially and individually. Why does such a sustained account matter? Because the recognition that the modern subject is a fossil fuel subject, categorically shaped by the energy it uses and resistant to change as a result, will complicate and reformulate the given and potential meanings of subjectivity today.[1]

The climate crisis is a crisis generated by our commitment to fossil fuel energy. If such commitment is not simply a matter of energy choices – of the meaning and import of energy in everyday life – but instead and more profoundly a core and constituent feature of the contemporary subject, then the prospect and stakes of energy transition shift significantly, expanding to require a thoroughgoing change in subjectivity, too. The point is twofold. The prospect of transforming our energy system is at once material – about the object matter fueling our ways of life – and ontological – about the subject form our modes of being take and might become. Concomitantly, the grave challenge posed by climate crisis is not soluble through technological ingenuity alone – it requires, much more dauntingly, an approach attuned to the quite comprehensive refashioning of our fundamental selves. While the attempt to posit a distinct energy subjectivity might seem to overstate the case (can giving subjects more energy really result in changes at the level of being?), we believe that understanding the problem of energy transition as one that also concerns subjects and subjectivity brings the full scope of the energy impasse we now face more clearly into view (Simpson and Szeman 2021).

To some, our claim that there is no existing description of an energy subject might come as a surprise. After all, most recent studies of energy (and specifically of fossil fuel energy), whether from within or beyond the energy humanities, do consider the impact of energy on modern life beyond a merely superficial level.[2] Brett Bloom's account of "petro-subjectivity" – the most declarative, forthright naming of energy subjectivity we know – usefully illustrates the way this impact is commonly framed:

> It is the presence of oil in your sense of the world and self. The conditions oil (fossil fuels) creates, through massive accretions of habit and influence from great to small, repeatedly over the course of seconds, minutes, hours, days, weeks, months, years, generations, in all of us gives immense force to our collective subjectivity. We repeat this collected totalizing gestalt of relationships every moment of the day, by ourselves and with others. I have been describing this precondition, the order of metaphorical relationships to the world, as 'petro-subjectivity' for lack of a better term or way of thinking about this problem. (2015: 18)

---

1   As this opening will indicate, we use energy subject and fossil fuel subject interchangeably, on the understanding that – for reasons elaborated as our argument proceeds – there is nothing like an energy subject prior to fossil fuels.

2   See, for example, Matt Huber's Lifeblood (2013), Stephanie LeMenager's Living Oil (2014), and Robert Johnson's Mineral Rites (2019).

Bloom describes petro-subjectivity as an existential "precondition," shaped and constrained by "the presence of oil" in one's sense of self and world, that affects not only our everyday "habit[s]" but "the order of metaphorical relationships to the world." According to Bloom, oil is embedded so thoroughly in modern life that it creates a "totalizing gestalt" – a constant, pervasive influence shaping our reality, so deeply ingrained that individuals are often unaware of it. Missing in such expansive claims, however, is any sustained, rigorous theoretical explication of the subjectivity in "petro-subjectivity." In a note glossing the book's initial invocation of its titular term, Bloom writes:

> The subject position or the subjectivity of individuals has long been debated by philosophers, psychologists, and others from Descartes to Freud, Marx, Heidegger, and most importantly for me Michel Foucault. Rather than entering that philosophical debate I would just like to clarify how I am using the term. For me subjectivity is a way to relate to the sense of self one has, regardless of what the processes are that produce this. I see and experience the results of how oil makes us relate to the world and this is wrapped up in how we talk about the world and act accordingly. The problem is as much one of ontology and philosophy as it is myth, metaphor and storytelling. (2015: 91)

As this passage will indicate, Bloom's use of subjectivity is gestural and rhetorical, not analytic: meant simply to evoke everyday experiences of the world (rather than, say, engaging with something like "everydayness" [Alltäglichkeit] as explored by Heidegger). Such a take on "petro-subjectivity" does little more than affirm that fossil fuel has had a big impact on modern life.

Other recent accounts offer more substantive and nuanced insight into the reciprocal relation among subjectivity, environment, and energy – and so come closer to the approach we believe is needed. Consider, for instance, the geographer Ludger Gailing's exploration of the politics of the Energiewende in Germany (2016). Gailing describes renewable energy developments as shifting not just energy sources but associated subject positions, thereby allowing individuals to adopt new roles as prosumers and active agents within energy networks – a dynamic process that suggests potential spaces of agency even within entrenched energy paradigms. The sociologist José Maurício Domingues (2023) and the political scientist Scott Hamilton (2019) likewise explore how imagining broader frameworks of collective and planetary subjectivity could offer insights into the complex relationality between individuals, society, and environmental crises. Domingues critiques the limited engagement of critical theory with climate change, proposing "collective subjectivity" as a concept that acknowledges the agency within communities, social structures, and even state institutions to recognize and address the material impacts of energy consumption. In analyzing the Anthropocene, Hamilton discusses a planetary "We" – an emergent, collective awareness that reframes humanity's agency at a planetary level. This collective subjectivity reframes individuals' roles from isolated "I" perspectives to a connected "We," a shift that constitutes, for Hamilton, an inevitable, unnerving outcome of human-produced climate change – yet that still could support more collective forms of environmental stewardship and responsibility.

Each of these approaches to the concept of the subject has benefits as well as limits – and there are certainly other examples we could add. But proliferating examples and assessing relative merits would only distract from the main point we want to make: that 'subject' as used in these texts implies positionality more than it does ontology. Even as, for these writers, subjects are formed by the force of social structures, state institutions, and energy systems, it nonetheless seems that subjectivity can easily change, whether through real world shifts in energy apparatus (in Gailing's argument) or else in new forms of subjectivity conceptualized to replace older ones (in the arguments of Domingues and Hamilton). These versions of the subject are fundamentally liberal ones, with the volitional capacity to take on new form by creating or imagining new social and political possibilities. Subjectivity, here, is flexible and fungible: easily modified, not obdurate or sedimented or enduring. The perspective makes it seem not just possible but straightforward to invent new subjectivities simply by identifying so as to surpass the limits of existing ones. By framing the issue of subjectivity in such terms, these accounts cannot really discern, let alone explain, the energy subject as one completely shaped, existentially and ontologically, by its experience with fossil fuels and its existence in a fossil fueled lifeworld: an energy subject so comprehensively molded by fuel that it persists in its fossil-fueled form even as new developments in renewable energy emerge and proliferate – and whether or not it works at 'prosuming' in new energy networks.

Necessary to substantiate the concept of energy subjectivity we call for here is a more sustained account of this deeper sense of the forces that make subjects what they are. Such an account will not disregard but instead regard as essential the processes that have produced and continue to produce energy subjects as specifically fossil fueled. We agree with Bloom that Michel Foucault has important insights to offer in understanding subjectivity philosophically. Unlike Bloom, though, we seek to engage those insights directly and explicitly, both to understand the processes at work in subject formation and to speculate on their potential consequence for questions of energy.

The Energy Subject and Power

Michel Foucault's The Subject and Power (1982) provides a generative overview of his unique understanding of how individuals are transformed into subjects via power. The basic terms of Foucault's theories about power, subjects, and their interrelation are by now well known. Power has been typically understood across the spectrum of political theory as the exertion of force by a group, class, or institution on individuals or on other groups, whether implicitly as threat or explicitly as violence. By contrast, Foucault argues that power must be understood as a relationship, a form of action that affects or impacts others by acting on their actions and doing so via the implementation of a diverse variety of techniques to shape and direct conduct.

The modern state is a key site and vector of power because its institutions, such as schools, hospitals, and prisons, actively shape the identities and behaviors of individuals to normalize and regulate their actions, rather than prohibit and impede them. Power relations must be understood as socially constitutive; as Foucault writes, "a society without power relations can only be an abstraction" (1982: 791). But Foucault is also careful to point out that the social reality of power relationships does not imply that they need take any of their extant forms. They can be – indeed, they always are – reshaped by struggles animated by "the recalcitrance of the will and the intransigence of freedom" (1982: 790). There is an agonistic relationship between techniques of power designed to organize the behavior, belief, and conduct of individuals and groups, on the one hand, and the resistance of those self-same groups to power on the other. It's why Foucault argues, at the outset of his essay, that the way to develop a "new economy of power relations [...] consists of taking the forms of resistance against different forms of power as a starting point" (1982: 780).

The process of acting on actions enables discourses and institutions to delineate what constitutes (for instance) sanity versus insanity, health versus illness, and legality versus illegality. It is because power relations have become increasingly 'governmentalized' that Foucault focuses on the analysis of state institutions in his work – in the examples just mentioned: mental institutions, hospitals, and prisons and legal systems. Fossil fuel energy certainly shapes the actions of subjects in determinate ways. But it's difficult to see why and how the force of fossil fuels could fit into Foucault's account of the development of modern subjectivity – an account with which we are largely sympathetic. Power relations develop out of institutional techniques to create subjects that act in determinate ways; they are also defined by the intransigence of subjects to do just that, due to their recognition that there are other ways of being and acting than those that states (or other institutions) wish to normalize. What is lacking in the development of fossil fuel subjects is any such intentionality on the part of either state institutions or subjects pushing back against power. During the modern era, bodies are not managed by states via delineations of legitimate or illegitimate, healthy or unhealthy forms of energy. And subjects have not, in the main, resisted fossil fuels, but have instead embraced their use. Many nations manage fossil fuel extraction and distribution via state energy institutions. Whatever power relations might emanate from such institutions, however, they do not involve making fossil fuel subjects – explicitly, directly, and with insistent force – and doing so against other forms of oppositional subjectivity, i.e., subjects disinclined to use the energies of fossil fuels. There is no need to. When it comes to the use of fossil fuels at a social level, nearly everyone has always already been on board; it is only very recently that there has been a desire by subjects to turn their backs on the daily use of fossil fuels, and this resistance has been carried out more in theory than in practice – it's simply not possible to live apart from, let alone renounce, fossil fuels in a substantive way.

One of the defining features of the fossil fuel era is thus, at the level of social practice and power, of actions and acting, what appears to be an unstated agreement about the legitimacy of fossil fuel subjectivity. But framing such legitimacy as an agreement – that is, as a mode of subjectivity about which there is no push-and-pull of agonistic struggle because of (something like) a pact made between opposing forces – is to miss the point. Energy subjectivity is fully absent from power relations, unrecognized and unrecognizable as a condition of social being; it constitutes the ground on which the exercise of power and the production of subjects takes place. The subjects being actively shaped by the actions of institutions such as schools, hospitals, and prisons in the modern era are always already fossil fuel subjects – healthy or ill fossil fuel subjects, sane or insane fossil fuel subjects, legal or illegal fossil fuel subjects. So, too, the subjects engaged in struggle against subjectivization: whereas people worldwide have routinely pushed against definitions and determinations of (say) illegality, there have been extremely limited questions raised about the legitimacy of the processes of subjection enabled by or of the subjects produced using fossil fuels. When energy humanists insist that fossil fuels have (until relatively recently) been invisible, the claim is not that there is no sense of their economic import, prominent role in geopolitics, or impact on communities near extraction sites. The point, rather, concerns the difficulty of recognizing the ontological significance of fossil fuels – a form of being that, while fully historical, nonetheless lies underneath the modern drama of subjectivity that has been front of mind in modern social and political analysis.

To assert that the modern subject is ipso facto a fossil fuel subject is, at one level, a banal claim. Insofar as the latter is effectively equivalent to the former, with every instance of modern subjectivity always already fossil fuel subjectivity, then adding fossil fuels to the dynamics of modern life might well have little impact on our understanding and analysis of power relations. Instead, the significance of fossil fuels might simply register as an element of "capacity," which Foucault identifies as the objective material and infrastructural basis for power relations (1982: 786–788). It is in the current passage from one energy system to another, however, that the critical and analytic importance of fossil fuel subjectivity becomes apparent. We now know that we have long been fossil fuel subjects; the environmental and climate crisis tell us we can no longer be such subjects. The ground on which all facets of our social and cultural practices, of our institutional and infrastructural relations, indeed of the various modes of liberal subjectivity have been constituted is thus quickly dissolving under our feet. With the disfiguration of fossil fuel subjectivity, our given systems of being, belonging, power, and resistance are under threat. With respect to some of these systems, we can say "good riddance!" But with many others, we are now faced with the task of re-examining and re-defining the deep, systemic, often unconscious attachments to the unique energy subjectivity defining modernity.

Work, Affluence, Freedom: The Fossil Fuel Subject

Energy is not merely a resource but a key force shaping subjectivity within industrial-capitalist society. And the resultant fossil fuel subjectivity constitutes, as we have argued, the ground on which the dramas of modern liberal subjectivity and subjection transpire. What, though, does it mean when making this argument to contend, as we do, that this sort of energy subjectivity is always already in place? What does always-alreadyness entail? How, historically, does it come to emerge? And what does it mean for living and being post-fossil fuels?

The material turn to fossil fuels at the start of the industrial era obviously constitutes the pivot point, a historically specific yet contingent shift that creates conditions of possibility for energy subjectivity to emerge and, increasingly, to become the grounding for liberal life in modernity. We recall here the important insight offered by Jean-Claude Debeir, Jean-Paul Deléage, and Daniel Hémery: "while there is no energy determinism there is a powerful energy determination at work in all societies [...] the energy determination is itself determined: it is the result of the interplay of economic, demographic, psychological, intellectual, social and political parameters operating in the various human societies" (1991: 13). The fossil turn exemplifies this double determination: a sedimented saturation spreading across industrializing societies that increasingly constitutes a kind of path dependency or infrastructural inertia. And the becoming-ground of the energy subjectivity that ensues – its given priority or always-alreadyness – is itself a consequence of the dialectical relation of material affordances of fossil power and more abstract commitments and ideals in liberal societies. In Dipesh Chakrabarty's incisive formulation: "The mansion of modern freedoms stands on an ever-expanding base of fossil-fuel use. Most of our freedoms so far have been energy-intensive" (2009: 208). The fossil fuel subject is, to recall Joseph Conrad's memorable phrase, the liberal subject's secret sharer.

Attention to the material dynamics of the processes we are describing complicates the prospect of "freedoms" by foregrounding issues of labor and class. Relevant, here, is Andreas Malm's influential account of fossil capital (2016). In the history Malm tells, England's cotton industrialists ventured in the 1830s to shift from water to coal in powering their mills, even though water was abundant, cheaper, and more potent, because coal as movable fuel – unlike geographically fixed waterways – enabled the relocation of manufacture into dense urban settings that offered a vital resource: numerous, cheap, exploitable laborers (perfect for sabotaging recent, hard-won victories by organized labor over work-time). Coal thus supplied the means by which capital could retool working subjects, acting on the actions of those employed in factories so as to solve a tangle of problems around labor, value, and profit. The purpose, we would stress, was not to fashion fossil fuel subjects as such – but the consequence has been exactly that, and the ensuing history of energy deepening, from coal to oil to diesel, has sedimented the fossil fuel subject as the constant ground for every subsequent retooling of (laboring as well as all other) subjectivities.[3] In effect, the historically specific and contingent but relatively constant and enduring ground supplied by fossil fuel subjectivity (not even rising to the level of recognized subjectivity as such) enables the unfolding of what liberalism idealizes as the volitional subject, one that we might understand instead as fungible, over the course of fossil fuel modernity. Fossil fuel subjectivity increasingly sets the conditions of possibility for acting on actions to form subjects in a modern era ever more saturated with fossil fuels.

We want to probe more fully the implications of these ideas for the understanding of energy subjectivity, holding in mind Foucault's account of the process of subject-formation while turning to another work with significant implications for our project: Pierre Charbonnier's *Affluence and Freedom: An Environmental History of Political Ideas* (2021). Rather than focusing explicitly on subjectivity, Charbonnier examines the historically evolving relationship between affluence and freedom. He argues that these ideas, deeply entwined with access to energy, underpin the specific political and social freedoms of the fossil fuel era. Through this lens, Charbonnier reveals how the fossil fuel regime has crafted a political-economic model where increased energy consumption equates to greater affluence and a promise of individual freedoms, the hallmarks of volitional subjectivity – a political-economic model that, though once celebrated, now reveals its environmental costs.

Charbonnier redirects attention from individual subject formation to broader configurations of wealth, liberty, and ecological cost. In his view, modernity's intertwined pursuits of affluence and freedom are fundamentally defined by the historical relationship between energy consumption and the promise of liberation from material constraints. In the fossil fuel era, energy abundance facilitated an unparalleled rise in affluence and personal freedom, shaping a social and political order that assumes both the necessity and the right to expand consumption indefinitely. Charbonnier argues that this paradigm has fostered an unsustainable expansion of 'freedom' through ecological exploitation, leading to environmental crisis. His approach allows us to understand the fossil fuel era not just as a period of heightened individualization or freedom but as a mode of environmental depletion intimately

---

3   Jeff Diamanti theorizes "energy deepening" as "capital's ever-increasing need for more and more physical energy, [which] results in the naturalization of fossil-fueled futures" (2021: 14).

tied to modern political ideals. It is this intersection of political freedom, affluence, and ecological constraint that Charbonnier unpacks, offering a critical lens through which to reassess the environmental impact of the freedoms won under the fossil fuel paradigm.

Charbonnier draws attention to the degree to which the constitution of liberal subjectivity is tied to the ever-expanding use of resources. In great detail, *Affluence and Freedom* traces shifts and developments in liberal political philosophy, attending to the decisive role played by resources in shaping the concepts that have defined liberalism, such as sovereignty, property, and, most importantly, autonomy or freedom. For such a complex history of ideas, the animating theme of the book is remarkably simple: the key liberal value of autonomy or freedom needs to be reimagined as "extraction-autonomy" (2021: 89) – an insight that, in his view, unnerves what we imagine as the ends of politics, and not only for liberals. Socialists, too, depend on extraction to achieve their ends. Even if their views of freedom might disavow some forms of affluence – ownership and property, for example – socialist freedom nevertheless requires the affluence of material abundance.[4]

There is a methodological imperative guiding Charbonnier's re-narration of liberal philosophy that, key to the argument he wishes to make, also acts as a measure of the success of his overall argument. He contrasts his analysis of the changing relationship between affluence and freedom with what he sees as the precepts guiding most approaches to ecological topics and issues. He emphasizes that what he offers is not a "history of environmental ideas" but rather "an environmental history of ideas" (2021: 15; original emphasis). The distinction is an important one. Histories of environmental ideas, Charbonnier insists, are normative. They start with a belief in right practices or principles (in this case, in relation to the environment) and then narrate how such principles arose or, perhaps, how principles now understood as correct – say, the necessity of a relation between human and non-human – once existed and were deferred or displaced. An environmental history of ideas, by contrast, does not focus on the environment as such. It foregrounds instead the import of the relationship between nature and society for all concepts and ideas. Charbonnier frames this project in the following terms:

> Rather than writing a brief, continuous history of environmental awareness, [...] I shall be writing the long, frequently interrupted history of the relationship between political thought and forms of subsistence, territoriality and ecological understanding. [...] [W]e will study several critical moments connected to such con-

---

4   Relevant here is Matt Huber's critique of degrowth theories on the eco-left: "A class analysis would always be premised on not the aggregate of society (and whether or not it needs to grow or degrow), but rather conflictual class divisions where a few have way too much and the majority have too little" (2019: n.p.).

cepts as property, production, waste, territory, risk and climate. These spaces of controversy jointly shape what could be called the environmental reflexivity of our societies. (2021: 16)

We live in a moment in which the excessive (and still expanding and increasing) use of resources has already rendered the world dangerous for many and uninhabitable for some. Recognizing that modern ideas of affluence and freedom are indelibly linked to resource extraction leaves such ideas, at least as now conceived, increasingly untenable. Thus, for Charbonnier, the environmental crisis means that freedom and political emancipation must be profoundly reimagined. "The conception of the social as an autonomous sphere," he writes, "progressively imposed itself in the wake of the Enlightenment as a central feature of societies that sought to be modern" (2021: 13). Such conception, dependent on affluence, becomes increasingly untenable after the recognition of climate crisis. And without affluence, modern understandings of the social, autonomy, and the freedom of citizen-subjects cannot continue.

For researchers in the energy humanities, such arguments will sound familiar, thematically and methodologically. (Their novelty for Charbonnier might suggest that he should read more widely.[5]) Indeed, the principal claim he advocates – that dominant political imaginaries are made possible only as a result of intensive resource use – is precisely what is captured by the term 'petroculture,' that is, the critical-analytic recognition that the culture of modernity, in all its aspects, is fundamentally animated and enabled by resource use. 'Petroculture' is an expansive and thus imprecise term – and deliberately so. It doesn't speak only to the conditions of liberalism and isn't limited to politics. It rather draws attention to how material 'affluence' conditions values, habits, affects, cultural practices, and social attachments – indeed, all social relations – in modern social practices and imaginaries, to determining (though not determinist) effect. The emphasis on energy isn't intended to suggest that material abundance is limited to the provisions of fossil fuels, but to insist on the latter's unique import, socially and materially, and the scale and intensity of the abundance it produces and represents.

Methodologically, too, the term 'petroculture' is offered as an invitation to engage in what, using Charbonnier's framing, could be described as an energy (instead of environmental) history of ideas, which insists on the need to attend to the impact and influence of energy on any relationship whatsoever.[6] If the energy humanities can periodically slip toward the normative – as for instance when framing pre- or

---

5   … perhaps beginning with the Chakrabarty essay we invoke above.
6   Cara Daggett's exploration of what she terms "energy-work bindings" – "the history of the capture of energy [...] by the logic of fossil-fueled work" – offers just one example of the insights that can emerge from such an analysis (2019: 4–5).

post-fossil fuel relationships as desirable or attuned to environmental limits while treating fossil fueled culture as an inconvenience to explain away, not a structuring feature of the modern that demands better understanding – nonetheless we more commonly see an increasing attunement to the complex character and experience of petrocultures in the plural: the global and local inequalities in material abundance generated by colonialism, imperialism, and dispossession, which have produced or inhibited the kinds of freedoms Charbonnier is intent on mapping. Even in times of supposed affluence, the freedoms associated with liberalism are far less common in reality than they are on a university whiteboard. All of which is to underscore the asymmetries and discontinuities attending affluence and freedom under the material conditions of petrocultural life.

Climate in Crisis: Unnerving the Energy Subject

Despite similarities to existing petrocultural perspectives and approaches – yet also blindspots to complexities raised by those perspectives and approaches – Charbonnier's analysis of the development of political subjectivity can nonetheless help to reframe the function of the energy subject within the critical practice of the energy humanities, particularly because affluence, due to its climate impact, is less and less tenable as the material basis of modern sociality. Especially relevant, here, is a core problem identified by Charbonnier about the misfit that has developed between modern subjectivity – the subject of affluence and freedom – and the world that has emerged from the processes making that subjectivity possible in the first place. The result is a gap or break that he frames, provocatively, in temporal terms:

> Sovereignty and property, abundance and scarcity, autonomy and extraction, market and production – these dimensions of modern political reflexivity are all undergoing profound changes. The world in which this repertoire of categories and institutions now has to function has changed so fundamentally since their establishment, and what is more under their direct or indirect influence, that it is imperative to take note of this transformation. However, curiously, and probably for the first time since humanity posed the question of the principles of its organization, our epistemo-political base has changed less quickly than the world it helped to build: the right to property, the productive schema, these cardinal elements in the arrangement between humans and nonhumans now prevalent in the world are all older than the geo-ecological reality that we inhabit. (2021: 238–239; emphasis added)

The myriad practices – capitalist accumulation and exchange, resource extraction, and so on – materializing the social conditions constitutive of affluence and freedom have produced environmental consequences that outstrip the subjectivity and the political categories they have served to enable. Affluence and freedom need each other, but the fossil-fueled means necessary for producing and reproducing afflu-ence have generated an externality – climate crisis – that imperils this relation. And while liberalism has tried and persists in trying to suture the resulting gap between affluence and freedom, the process of doing so only exacerbates the climactic prob-lem it's intended to fix. The contradiction is insoluble, and chronic: the cherished values key to the liberal 'good life' depend on material expenditure – burning fossil fuels – that, in its effect on the climate, jeopardizes life as such.

For thinkers in the energy humanities, Charbonnier's framing of modern sub-jectivity and its rupture poses a generative challenge. We have tended to understand problems of belatedness with reference to long-since burnt carbon haunting the fu-ture as well as the present: what Andreas Malm terms "all those historical fires, [...] the cumulative emissions, the pulses of CO_2 stacked on top of each other" (2018: 5). Against such belatedness, we have endeavored to conceptualize transition in terms of a passage from one energy system to another that, whether explicitly or only tac-itly, presupposes – which is to say takes as given without really theorizing – a refash-ioned subjectivity. Charbonnier's account inverts these coordinates by conceptual-izing the modern subject as itself obdurate and belated: the locus of what we could call a type of subjectivity deepening over modernity's long unfolding, and as such entirely consonant with a modern energy history characterized not by transition, by changes from one energy form to another, but by accumulation, by the accretive piling on of ever more fuels in the energy mix.[7]

Translated into an energy humanities idiom, in which energy is front and centre, we might say that the subject of affluence and freedom is constitutively and always already a fossil fuel subject, yet one that is unknowing and unaware of its existence and ontology as such a subject. Energy subjectivity remains internal to the dialectic of affluence and freedom necessary for such subjectivity's deepening, normaliza-tion, and very possibility as a condition of being. Today, though, this energy subject is also and inextricably a climate subject: one all too aware and indeed incapable of not knowing its genesis in the externality constituted by climate crisis (a recogni-tion that will recast postures and practices of explicit climate denial and petro-mas-culine excess as themselves dysfunctional modes of such incapacity not to know). This climate subject is still and inescapably a fossil fuel subject. But it has become

---

7   Our invocation of subjectivity deepening recalls Diamanti's account of "energy deepening" cited earlier. Christophe Bonneuil and Jean-Baptiste Fressoz vividly explain the fallacy of en-ergy transition as phrase and concept: "if history teaches us one thing, it is that there never has been an energy transition. There was not a movement from wood to coal, then from coal to oil, then from oil to nuclear. The history of energy is not one of transitions, but rather of successive additions of new sources of primary energy" (2017: 101). At stake in such addition is energy intensification: a measure of Jevons paradox (efficiency does not lead to less con-sumption but to rising demand) exemplified, today, by the voracious energy hunger of A.I.

a fossil fuel subject reconstituted, even transmuted through its climate encounter: a subject now simultaneously internal and external to the dialectic of affluence and freedom that has to recognize, because it cannot avoid experiencing, its subjection to energy through the material consequences of fossil fueled power registered in climate catastrophe and ecological collapse. Ground, one might say, has unnervingly become figure.[8]

For his part, Charbonnier sees the gap or break he identifies as a problem in need of solution (an instinct that is understandable and unsurprising, given how dire the problem is). "We inherit a world," he observes, "that no available political category is designed to manage, and therefore we are faced with a seemingly impossible task" (2021: 261). Charbonnier nonetheless finds within this daunting semblance the seeds of a cautious optimism, as he goes on to elaborate:

> This historic loneliness, the fact that the past and the future seem definitively lost to us, and the discouragement that may ensue, can nevertheless be tempered if we manage to tell the story of our recent history and to organize the map of our attachments so that politics and the use of the Earth are no longer heterogeneous. (2021: 261)

Given Charbonnier's methodological commitments, this stated desire to somehow suture the rift that has developed between freedom and affluence, the former dragging behind as the latter races ahead, comes as a surprise. Within the larger arc of Charbonnier's argument, it constitutes a methodological about-face, with implications for the account he wishes to offer. Recall a key point we noted earlier: that Charbonnier prefers to compose an environmental history of ideas rather than a history of environmental ideas because, for him, the latter is normative, driven by principles, a "philosophical anteriority, converted into a moral priority" (2021: 20). Yet in our reading of his argument's dénouement the effort to suture the break introduced by climate crisis so as to renovate the subject of affluence and freedom beyond its rupture is fully normative as a matter of political method. Posed as a question: does the conditional form of narrative management proposed by Charbonnier in the passage from the conclusion of his study quoted above mean that the story he tells breaks with the impulses guiding an environmental history of ideas to become a history of environmental ideas after all? Why is the rift or break framed as a problem in need of a solution, instead of an assessment of new material conditions for political subjectivity, whose consequences will be decided by history?

What if the gap that Charbonnier seeks to close, the rift in subjectivity created by the dislocation of freedom from affluence that he strives to suture, were taken in-

---

8   We draw inspiration from the brilliant analysis by Jennifer Wenzel (2022) of the figure-ground relation at work in energy infrastructure (157–159).

stead as an analytic opening? The question is foremost a methodological one. Reading the rift or break to offer an opening means resisting the normative and advancing, instead, the analytic. And to us, the prospect of energy subjectivity is most interesting and most generative as a means of and to analysis: not a matter of this or that content, of various distinctive characteristics, and still less a matter of principle, of what to do and how to do it, but instead a position or parametric with and through which we can assess the coordinates of the present conjuncture.

"We are citizens and subjects of fossil fuels through and through, whether we know it or not. And so any meaningful response to climate change will have to tarry with the world and the people that have been made from oil" (Szeman and Boyer, 2017: 1). We began by noting the absence of any sustained account of the fossil fuel subject, even though appeals to it are frequently made (if usually off-handedly and often for rhetorical purposes, rather than analytic ones). The attempt to provide such an account reveals the conditions for the politics of energy at the present time. Were one to identify a proper energy subject, a first and perhaps most obvious approach would be empirical, involving the creation of a list of qualities or characteristics that distinguish the fossil fuel subject from others. But this approach runs into immediate problems, precisely because as we have argued here all subjects are energy subjects, immanent to and an expression of their socio-historical circumstances, both result and process in a properly Hegelian fashion. While one might manage to identify different capacities and possibilities attendant to levels of available resources, doing so would only reaffirm the immanence of subjects with energy in the fossil fuel era.

The approach we've taken here, by contrast, works to unnerve not reaffirm such immanence. The moment when energy subjects are no longer immanent to modernity's fossil fueled history is when they fully recognize how and why they are subjects constituted by energy. And this recognition only happens when they come to understand a limit outside of the system that sustains them, one that threatens the continuation of their circumstances and capacities. A break or rupture in the immanent relationship between energy subject and energy reality is needed to expose what has been obscured within the latter: recognition and understanding of the consequences of climate crisis and environmental devastation. Charbonnier wants to sustain the liberal freedoms produced by high-energy social life by refiguring affluence, making certain that it no longer has climate implications. Such refiguration would preserve the immanence of the energy subject, leaving intact and unseen its status as the ground on which the dramas of liberal, volitional subjectivity and subjection continue to unfold. By occluding the status of energy subjectivity as a fundamental mode of subjection inextricable from climate crisis and the subjectivity it provokes into being, any refiguration of affluence will only close the opening, and thereby jeopardize potent critical and political capacities, afforded once we come to recognize the inextricable entanglement of energy subject with climate subject, energy reality with climate catastrophe.

Why there hasn't been an account of the energy subject to date is perhaps because we don't need it. The moment when the energy subject comes to understand itself as such, when its immanence with the affluence of energy has been shattered, it becomes something else: what we here have named the climate subject. This climate subject, we want to emphasize, is very different from the planetary subject critiqued so witheringly by Peter Osborne, precisely because it signifies not the climate as subject, but human subjection by and to the climate (a prospect and process that is, to use the charge leveled by Bruno Latour against Marxism that Osborne reiterates with irony in his essay, excessively social) (2024: 7, 12, 14). The political challenge we face is not to rush to close the gap between freedom and affluence that so troubles Charbonnier, but to understand the impact of our ongoing commitments to modern notions of either freedom or affluence, or both. The two might need to change, separately or in concert. And the degree to which they might need to do so, and how and to what ends, will require measurement not in terms of per capita energy use, but by degrees Celsius of a planetary warming.

Bibliography

Adorno, Theodor W. (2003): "Progress (For Jacob König)," trans. Henry W. Pickford. In: Rolf Tiedemann (ed.): Can One Live After Auschwitz? A Philosophical Reader, Palo Alto: Stanford University Press, pp. 126–145.

Bloom, Brett (2015): Petro-Subjectivity. De-Industrializing Our Sense of Self, Ft. Wayne, IN: Breakdown Break Down Press.

Bonneuil, Christope and Jean-Baptiste Fressoz (2017): The Shock of the Anthropocene, trans. David Fernbach, London: Verso.

Chakrabarty, Dipesh (2009): "The Climate of History: Four Theses." In: Critical Inquiry 35/2, pp. 197–222.

Charbonnier, Pierre (2021): Affluence and Freedom: An Environmental History of Political Ideas, trans. Andrew Brown, Cambridge: Polity.

Conrad, Joseph (1910): "The Secret Sharer." In: Harper's Monthly Magazine 121/723 + 724, pp. 349–361, 530–542.

Daggett, Cara (2019): The Birth of Energy: Fossil Fuels, Thermodynamics, and the Politics of Work, Durham: Duke University Press.

Debeir, Jean-Claude, Jean-Paul Deléage, and Daniel Hémery (1991): In the Servitude of Power: Energy and Civilization Through the Ages, London: Zed Books.

Diamanti, Jeff (2021): Climate and Capital in the Age of Petroleum: Locating Terminal Landscapes, London: Bloomsbury.

Domingues, José Maurício (2023): "Critical Theory and Climate Change: Collective Subjectivity, Evolution and Modernity." In: International Journal of Politics, Culture, and Society 37/4: 459–475. https://doi.org/10.1007/s10767-023-09462-1.

Foucault, Michel (1982): "The Subject and Power," trans. Leslie Sawyer. In: Critical Inquiry 8/4, pp. 777–795. https://doi.org/10.1086/448181.

Gailing, Ludger (2016): "Transforming Energy Systems by Transforming Power Relations: Insights from Dispositive Thinking and Governmentality Studies." In: Innovation: The European Journal of Social Science Research, 29/3, pp. 243–261. https://doi.org/10.1080/13511610.2016.1201650.

Hamilton, Scott (2019): "I Am Uncertain, But We Are Not: A new Subjectivity of the Anthropocene." In: Review of International Studies 45/4, pp. 607–626. https://doi.org/10.1017/S0260210519000135.

Huber, Matt (2013): Lifeblood: Oil, Freedom, and the Forces of Capital, Minneapolis: University of Minnesota Press.

Huber, Matt (2019): "Ecological Politics for the Working Class." In: Catalyst 3/1. https://catalyst-journal.com/2019/07/ecological-politics-for-the-working-class.

Johnson, Robert (2019): Mineral Rites: An Archaeology of the Fossil Economy, Baltimore: Johns Hopkins University Press.

LeMenager, Stephanie (2014): Living Oil: Petroleum Culture in the American Century, New York: Oxford University Press.

Malm, Andreas (2016): Fossil Capital: The Rise of Steam Power and the Roots of Global Warming, New York: Verso.

Malm, Andreas (2018): The Progress of This Storm: Nature and Society in a Warming World, New York: Verso.

Osborne, Peter (2024): "The Planet as Political Subject?" In: New Left Review 145, pp. 1–14.

Simpson, Mark and Imre Szeman (2021): "Impasse Time." In: South Atlantic Quarterly 120/1, pp. 77–89. https://doi.org/10.1215/00382876-8795730.

Szeman, Imre and Dominic Boyer (2017): "Introduction: On the Energy Humanities." In: Energy Humanities: An Anthology, Baltimore: Johns Hopkins University Press, pp. 1–13.

Wenzel, Jennifer (2022): "Forms of Life: Thinking Fossil Infrastructure and Its Narrative Grammar." In: Social Text 40/4 (153), pp. 153–179. https://doi.org/10.1215/01642472-10013360.

The Cultural Processing of Oil: Between Greed and Messianism
Interview with Angelina Davydova

Ilya Kalinin

Angelina Davydova: Oil and other fossil fuels have had an uneasy reputation and predominantly a bad image over the past decades, being considered the main culprits of the climate crisis, the extractivist model, inequality, and suffering. But can we really consider them to be autonomous non-human agents, or do you see their agency as always tied to human activity (corporate, profit-driven, etc.)?

Ilya Kalinin: Regardless of how we resolve the question of the autonomous agency of oil and other fossil fuels, the primary culprit behind the climate crisis, growing inequality, and other socio-political problems associated with the extractivist economic model is the human being. Any type of fossil fuel, until it is extracted and integrated into technological chains for energy production, is essentially neither "fossil" (the word derives from Latin *fossilis*, "dug up") nor "fuel" (from Latin *focus*, "hearth, fireplace").

From a non-human perspective, oil and other hydrocarbon compounds are elements of the Earth's geological structure, each with its own formation history, combining in various ways with other elements (geological formations), and governed by physical and chemical laws. The nature of these laws fundamentally differs from the socio-historical patterns characteristic of human societies: they operate on different temporalities, have different organizational forms, and follow different principles of functioning. However, this does not exclude the reciprocal influence of humans on the laws of nature—something Vladimir Vernadsky already wrote about in the 1930s in his work *Scientific Thought as a Planetary Phenomenon*.

For the ancient Zoroastrians of the Caspian region, oil and the accompanying gas were sacred substances, associated with fire, which they worshipped by building temples at sites where these substances naturally emerged at the surface. One such temple is Ateshgah, located 30 km from modern-day Baku. The literal translation of its name is "House of Fire." For thousands of years, underground gas would erupt to the surface here and ignite upon contact with oxygen—making the site particularly significant for Zoroastrians. In the 1850s, oil fields were discovered there, and a refinery was built near the temple. As a result, pressure dropped, the natural gas seepage ceased, and the temple fires gradually dwindled. Rational technologies replaced ritual practices; the refinery claimed what once belonged to the temple; the emanation of the divine was turned into a natural resource. The religious community saw a disappearance of the fires as a heavenly "oil curse" and slowly abandoned Ateshgah. In 1880, the last Hindu living there returned to India, and in 1902, the last flame went out.

This is a story about how oil and gas, once seen as emanations of divine grandeur, became sources of material prosperity through their integration into a different type of socio-cultural relations. But this wasn't their final transformation. In the 21st century, the temple was restored, and its "sacred" fires now burn again—fueled by gas specifically piped to the altars. However, these gas flames now refer less to religious origins and more to the idea of cultural heritage and the pragmatics of the tourism industry.

Seen through the eyes of modern humans, oil becomes a resource—a pure potentiality that can be technologically utilized and transformed into energy or the physical base of various synthetic materials. Concentrating in itself the work of nature that took millions of geological years, oil becomes not only a source of energy but also a source of temptation. The alluring possibility of appropriating this work of nature leads to consequences that say more about humans than about oil (and the same can be said of other mineral resources, although oil can be seen as their exemplary case in many respects).

On one hand, the technologies that trigger the energetic and chemical transformations of oil help solve many social problems and improve living standards by providing access to cheap energy and inexpensive synthetic materials. On the other hand, while solving some social problems, these very technologies create new ones—not only social but also ecological. Hydrocarbon energy can combat poverty, but it can also produce it; it can reduce inequality or intensify it; it can stimulate or block any useful creative activity. Once again, oil is a temptation, grounded in the possibility of appropriating massive volumes of someone else's labour. This is an instance of appropriation or alienation that fails to recognise its own character as such—since it is the appropriation of labour performed by nature. Yet at the same time, oil is a challenge—a challenge that can be met with resistance to this temptation.

In the end, the possibility of transitioning to other energy sources not based on hydrocarbons also becomes feasible thanks to the level of development achieved through hydrocarbons (coal, peat, oil, gas). The prospect of global ecological catastrophe raises the stakes of this evolutionary dialectic to the highest level. The question becomes one of choosing between denying the hydrocarbon foundations of modern civilization and denying humanity itself. Thus, the agency of oil is that of a mirror—one in which humanity can see a reflection of its desires and fears. It is the non-human that allows us to recognize the human, all too human (*Menschliches, Allzumenschliches*)—in the critical sense Nietzsche meant in the title of his book.

AD: What role do you think oil plays in global culture? Would that role be different in oil-extracting and exporting countries like Russia?

IK: Having become the primary economic resource of the past century, oil inevitably also became a significant object of cultural reflection. In a sense, one could say that oil is not only processed in cracking plants and used to fuel internal combustion engines—it also undergoes profound symbolic processing once it enters the realm of cultural representation. The outcomes of this cultural oil refining are even more diverse than the material products resulting from the physical and chemical transformation of hydrocarbon bonds. The specific nature of these cultural petro-products depends on the political identity of their producers; it is rooted in the particular languages of cultural traditions used in their production; it acquires distinctive shades shaped by the ideological or religious preferences of their consumers. The cultural byproducts of oil—literary texts, feature and documentary films, works of visual art, advertisements and social posters, journalistic reports and opinion essays—created by American conservatives will differ from those produced by left-liberal circles in Canada or Norway. The cultural petro-products of Middle East Islamists are unmistakably different from the oil-related narratives of Latin American leftists. Reflections on oil mediated by the interests of transnational corporations are fundamentally different from those expressed by local and ethnic communities living in oil-producing territories. The list of possible combinations—comprising political, ideological, and cultural coordinates—is open-ended.

As for the volume of cultural processing, it tends to correlate with whether a country is an oil producer or merely a consumer. In Russia, the specifics of cultural engagement with oil are deeply rooted in the long and eventful history of the industry itself, which has undergone several boom periods, each aligned with different political eras of Russian statehood. One can find in this history examples of revolutionary critiques of the oil fever that gripped the Russian Empire in its final decades; celebratory portrayals of Soviet oil as emancipated from exploitation and unleashing energy for socialist construction; and triumphant odes to West Siberian oil, whose rich deposits allowed the USSR by 1975 to become the world's leading oil producer, rapidly expand its oil exports, and secure that particular blend of geopolitical power and relative consumer prosperity characteristic of the late socialist period.

This enthusiasm gave way to a widespread oil-related ressentiment in the late 1980s and 1990s—a tightly woven tangle of lamentations over oil dependence and accusations against the West for crashing global oil prices. Over the past few decades, under Putin's uninterrupted leadership, two main vectors of cultural oil-processing have emerged, closely interlinked. The first trend can be described as postmodern and neoliberal: oil is portrayed as an endlessly metamorphosing substance whose transformations promise personal wealth. In this view, oil becomes the embodiment of human libido, a symbol of desire for possession, a cynical justification of greed and the pursuit of limitless profit. The second trend can be seen as a conservative version of oil-processing: oil is framed as a resource of state patriotism and a national idea. It becomes a sign of the nation's historical chosenness, a natural proof of its right to geopolitical dominance, a geological foundation for political sovereignty. These two trends coexist like the two heads of the eagle on the Russian imperial coat of arms. They are two sides of the Putin regime—its real raison d'être and its official image.

AD: Have cultural perceptions of oil changed from the times of the Soviet Union to post-Soviet Russia? And since the beginning of the full-scale war in Ukraine in 2022?

IK: First of all, it's important to note that cultural reception of oil was never homogeneous, not even during the Soviet period—and it certainly isn't today. However, if we are to outline the most general dominant narratives characteristic of the official versions of Soviet and post-Soviet petrocultures, we can say the following: The mainstream of Soviet oil representation emphasized its connection to modernization, the movement toward the horizon of socialism, the overcoming of economic and cultural backwardness caused by colonial oppression in the imperial peripheries, and proletarian internationalism. A key mechanism of this discursive transformation was the industrial conversion of a dark geological past into the bright future of communism. Oil was defined not in terms of a commodity, but as a productive force, participating in the construction of a new world on par with the working class. Official Post-Soviet mainstream of oil representation identify it with national tradition, a rich natural inheritance granted to Russia so that it may fulfil its historical mission. The inner tension that this official discourse of natural heritage—symbolically aligned with traditional values rooted in national soil—tries to conceal lies in the dual nature of legal ownership over subsoil resources. On the one hand, under the law, Russia's subsoil resources belong to the Russian state (the people of Russia); on the other, they are in the temporary use of private companies and state corporations, whose profits are used for the personal enrichment of those within Putin's inner circle. This effective monopolization of access to natural resources—entirely controlled by the political regime and its constituent interest groups—gives rise to a specific form of oil fetishism, intertwining the pursuit of property with the pursuit of power. Possessing oil as a commodity that brings personal wealth fuels the obsession with oil as a resource that guarantees the political power of the state—and vice versa. This blend of personal greed and historical messianism forms the magical power of oil that internally consolidates the Putin regime.

The invasion of Ukraine and the sanctions imposed by the US and EU on Russian oil trade have changed the directions of export routes and the logistics of its transportation. Oil sold on foreign markets now resembles contraband: its flows are concealed, volumes kept secret, and the tankers that carry it operate in a legal grey zone—forming a "shadow" or "dark" fleet reminiscent of pirate squadrons of the past. (It is only now that the violence carried by these ships does not take the form of a crew of ruthless people outside the reach of the law. Instead, this violence is in the form of oil, which also cannot be controlled by the law, but allows a particular state to finance its war.) Like all that is hidden, obscured from view, and kept secret, this ghostly existence of Russian oil endows it with even greater symbolic significance—not only in the economic logic of war but also in the political unconscious, both of Russia and of the world. The ghost of Russian oil haunts not only Southeast Asia but also Europe, seductively reminding elites of their recent prosperity and testing the EU's future resilience.

For those countries and companies that continue to purchase Russian oil or liquefied gas, this trade has come to resemble a kind of guilty pleasure: the price compels them to turn a blind eye to the source of the desired commodity, the semi- or outright illegal methods of its delivery and payment, and the environmental risks associated with the tankers' technical condition. This guilty pleasure concentrates a whole range of problems and consequences: the world market's unwillingness to let go of Russia's share of hydrocarbons; the understanding that their purchase directly finances the war; a conscious or unconscious sense of guilt among those who politically oppose the war; and an even deeper demonization of Russia, fueled by this internal guilt of complicity in its financial support.

Meanwhile, for many Global South countries, the refusal to support anti-Russian sanctions becomes a way to signal their dissatisfaction with the existing global order— what allows the Russian leadership to indulge in the hope that Russia can become the leader of this movement. In this sense, the willingness to deal with Russian oil becomes an important marker of the desire to revise the current world order and its power structures.

For Russia itself, the redirection of oil flows from West to East, accompanied by a move into opacity, serves as a narrative for justifying not only an economic and political but also a cultural and civilizational turn. In his speeches, Putin frequently invokes the figure of Prince Alexander Nevsky, who in the mid-13th century fought Danish and German knightly orders while remaining loyal to the Mongol Golden Horde. Nevsky was canonized during the reign of Ivan the Terrible and became an icon of national patriotism, revived again under Peter the First and Stalin. In Putin's interpretation, Nevsky's political choice stemmed from the fact that Mongol military dominance did not involve attempts to strip the Russian people of their civilizational identity, whereas Europeans always sought to impose their cultural values on Russia. These references to a particular reading of the past transparently justify the turn that both Putin and the country he governs are now undertaking. The message is a tacit acknowledgment of China's economic and political dominance—one Russia recognizes and is nearly prepared to formally submit to.

Despite being economically unfavourable for Russia, trade with China under the latter's conditions is, in Putin's logic, strategically more appropriate than the formerly mutually beneficial trade with Europe. His argument might be reconstructed as follows: Previously, Russian oil sold to the West was exchanged not only for dollars and euros, but also for 'Western values'—liberal democracy, the supremacy of international law over national one, LGBT rights, and so on. In other words, along with exported oil, Russia was losing its traditional national values. Shared political and cultural values formed the informal yet essential condition of a shared market—thus, the western vector of Russian oil exports led to reciprocal Westernization of Russia.

Now, the situation has changed drastically. China buys Russian oil cheaply but does not attempt to impose its civilizational norms on Russia. Yes, Russian oil is sold to China at a discount, and much of the yuan received remains in Chinese banks—but in exchange, China sells Russia just goods, not values. So now, by selling its oil to the East, Russia does not lose its unique national identity; on the contrary, it can reinforce it—using the money and goods received from the East to do so.

AD: How can one convey or communicate the need to abandon oil ("leave it in the ground") to economic and political systems and societies whose wellbeing is tied to oil extraction?

IK: If abandoning oil simply required the creation of compelling images and narratives demonstrating the positive outcomes of doing so—and the catastrophic consequences of continuing extraction—then oil would have long since been peacefully left in the ground. As long as oil-producing countries have buyers, extraction will continue, bringing with it both prosperity and all the socio-political problems encompassed by the term "resource curse" as well as ecological disasters and climate changes.

Of course, the way ideas are articulated affects how they influence people's perceptions and imaginations—and thereby public opinion as a whole. But oil will only stay in the ground when humanity no longer needs it above. In this regard, turning to the classic Marxist framework of base and superstructure is entirely appropriate. As long as the oil business remains one of the most profitable sectors, even the most rational arguments, vivid imagery, and emotionally powerful stories advocating the necessity of abandoning intensive oil extraction will persuade everyone—except those directly tied to the business and its superprofits.

However, what we are now witnessing is a transformation of the very economic base linked to oil extraction and processing. There is hope that green technologies will significantly reduce (and eventually eliminate) the use of hydrocarbons in energy production. The horizon for phasing out internal combustion engines in road transportation already appears attainable. The development of hydrogen-powered engines for aviation is constantly postponed, but movement in that direction has begun. Most likely, hydrocarbons will still be needed for the production of synthetic materials. But removing them from the energy sector—along with phasing out internal combustion engines—would drastically reduce their overall consumption, and thus CO_2 emissions into the atmosphere (with the alternative possibility of directing CO_2 into agricultural greenhouses to stimulate plant growth).

Still, the logic of capitalism—difficult to imagine without the imperative of economic growth fueled by increased consumption—will continue to leave room for the temptation to tap nature's reserves, drawing on minerals accumulated through its labour. So, the key question becomes either the rejection of the very idea of economic growth, or the decoupling of growth mechanisms from the volume of extracted resources—which are nothing other than products of non-human labour. And these products are alienated from nature by humans without even a thought of compensation for the work done—unlike the case of capitalist exploitation of humans by other humans.

AD: How has the representation of oil and human activities connected to oil been portrayed in international cinema and in recent Russian cinema?

IK: One might intuitively assume a direct correlation between a country's high economic dependence on oil extraction and the way this extraction is portrayed in its national cinema—specifically, the extent to which oil is mythologized positively. However, tracing this correlation proves difficult, as only a few countries meet the necessary conditions: state control over oil-producing companies and a well-developed national film industry funded by the state. In most countries, both the oil business and film production are driven by private commercial interests, making their agendas nearly impossible to align. The former caters to a narrow circle of direct beneficiaries and industry insiders, while the latter targets a broader audience—one that may benefit daily from the comforts of the hydrocarbon civilization, but is not a direct recipient of oil rents and is increasingly aware of this civilization's environmental and social costs. These structural conditions likely help explain the consistent critical stance cinema has taken toward oil, and the dark imprint it leaves on people and landscapes tied to its production.

Western cinema has reproduced this critical gaze toward oil infrastructure—extraction, transport, and refinement—at least since the 1920s. Global cinema, however, also contains alternative portrayals and modes of representing oil. Positive mythologization of extractive labor—in film and cultural production more broadly—was typical of many developing and socialist countries where industrialization overlapped with ideological narratives of national and/or class liberation. A model for this mythology of emancipated labor, drawing forth underground riches "belonging to the people," was Soviet culture. In 1927, Moscow's Sovkino studio released the cultural-educational film OIL (dir. N. Lebedev, A. Litvinov), which, according to a Soviet film critic, "had the good fortune to reveal our oil power," ensuring that "both we and foreigners would see the unlimited potential of the USSR." In the 1950s, Roman Karmen directed two documentaries—THE STORY OF THE CASPIAN OIL WORKERS (1953) and CONQUERORS OF THE SEA (1959)—marking a shift from Stalinist socialist realism to the lyrical cinema of the Thaw. In the first film, oil is embedded in a heroic narrative, steeped in collectivist techno-optimism and the political program of late Stalinism; in the second, industrial oil production is portrayed through interest in the everyday lives of workers and the surrounding natural elements. In 1958, FIRES OF BAKU (dir. A. Zarkhi, I. Kheifits, R. Takhmasib) came out, embedding the story of Caspian oil into the larger history of the 20th century: the revolutionary movement, civil war, 1930s industrialization, and World War II. The film's screen history itself reflected the ironic twists of Soviet political dynamics. While the film's central subject matter – oil – remained unchanged, its central political protagonists were subjected to a gradual censorship that reflected the political dynamics of the era. It was shot in 1950 under Stalin, with bloody people's commissar of internal affairs Lavrentiy Beria—then head of the oil indus-try—featuring prominently. Both Stalin, who led the Bolshevik underground in Baku during the first Russian revolution of 1905–1907, and Beria occupied a signif-icant place in the patriotic narrative about Soviet oil. But by the time of the film's release, Beria had been executed, and his scenes were cut. Then, in 1968, Stalin's character was also removed, further 'purifying' the oil mythology.

In 1978, two major films about the discovery of West Siberian oil appeared: SIBERIADE, a four-part epic by A. Konchalovsky (Grand Prix, Cannes 1979), and STRATEGY OF RISK, a three-part television film by A. Proshkin. In 1983, A. Granik's THE SCENE OF ACTION continued this theme, based on Alexander Prokhanov's novel about building a major refinery in a Siberian city (modeled on Tobolsk). These films used industrial narratives of exploration and refining, interwoven with melodramatic conflicts and love stories, transforming hydrocarbon energy into the energies of Eros and Thanatos. Beyond industrial and historical genres, oil also appeared in popular genres like comedy and action, as in the hit Thaw-era comedy THE GAS STATION QUEEN (1962, dir. A. Mishurin, N. Litus) and the Azerbaijani-shot action-comedy DON'T BE AFRAID, I'M WITH YOU (1981, dir. Y. Gusman). Thus, late Soviet cinema linked oil not just with labour, but also with leisure, turning its fluid substance into 'humor' (Latin *humor* = moisture), and a resource for both comedic and dramatic plotlines.

By the Perestroika era, cinema largely abandoned oil. Plummeting oil prices and declining extraction in the mid-1980s intensified the USSR's economic collapse and political destabilization. Oil's blackness came to signify not 'black gold,' but the bleak realism of *chernukha* (the notion derived from the Russian word for 'black' – *cherny*), a genre depicting the grim disintegration of late-Soviet life. Aesthetically powerful and socially unforgiving, Pyotr Lutsik's Outskirts (1998) stands as perhaps the only Russian film offering a deeply critical cinematic reflection on oil's role in wealth accumulation. Its critique centers on the vampiric political economy of wealth built on predatory privatization and the conversion of public good into private capital. This tone—giving the oil magnate infernal, devilish traits—anticipates the thematic treatment of oil in THERE WILL BE BLOOD a decade later (notably, Lutsik's team may have been familiar with Upton Sinclair's 1927 novel *Oil!*, the source for Anderson's film). Outskirts' dark and grotesque aesthetic places oil at the heart of artistic reckoning with the destruction of social worlds by 1990s neoliberal reforms. The film portrays oil as the essence of a fluid modernity in which total economization strips life of its ontological, ethical, and existential foundations—reducing societal interaction to a duel between vampire capital and the dispossessed, cast to the margins but ready to fight for justice. Their bloody social revenge takes form in a zombie uprising. Finally, the last major post-Soviet representation of oil—reflecting Putin-era patriotic revalorization of the Soviet past—is the TV series BIG OIL (dir. A. Cherkasov, 2009). Its depiction of oil development in West Siberia during the 1960s–1980s is filtered through the ideological lens of 2000s Russia, centred on the desire to restore the USSR's lost strategic might by transforming into an energy superpower.

AD: Being a fossil fuel, in what way is oil connected to the concepts of death and resurrection, or new life, within the Russian (or perhaps also global) political and cultural context?

IK: The burning oil torches erupting from the ground in the Caspian region—around which Zoroastrians built temple complexes—were sites where the sacred and the profane intersected, linking the earthly and the otherworldly. The religious rituals performed around these oil altars mediated communication between humans and gods, between cycles of earthly life and the eternal struggle between good and evil, creation and destruction. In this sense, oil has long been embedded in those systems of exchange that Georges Bataille termed "general economy"—a realm that encompasses not only the material but also the symbolic, and whose law includes not only accumulation but also expenditure: sacrifice and destruction of surplus.

Human history, therefore, has long transformed the material substance of oil into an element of magical dialogue between humans and the Other—death, rebirth, transition into a new state.

On a more literal and direct level, oil and death have gone hand in hand ever since oil began to be used not only in pharmaceuticals (a practice that dates back to ancient

Babylon), but also in internal combustion engines. From that point onward, oil became not only the object of war but also a significant factor in its course—and even
its source. Oil powers not only engines of war machines but also fuels the "war machine" in the Deleuzian sense (machine as a system for channeling and processing all
forms of energy), which Iranian philosopher Reza Negarestani explores in *Cyclono-
pedia* (2008). Thus, since the 20th century, the link between oil and war (i.e., death)
can be described not only in terms of material struggles over strategic resources, but
also in a structural sense—a homology between substance of energy concentration
(oil) and ways to utilize huge amounts of energy (war).

In Soviet and Russian cultural reflection on oil, we see a specific emphasis on
its fundamental connection to threshold moments of human existence. Perhaps the
symbolic economy of oil was initially inspired by the phonetic rhyme in the Russian language between *neft'* (oil) and *smert'* (death). This sonic echo was reinforced
by oil's foundational role in both the Soviet economy—which grew increasingly oil-
dependent from the 1970s and for which oil was partly responsible for both citizens'
relative material wellbeing and the ultimate collapse (death) of Soviet society—and
in the post-Soviet Russian economy, where oil prices became arguably the main de-
terminant of national prosperity; access to hydrocarbon resources and the distribution of oil rents formed the basis of governance mechanisms linking the state,
elites, and society; export volumes and routes shaped the geopolitical framework of
foreign policy. As a result, *neft'* and *smert'* evolved from lexical elements that could
simply rhyme into conceptual motifs at the heart of philosophical reflection on human existence in the face of death. In this cultural context, oil became an ontological
operator of *Sein zum Tode*—Heidegger's "being-toward-death."

The history of Soviet and post-Soviet cinematic representations of oil illustrates
a mythological epic tracing the decline of oil's existential potential—once invested
in the metaphysical task of human salvation. (This is a topic I am currently writing
a dedicated study on.) Roman Karmen's THE STORY OF THE CASPIAN OIL WORKERS
(1953), a prime example of Stalinist high culture, portrays its protagonists as semi-
divine heroes. Under the guidance of the immortal leader, they achieve technological
triumph over natural elements and themselves become immortal through the socialist liturgy (Greek: "public service") of heroic labour. Andrei Konchalovsky's SIBERI-
ADE (1978) links the historical saga of discovering West Siberian oil to the meta-his-
torical philosophy of Russian cosmism—particularly the work of Nikolai Fedorov
(1829–1903), who proposed that humanity's salvation was impossible without the
resurrection of the dead. The film's finale depicts such a resurrection: as oil bursts
into flames, the ancestors of Soviet oil workers rise from their burning graves. Pyotr
Lutsik's OUTSKIRTS (1998) features protagonists who—having been dispossessed of
their former collective farmland, privatized by a 'New Russian' oligarch to exploit a
newly discovered oil field—appear as zombies: the dead who have not been buried.
At the core of this post-Soviet oil narrative is a story of repression (in both psycho-

analytic and socio-economic senses), wherein 1990s neoliberal capitalism repressed former social structures and the bearers of historical memory about this past. The TV series BIG OIL (2009) attempts to revive this memory of the Soviet past, but does so through the discursive templates of patriotic glorification typical of Putin-era historical politics since the mid-2000s. The result is a wax museum—a self-parodying attempt to breathe life into puppet-like characters. The viewer sees a parade of clumsy, grotesque imitations of socialist realist narrative forms in their most hollow and ritualized versions.

This interplay between material and symbolic economies reflects a peculiar symmetry: just as the post-Soviet oil business parasitizes the legacy of the Soviet oil industry, so does post-Soviet cinematic staging of this industry rely on lifeless and stillborn characters who—with comedic seriousness—try to parasitize the cultural legacy of socialist realism. In schematic terms, the historical dialectic outlined above—where oil functions as a driver of metaphysical transformations of human existence—can be summarized as follows: immortality → death and resurrection → return of the unburied (zombies) → parade of the stillborn (*nature morte* instead of portrait).

AD: Can you imagine a post-fossil future for oil? What could its cultural importance be?

IK: Of course, it's tempting to dream of a future in which fossil fuels are primarily used as materials for contemporary art or as exhibition pieces in museums of industrial heritage. Perhaps it will be precisely the current artistic representation of the social and ecological effects of the hydrocarbon civilization—whose impact on humanity and the planet is broader and more dramatic than the direct consequences of the so-called 'resource curse,' which mainly affects producer countries—that will hasten the transformation of internal combustion engines into museum artifacts. It's unlikely that oil will be completely replaced as a raw material for the chemical industry, but the advancement of waste collection practices and recycling technologies could significantly reduce the sector's reliance on primary hydrocarbon feedstocks. All of this could lead to a radical reduction in oil extraction: the conservation of existing fields, a halt to the development of new or hard-to-reach reserves—especially in regions like the Arctic, where fragile ecosystems are at risk of collapse with global consequences.

If these goals can be achieved—if oil extraction and carbon emissions are substantially reduced—it would help resolve a significant portion of both environmental and political problems. Capital would have to curb its appetite and seek out alternative areas of investment—less profitable for itself, but also less destructive to the natural and social environments. Autocracies, having lost their source of natural rent, would become more dependent on tax revenues and would thus be compelled to respond to public demands for political representation. A general decline in dependence on oil and other fossil fuels could open the door to overcoming the extractivist development model in regions where it currently dominates. In turn, moving away from extractivism—the most raw and brutal form of capitalism—could enable a reevaluation and transformation of the fundamental mechanisms of exploitation and alienation that underpin it, potentially altering not only the relationship between humans and nature but also between humans themselves.

If humanity's future becomes less fixated on the Earth's geological past—encapsulated in fossil fuels—then the narrative frameworks used to represent oil, which have dominated the past century, may also shift. Dystopian scenarios, depictions of man-made disasters, parables of greed unraveling the fabric of human relationships, and post-apocalyptic stories about wars over resources may give way to a historicizing mode of storytelling—about dangers that were faced and overcome. Oil, once a substance of temptation, could become an example of a hard-learned lesson and hard-won experience. Otherwise, the fictional modality of warning and worst-case visualization—so characteristic of contemporary petropoetics—may transform into a documentary one, in which that worst-case scenario has already become the present.

AD: On a cultural and psychological level, how would you describe the relationship and interaction between oil and humans in various societal and cultural contexts?

IK: The social meaning of oil—which is not identical to its technological or economic functionality—is always derived from the context in which it exists. These meanings are products of a kind of 'oil refinement' carried out by human culture. Depending on the social exchanges and political-economic transformations into which the materiality of oil is inserted, it gives rise to various "semiotic f(r)actions." In other words, once designated a resource, the material totality of oil begins to fragment, generating a spectrum of meanings. This semiotic fragmentation of the original whole is initiated by the very act of defining something as a resource. A resource is, by definition, a part—an extracted, valuable part. The whole from which that part has been removed becomes devalued—a useless remnant, a pile of exhausted matter. In this sense, the ontology of natural resources, of mineral fossils is grounded in a mode of devaluation—of nature as a unified whole—since it relies on a perspective that separates what is 'valuable' (the resource) from what is not.

Russian philosopher Vladimir Bibikhin (1938–2004) offered a brief but profound commentary on the wound inflicted on nature when a part of it is extracted and turned into a resource. Echoing late Heidegger (whom Bibikhin translated), he writes: "The part, before it was taken to be used, passed through a traumatic path of the whole's disfigurement. Oil extracted in Tyumen, before it was pumped from the earth and made into industrial raw material, had already been dissected by a scientific worldview that promised it to the masses as a gift of nature... For millennia, oil—like many other things—belonged to the whole of nature precisely in its uselessness to the economy. And yet it increasingly belonged to a whole that once existed, but no longer does. The [scientific] worldview has no doubt about the irreversibility of this lost whole. In that certainty it justifies its dominion." Thus, the central question of a fundamental ontology that interrogates the relationship between nature, humanity, and natural resources is the reflection on the wound—the trauma inflicted on the being of the whole by the extraction of a part deemed meaningful for human progress. We must ask whether the extractive logic of human development is, in fact, a threat to humanity's own reproduction—since in utilizing the part, it may destroy the whole.

Once extracted from the earth, oil becomes as semantically protean as its physical form is fluid. It can be perceived as both curse and salvation, threat and gift, mark of the devil and sign of divine favour. The mythological charge concentrated in the cultural motif of oil is comparable to the energy condensed in its chemical formula. Regardless of the value orientation—whether oil is seen as good or evil—its symbolic field exerts exceptional gravitational force. It distorts critical reason, arouses desire, and generates phantasmatic visions and mirages akin to optical illusions produced by oil vapors. A brilliant deconstruction of these sexualized oil fantasies can be found in Polish journalist Ryszard Kapuściński's *Shah of Shahs* (1982), about the Islamic Revolution in Iran: "Oil provokes extraordinary emotions and passions, because oil is above all a colossal temptation. It promises easy, insane wealth, happiness, power. It is a filthy, stinking sludge that gushes from the ground and falls back to earth as a rain of money... [The one who finds oil] doesn't just become rich—he acquires a mystical belief that some higher force, ignoring all others, has chosen him as its favourite... Oil is a substance that poisons the mind, clouds the eyes, and has a demoralizing effect."

Beyond this mystical theology of oil—entwined with the libidinal economy—another interpretive approach emerges through Marxist political economy. Oil, as a real commodity, an imagined object of desire, and a theoretical construct, has become a universal equivalent of value, replacing the role once held by money. This convergence is evident in the perspective of global oil magnates (Robert O. Anderson, founder of ARCO, once said "oil is already almost money") and in the linguistic amalgam of everyday terms like 'petrodollars.' In effect, oil has become the structural core—or more precisely, the fluid substance—of an economy based on the free circulation of capital and commodities. The San Francisco-based leftist collective Retort describes the relationship this way: "If goods are the economic cellular form of capitalism, then oil is the perfect example of that cellular form." Oil exemplifies the commodity form not only through its almost absolute protean capacity to become anything—like money—but also because it embodies both aspects Marx identified in every commodity: its use-value as a concrete good (fuel, plastic, etc.) and its abstract value-function, serving as the material depositary that grounds all exchange. In this sense, the oil molecule is capitalism's primordial cell, synthesizing both the consumable and the structural logic of global trade. By contrast, in socialist petro-discourse, oil was not described as a commodity or as capital, but as a productive force, on par with the working class emancipated from exploitation. The horizon of class struggle reframed geological oil formations as "socially allied laboring elements"—comrades in the fight against capitalism. Planned development of oil fields—made possible by socialist production relations—was depicted as the liberation of the subsoil from the predatory over-exploitation it suffered under capitalism.

Ivan Gubkin (1871–1939), founder of Soviet geology and of the Moscow Oil Institute, wrote: "Capitalism cannot properly develop natural wealth. Its inherent tendency is to plunder. It squanders living labor, accumulated past labor, and natural resources" (*Policy of planned exploration of oil fields in the USSR*, 1933). His argument can be interpreted as follows: private property, by dividing oil fields into parcels owned by different stakeholders, leads to chaotic drilling, uncoordinated development, and the fragmentation of natural unity by conflicting capitalist interests. Even when monopolies enable coordinated exploitation, their competitive pressures redirect investment to newer, richer sites, abandoning previous fields unfinished. Geological strata are thus fundamentally anisomorphic to the capitalist socio-economic formation. The logic of geological layers, their deep time and systemic integrity, contradicts the 'anarchic' laws of market capitalism. The nomos of the Earth can only be spoken in the rational language of a planned socialist economy; market dynamics, driven solely by profit, distort the constitution of nature. Ironically, the Soviet geologic discourse defending planned development relied on the same topoi of wholeness, shared origin, and vital energy from nature's accumulated labor that are now echoed in contemporary geophilosophy (new materialism, speculative realism, flat ontologies)—which imbue non-human entities with autonomous agency. As Gubkin put it: "In place of exploitation and squandering of the Earth's forces comes proper use of nature's power."

The debate was whether forced development served or violated the 'interests of the resource.' The conclusion of engineers and scientists at the time was that "rapid extraction does not contradict the interests of the deposit." Thus, the class interests of workers and peasants aligned with the 'interests of the resource' (which consisted in the fact that the maximum volumes of energy were extracted to the surface) – merged into a common symphony of labor. Yet the real history of real socialism tells a different story. Forced industrialization, war, postwar recovery, and the USSR's growing dependence on oil exports in its final decades meant that the 'interests of the deposit'—as well as those of the environment and Indigenous communities living near oil fields—were routinely ignored.

Still, the discursive framework developed in the 1920s–30s to understand the relationship between Soviet oil and socialist society may offer the right direction. It calls for viewing natural resources as productive forces, recognizing in them the embodiment of nature's accumulated labor, and caring for the 'interests of the resource.' The grammar of this socialist discourse implied agency for non-human actors—and therefore the presence of their rights and interests. The task is to realize this grammar in practice. As is well known, the European integration process began after WWII with the formation of the European Coal and Steel Community. Why not take that name literally and imagine a community—a union—not of particular industrial sectors, but of the very materials themselves: coal, oil, iron ore, and other natural resources? And why wait for World War III to do so—when such a shift might help to prevent it?

Look Who's Talking (about the Climate Crisis)!
The Cinematic Climatic Subject and its Others

Matthias Grotkopp

The climate crisis is not just an ecological, technological problem but it is also a question of basic injustices. The ongoing inability of the main polluting countries to implement effective measures of mitigation and adaptation or loss and damage mechanisms at the same time points to a fundamental crisis of Western ideas of how scientific knowledge, political action and everyday life are related – or are supposed to be related. The experience of the last decades tells us that the distribution of labor between science, mass media and politics has become dysfunctional. But how can the image of knowledge and action be shaped differently by media and arts in general and by audiovisual media in particular?

This essay will sketch a speculative cinematic biography of a Western climatic subject that undergoes a transformation in the representation of the climate crisis. This speculative viewing biography also implicitly accompanies a research and teaching biography of myself as a European academic, striving to be aware of my privileged position and complicity in the system and finding ways to use this privilege to create meaningful spaces within the university and the climate justice movement. What kinds of subjectivation effects can be ascribed when one follows a shift in the audiovisual discourse away from the usual disaster movies and the numerous documentaries explaining the physical causes and consequences of the climate crisis as if these were mere abstract information to be processed? How does one's perspective change if one not only includes the global institutional processes, technological solutions but starts to foreground local struggles of climate justice, direct action, conflict, and alliance building in activism and solidarity with Indigenous communities[1] and the most affected people? Starting from a change in the kinds of experts and

---

1   Following the definition of Shaw et al. (2006: 268), I use the term Indigenous to designate "groups with ancestral and often spiritual ties to particular land, and whose ancestors held that land prior to colonization by outside powers, and whose nations remain submerged within the states created by those powers." This term is not meant to construct a general, universal Indigeneity simply defined in opposition to hegemonic societies or the "Global North" but assembles heterogenous histories, experiences and struggles.

different cultures of knowledge practices there is also a movement towards different narratives and a different (audio-)visuality of the climate crisis. How do certain films project a different world, alternative scenarios of being in solidarity with other humans and with more-than-human others? How do they make their audiences realize that when everyone becomes a scientist – in the sense of an empirical and emphatic relationship to one's environment (Battiste/Henderson 2000: 45) – and when every scientist becomes an activist – in the sense of actively engaging to preserve livelihoods and the rights of humans and more-than-humans – this different world can be achieved?

1. The Climate as Graph and Special Effect

Two films are generally regarded as the paradigm setting examples of depicting the climate emergency: THE DAY AFTER TOMORROW (Roland Emmerich, USA 2004) and AN INCONVENIENT TRUTH (Davis Guggenheim, USA 2006). Twenty years later, it is important to both acknowledge their impact but also to critically historicize their modes of audiovisual projection of the climate crisis – the way they approach knowledge transfer through visualization and speculative fictionalization – as well as the kinds of solution and attitudes they suggest.

AN INCONVENIENT TRUTH is a prime example for the proposition that 'climate' as a hyperobject (Morton 2013) is beyond the spatial, temporal, and causal frames of ordinary perception and cognition. Visualizations like maps, graphs and charts are therefore not just necessary mediators between abstract measurement data and embodied perception (Schneider/Nocke 2014: 13), but they become the thing that climate is according to the poetic logic of the film. The film also refers to the visible effects of the climate crisis, most notably the melting of glaciers, but these and other evidence – like high temperatures affecting people's health, shifting patterns in animal behavior or rising sea levels – are primarily filtered through the diagrammatic as well. And this has consequences for the kind of knowledge and the kind of experts that are competent and entitled to talk about the climate, since this is a decidedly western, male, instrumentally rational mode of being.

The way AN INCONVENIENT TRUTH thinks its own place in historical time is to regard itself an technocratic intervention into the projected graphs. It absolves the audience of any previous wrong-doing, based on their presumed unawareness, and sets itself as the turning point. But it is an intervention that fails to see beyond its epistemic frame and the underlying hierarchies of knowledge and action and therefore simply offers a kind of green(-ish) consumerism as the answer: "But each of us can make choices to change that. With the things we buy, the electricity we use, the cars we drive. We can make choices to bring our individual carbon emissions to zero." (Min. 81).

A similar problem can be detected in the approach of THE DAY AFTER TOMORROW both on the surface level of ethnic and gender stereotypes and the kinds of agency attached to them but also on the level of narrative and aesthetic structure. By insisting on giving its audience a spectacular event-shaped idea of climate change as a direct image, the film short circuits the natural sublime, the technological sublime of tools and data, and its own celebration of special effects imagery (Ivakhiv 2013: 258–275). It is the illusion of having access to the whole that at the same time excludes human agency and the forces of fossil lifestyles. The narrative closure of the melodramatic action that reunites the patriarchal, heteronormative family finally undermines any understanding and affective realization of the ongoingness of the climate crisis.

Another word for this kind of change, that is not changing, action that is not acting, is: Deferral. It leads to a specific kind of aesthetic pleasure of imagining yourself in a special time of transition. More than just being before something that is going to happen, it means being in a privileged relation to that future. At the same time AN INCONVENIENT TRUTH and THE DAY AFTER TOMORROW are eminently nostalgic in the sense of a restorative nostalgia (Boym 2001) that frames the way forward as the return to a state of innocence.

On the one hand, both film's commercial and public success is therefore an accomplishment in the need to make science accessible and appealing that had a strong short-term effect on its audience's intentions and attitudes (Leiserowitz 2004; Nolan 2010; Beattie et al. 2011) and that can be argued to have made other films possible:

> This rise in 'visual' media coverage suggests that in the last decade the 'availability heuristics', such as melting mountain glaciers and Arctic ice sheets, stranded polar bears and flooded river basins and coastal zones, for promoting public understanding of climate change have risen dramatically. (Corfee-Morlot et al. 2007: 2765)

On the other hand, the images and models of experts, nexuses and actions that these films propose – neglecting systemic relations of consumerism, capitalism and the fossil fuel industry – has dominated the audiovisual discourse and in the long term can be argued to have led to an "acute disempowerment and disengagement with environmental politics altogether" (Yuen 2012: 19). This may also be the result of other films that follow the assumptions that many of the problems that threaten the planetary boundaries have already solutions available but that are just not deployed. Films like 2040 (Damon Gamon, Australia 2019) or DEMAIN/TOMORROW (Cyril Dion and Mélanie Laurent, France 2015) show many of the technological and behavioral changes that reduce greenhouse emissions and other impacts of Western industrial lifestyles but they shy away from both showing concrete pathways to their global implementation and a honest and clear view of the deep transformation of social and political organization that scaling-up these solutions would have as a condition.

The rhetorical trap of AN INCONVENIENT TRUTH, and one that many other films fall into, is that transformations are dangerous and threatening and that only a certain kind of change is good, which is the change that leads to a return to a stable condition of normality. And this is contrary to the first thing that any subjectivity adequate to the climate reality has to accept: "the end of the world has already happened, if by world we mean a stable set of reference points that guide our action" (Morton 2019: 155). The end of the world, in the sense of an environmental scaffolding of life, labor and culture, is not lurking at the horizon of expectations (Koselleck 2004 [orig. 1979]) but is already here and has shattered this horizon altogether.

This realization of living after the end of the world, is one of the central lessons that may be learned from listening to BIPoC-people: "Imperialism and ongoing (settler) colonialisms have been ending worlds for as long as they have been in existence" (Yusoff 2018: xiii). Can listening to the voices and stories of Indigenous people lead towards accepting the climate crisis not as an outside event but as an integral part of cultural self-description and therefore also to a different kind of audiovisuality of the climate crisis?

2. In Defense of Talking Heads

In cinematic terms, the task of listening to voices is conventionally ascribed to the audiovisual procedure of the 'talking head.' There are huge differences, however, in the way films can put this into action. For example, a film like THE 11th HOUR (Leila and Nadia Connors, USA 2007) translates the tendency towards abstraction, which is inherent in the conceptualization of climate as an aggregated data set, into the worldlessness of its speaking experts. More than 50 persons are shown talking to the film-makers, most of them read as white and male, some very famous like Stephen Hawking and Michail Gorbachev, but also including influential BIPoC spokespersons and activists like Oren Lyons, Wangari Maathai and Sheila Watt-Cloutier – they are alle positioned in front of the same dark blue, velvet background, giving short snippets of their insights to be woven into a somehow placeless, abstracted discourse on the environmental emergency.

If one compares this to the use of the same technique in QAPIRANGAJUQ: INUIT KNOWLEDGE AND CLIMATE CHANGE (CAN 2010) by Zacharias Kunuk, an Inuit film-maker, and Ian Mauro, a Canadian environmental geographer and filmmaker who lived with Inuit communities for years before shooting the film (Bloom 2022: 87–88), one can see very different kinds of talking heads. The interviews collect the personal accounts of Inuit living in Inuit Nunangat, almost exclusively in their native language, Inuktitut, and are filmed in their immediate surroundings: personal objects, family photographs and kitsch as well as historical documents, old images of glaciers. The film sometimes subtly juxtaposes artifacts of traditional technologies in the frame with modern objects, like tending a Qulliq, a lamp made of stone, burning seal- or whale-oil, with one hand, whilst on the other hand there is a digital wristwatch.

Overall, there is a concrete sense of spatio-temporal continuity of the talking heads' spaces with the exterior shots and the archive footage that is absent in the more metonymic or purely symbolic shots that accompany the statements in THE 11th HOUR. It is as if the main driver of the images in THE 11th HOUR is a fear of boredom and a fear of the prejudice against talking heads as uncinematic and too close to the appearance of television in its lowest form: radio with merely optional images. This is partly a side effect of the dominance of visuality in Western epistemology and aesthetics and one could attribute the fact that the talking heads in Qapirangajuq are differently placed to a culture based on oral traditions. The absence of any expository voice-over also distinguishes this film from an earlier film – SILA ALANGOTOK: INUIT OBSERVATIONS ON CLIMATE CHANGE (Bonnie Dickie/Terry Woolf, CAN 2000) – that does not fully trust the words of the Inuit elders to stand on their own in the same way (MacKenzie /Westerstahl Stenport 2022: 73).

QAPIRANGAJUQ therefore not only positions a different kind of expert voices, but it also locates these voices differently. In this way, it provides a counterpoise to the audiovisual discourse on the climate crisis, because it shows how this expertise is derived from an intense mutuality with the land, the ice, the wind and with other species. Knowledge is shown to be based on qualities that Indigenous scholar Kyle Whyte uses to describe kinship: "reciprocity, consent, trust, transparency, and confidentiality, among others" (Whyte 2021: 48). The polar region, with all its harshness, is not an empty 'out there' only accessible to male, white explorers and the cameramen of the BBC's Nature History Unit, but it is a place of human, cultural meaning.

QAPIRANGAJUQ centres the everyday experience of living in an Arctic environment and depicts the reality of the climate crisis through the patience and observational skills needed for dealing with rapidly changing relationships with land, ice and animals and not through a spectacular, cataclysmic event. Views of polar bears and walruses are not shot by helicopters flying over vast, empty landscapes, but related back to the humans looking at them. The same can be said about the icebergs and melting glaciers always filmed from concrete points-of-view instead of disembodied omniscience. The opening shots already create a precise argument in a straightforward rhythm of images and speech, with each cut working as a grammatical conjunction: A slow pan to the left is showing a bay with hills in the background and a small settlement at the bottom of the image, the sun and the clouds are forming an impressive, darkening twilight atmosphere. The witness voice explains that the sky and the clouds were used to predict the weather. But: A group of birds is flying toward the camera in a telephoto lens, the warm light of the sky contrasts with the grey clouds of the previous shot and the voice claims, that it is different now. Therefore: A wide shot of a group of people against the light. They are standing and walking on a rocky slope and then a single person is shown closer, walking to the right while the voice talks about the unpredictability of cloud movements. It is as if the figures were re-enacting this unforeseeable motion in order to attain some knowledge of it. But still: A fifth shot is showing the same person from behind, at a low angle. The person is standing on a small rock and looks to the left, away from the camera, taking binoculars to see further. Yet it is not a romantic back-figure image composition as in a Caspar David Friedrich painting, where the audience is put in the position of seeing the observer from behind and the observed landscape as well. The position of the camera makes it impossible to see what there is to be seen at the horizon. And the voice is silent.

Fig. 1: Stills from Qapirangajuq – Inuit Knowledge and climate change.

The remainder of the film is working on making this interruption of patterns established since time immemorial felt as well as the communal work of repair and care that comes with it. Every piece of observation and knowledge is fed back into the community and there are many images of intergenerational exchange around the daily and seasonal rhythms, food preparation and traditional handicrafts. In contrast to Western media's portrayal of polar regions, with melting glaciers and struggling polar bears as mere symbols of the climate crisis with no significance to everyday life, the images here are populated with landscapes, animals and people and all of them affecting each other. The Inuit's reliance on observing the weather, the animals, their surroundings, as well as the passing down of knowledge through generations challenges a Western perception of "human interaction with the natural environment and privileges other ways of seeing and knowing besides the scientific" (Bloom 2022: 88). Furthermore, these oral testimonies can be seen as an act of media sovereignty (Rickard 1995; Ginsburg 2016) as the interviewees reclaim agency over the stories and histories told; and thereby cultivate a concept of knowledge primarily based on connection, on storytelling and listening, that challenges a dominance of visuality and distancing in Western epistemologies, both in general and in regard to the discourse of the climate crisis (MacKenzie /Westerstahl Stenport 2022: 75).

3. Land, Water and Image Protectors

For many Inuit communities the detrimental environmental processes are originating from sources far away in what they call the South and reaches them through the atmosphere and the water. This is also true for the people living on the low islands of the Indian or Pacific Ocean, who's lives and cultures are destroyed by rising sea levels. For them, questions of media sovereignty are closely tied to more and more desperate and angry appeals to international solidarity. This can be seen in THE ISLAND PRESIDENT (Jon Shenk, USA 2011) that follows the campaigns of the then President of the Maldives, Mohamed Nasheed, for stronger and binding international rules to reduce greenhouse gases or in ONE WORD (Viviana Uriona, Germany 2020), that used a participatory approach to collect the first-hand experiences and observations of the people from the Marshall Islands.

A different kind of urgency and media sovereignty is expressed by those Indigenous groups and allied activists who are fighting at the concrete crime scenes of ecocide, at the sacrifice zones and against the infrastructures of extraction. Documentary filmmaking is here considered a key component of continuing the actions of land and water protectors. It is also a riposte to prevailing images and narratives of ecological destruction in Western media. These depictions of the climate, biodiversity and pollution crisis often use images that are too spectacular and distanced (Grotkopp 2023) and therefore aestheticizing their audience's own relationship to it (Demos 2017: 70), as for example in films like ANTHROPOCENE – THE HUMAN EPOCH (Jennifer Baichwal et al., Canada 2018). But there is also the problem of many news media who are aiming for restraint and balance and thus inadvertently contribute to normalizing the ruination and the economic and political conditions that make it possible (Sholette/Ressler 2013). In contrast to these pitfalls, there is a growing tendency in films to embrace activism and to foreground the systemic nexus that connects the destruction of nature to the destruction of human health and well-being and to the ongoing violations of fundamental rights that are perpetrated at various places of resistance around the world.

On the one hand, these films act as witness to the destruction of habitats, earth and water bodies as well as to the violence perpetrated by police and private security companies against activists. On the other hand, they are showing the autonomous zones and resistance camps as practical examples of alternative ways of living. These can be both the very concrete everyday practices of organizing labor and consumption differently as well as the techniques of dissent and disobedience. Through their emphasis on place and community, films like VERGISS MEYN Nicht (Fabiana Fragale, Kilian Kuhlendahl and Jens Mühlhoff, Germany 2023) or DIRECT ACTION (Guillaume Cailleau and Ben Russell, France/Germany 2024) also aim at a different kind of climatic and environmentalist subjectivity that has incorporated the slogans and political analyses and that emerges from a different engagement with the materialities of land and sea, with collectivity and with other species. And they ask fundamental questions about the means and ends of political action.

Among this cycle of films there is again a specific stake emphasized by Indigenous activists and filmmakers, which does not start from the evidence of pollution, destruction and extinction but roots its arguments in challenging the underlying epistemologies and in emphasizing the aspect of justice that unites ecological with social and political struggles:

> There is no hope for restoring the planet's fragile and dying eco-systems without Indigenous liberation. This is not an exaggeration. [...] Indigenous people understand the choice that confronts us: decolonization or extinction. (The Red Nation 2021: 108)

Films like KANEHSATAKE – 270 YEARS OF RESISTANCE (Alanis Obomsawin, Canada 1993), HUICHOLES: LOS ÚLTIMOS GUARDIANES DEL PEYOTE (Hernán Vilchez, Mexico 2014) or LAKOTA NATION VS. UNITED STATES (Jesse Short Bull, Laura Tomaselli, USA 2022) embed contemporary struggles within the long histories of colonial violence and Indigenous resistance, but they also directly contest hegemonic, western conceptions of land ownership and exploitation and they employ the wisdoms of animistic worldviews and modes of Traditional Ecologic Knowledge (Pierotti/Wildcat 2000; Kimmerer 2015). The poetic logic of these films is to connect Indigenous ideas of kinship (Van Horn et al. 2021) between humans, land, water, other beings, objects and cultural practices to the concrete struggles at the frontlines of the climate emergency and the infamous actions of industries and governments. These films create distinctive experiences of visual and auditory territories that are not static boundaries carved onto the land but lived interactions with land, water and the more-than-human (Robinson 2020: 53–54). At the same time, there is also a reluctance and an awareness of incommensurability when it comes to making this knowledge transparent for a wider audience. For this reason AWAKE – A DREAM FROM STANDING ROCK (Myron Dewey, Josh Fox, James Spione, USA, 2015) does not only document the resistance against the Dakota Access Pipeline and the spiritual and cultural practices of the water protectors but – being a collaborative work between Indigenous and white filmmakers – it also self-reflexively presents and enacts a protocol for allies engaging with Indigenous struggles and makes the audience aware of its pluralized, multi-tiered address to the people who were present at Standing Rock, to other Indigenous groups, to those who consider themselves allies and to a general public sphere. With regard to the latter two it is necessary to develop a certain ethics of being an audience to words, songs, actions and narratives that are not meant for you and to resist the urge to make their meanings transparently accessible and instead accept Indigenous people's right to opacity as theorized by Édouard Glissant (1997 [orig. 1990].

4. Experimental Constellations of Climate Dislocation

The Indigenous artist and experimental filmmaker Sky Hopinka reacted to the unease of mediation and the potential loss of sovereignty over the image of Standing Rock, as it was slowly turning into a resource for other groups. His short film DISLOCATION BLUES (USA 2017) is similar to AWAKE – A DREAM FROM STANDING ROCK in the way it keeps these different perspectives suspended. But instead of stretching out the protest of a specific place and time towards a montage of global solidarity and replication, as the Coda of AWAKE does, Hopinka emphasizes the loose ends and leaves wide open the question of what Standing Rock will have meant in the future. The final scenes of his film push the depiction of activism and resistance further from a documentary or even essayistic-contemplative mode into the realm of experimental, avant-garde art.

The film, as typical for Hopinka's approach, starts with a deceptively simple syntax of sound/language and images that however never settles into a system but always remains open to contingency and capriciousness. It mainly consists of two interviews, with one of the interviewees (Terry Running Wild) only audible and the other one (Cleo Keahna) only visible on a laptop screen during a video call. The images of the camp neither simply illustrate their reflections on roles, pressures and liberation, on the insecurities of Indigeneity nor do they focus the moments of confrontation and violence but they show the resistance camp as a place of quiet and possibilities. With Keahna's refusal towards the end to translate the experience into words and to claim any authority to speak for the whole, the film shifts into a different mode and also enacts a poetic, audiovisual multitude in which the style of the images keeps changing unpredictably: At first, a forty-second-long shot shows a group of protesters passing by from left to right as the song "Not for me" by Bobby Darin from the 1960s sets in. But the framing of the shot is so that one only sees the individual people for a very short time before they leave the frame and one can never settle on observing or classifying them. Also, a second voice starts singing with the song, first softly, as if only for itself, later it becomes more present but never drowning out the original song. The impression of people rushing by is then enhanced by a move to abstraction, blurred patches of blue and white light flicker on the screen as if the camera is looking at the sun through a thick fabric. After shortly returning to the parade of people and a view of a night scene at the camp, with a campfire in the foreground, comes one of the iconic images from Standing Rock: a group of young warriors on horses, with one chief in full headdress at their center. But instead of settling with either abstraction or iconicity the final shot of DISLOCATION BLUES shows a spatialized composite image that is only slowly deciphered: It starts with a tracking shot from the rear of a driving car, with teepees and cars in the background. The image quickly gets creases, and mysterious shadows move over it. As the camera moves back, it is revealed that the shot from the car was actually projected onto a crumbled screen and then, as the camera moves further back and pans to the left, another screen comes into view, straight and smooth, onto which the same shot is projected. The camera moves back further still to show the dark studio setting with the song ending and the two types of screens silently contradicting, completing, commenting each other.

It seems that films like DISLOCATION BLUES ask the question if the world really needs more images of the climate crisis or if it does not rather need a climate crisis of images in which visual and audiovisual interventions into the depiction of the climate crisis make explicit the relation and disproportion between the visible and the visualized, the abstract data and the thinking-feeling of everyday action. Of course, there are important differences between common notions about the historical development of the Western, European avant-gardes of the early- and mid-20th century and the work of contemporary Indigenous artists. But if one leaves aside the problematic tendencies of certain movements, like the Italian futurists and other proponents of a heroic-masculine destructive approach and puts the spotlight on different "Moments and Temporalities of the Avant-Garde" (Pollock 2010), then the procedures and goals of the Avant-garde to attain a different sensuality in culture and an entirely different status of art can be reconciled with practices of care and kinship.

Fig. 2: Stills from Dislocation Blues.

5. Cinematic Climate Realism

The artistic practices of experimentation and lyricism can be important voices in grasping the way the environmental crisis is more than just a linear change in data but that it is shattering the scaffolding and the traditional frameworks within which change can be accommodated, grasped, and processed. Like the centuries old vocabulary for haiku poetry in Japan, where the climatic and ecological phenomena typical for the course of the seasons are condensed in single words, words that no longer provide adequate descriptions but rather accentuate the disruptions by becoming incongruous (McCurry 2023).

A cinematic subjectivity for climate cultures that has travelled through audiovisual worlds of data and visualization, spectacle, witnessing and resistance, experimentation and dislocation may get closer to a point of climate realism, where every narrative and every visual or acoustic work directly connects to changes in the patterns of life on this planet. The labels of climate fiction or eco-media will become obsolete because they become synonymous with the representation of the world:

"Those works that portray a stable climate as the mute and reliable background to human drama might then be considered, in an ironic reversal, to be mere fantasy, or historical fiction" (Schneider-Mayerson 2017: 318). There are glimpses of this realism when films make the audience feel the many contradictions and dissonances of the climate crisis and the unreality of everyday so-called normality like Night Moves (Kelly Reichardt, USA 2014) or films that make them see people's inability to see the evidence of the crisis around them like Roter Himmel (Christian Petzold, Germany 2023).

In the meantime, there is a special need for cultural processes that confront the climatic subjects with it's others because there is a need for a deep transformation of Western societies that for the moment of this viewing and writing is only prefigured in radical acts of disobedience and in encounters with and acts of listening to Indigenous people, affected people, spokespersons for other species and for other beings like rivers and mountains:

> Because all it takes is such a small gesture that you see or feel or watch or experience that activates something in yourself that makes you want to do something, or question what you've been boing. Like any other sort of resistance it starts with something outside your own. (Rabinowitz/Hopinka 2021: 85)

Bibliography

Battiste, Marie, Youngblood Henderson (Sa'ke'j) James (2000): Protecting Indigenous Knowledge and Heritage. A Global Challenge, Vancouver: UBC Press.

Beattie, Geoffrey, Laura Sale, and Laura McGuire (2011): "An inconvenient truth? Can a film really affect psychological mood and our explicit attitudes towards climate change?" In: Semiotica 187, pp. 105–125.

Bloom Lisa E. (2022): Climate Change and the New Polar Aesthetics: Artists Reimagine the Arctic and Antarctic, Durham/London: Duke University Press.

Boym, Svetlana (2001): The Future of Nostalgia, New York: Basic Books.

Corfee-Morlot Jan/Maslin, Mark/Burgess, Jacquelin (2007): "Global warming in the public sphere." In: Philosophical Transactions of the Royal Society A 365, pp. 2741–2776, https://doi.org/10.1098/rsta.2007.2084.

Demos, T. J. (2017): Against the Anthropocene: Visual Culture and Environment Today, London: Sternberg Press.

Ginsburg, Faye (2016): "Indigenous Media from U-Matic to Youtube: Media Sovereignty in the Digital Age." In: Sociologia & Antropologia 6/3, pp. 581–99, https://doi.org/10.1590/2238-38752016v632.

Glissant, Édouard (1997 [orig. 1990]): Poetics of Relation, trans. Betsy Wing, Ann Arbor: University of Michigan Press.

Grotkopp, Matthias (2023): "Tipping the scales. The Interfering Worlds of Anthropocene: The Human Epoch." In: Interfaces 50, https://doi.org/10.4000/interfaces.8114.

Ivakhiv, Adrian (2013): Ecologies of the Moving Image, Waterloo (Ontario): Wilfrid Lauruer University Press.

Kimmerer, Robin Wall (2015): Braiding Sweetgrass. Indigenous Wisdom, Scientific Knowledge and the Teachings of Plants, Minneapolis: Milkweed Editions.

Reinhart Koselleck (2004 [orig. 1979]): "'Space of Experience' and 'Horizon of Expectation': Two Historical Categories." In: Reinhart Koselleck: Futures Past. On the Semantics of Historical Time, New York: Columbia University Press, pp. 255–275.

Leiserowitz, Anthony A. (2004): "Before and after the day after tomorrow: a US study of climate risk perception." In: Environment: Science and Policy for Sustainable Development 46/9, pp. 22–37.

MacKenzie, Scott/Westerstahl Stenport, Anna (2023): New Arctic Cinemas, Oakland: University of California Press.

McCurry, Justin (2023): "Japan's haiku poets lost for words as climate crisis disrupts seasons," In: The Guardian, November 14, https://www.theguardian.com/environment/2023/nov/14/lost-to-the-climate-crisis-japan-haiku-poets.

Morton, Timothy (2013): Hyperobjects. Philosophy and Ecology after the End of the World, Minneapolis: University of Minnesota Press.

Morton, Timothy (2019): Being Ecological, Cambridge (MA): MIT Press.

Nolan, Jessica. (2010). "An Inconvenient Truth" Increases Knowledge, Concern, and Willingness to Reduce Greenhouse Gases." In: Environment and Behavior 42/5, pp. 643–658. 10.1177/0013916509357696.

Pierotti, Raymond/Wildcat, Daniel (2000): "Traditional Ecological Knowledge: The Third Alternative (Commentary)." In: Ecological Applications 10/5, pp. 1333–1340.

Pollock, Griselda (2010): "Moments and Temporalities of the Avant-Garde 'in, of, and from the Feminine'." In: New Literary History 41/4, pp. 795–820.

Rabinowitz, Michael/Hopinka, Sky (2021): "Front: Artist Conversations." In: Joe Riepenhoff (ed.), Sky Hopinka, Manawa: Poor Farm Press, pp. 69–97.

The Red Nation (2021): The Red Deal. Brooklyn / Philadelphia: Common Notions.

Rickard, Jolene (1995): "Sovereignty: A line in the sand. Photographs by George Longfish, Zig Jackson, Pamela Shields Carroll, Ron Carraher, and Hulleah Tsinhnahjinnie." In: Aperture 139, pp. 50–59.

Robinson, Dylan (2020): Hungry Listening: Resonant Theory for Indigenous Sound Studies, Minneapolis: University of Minnesota Press.

Schneider, Birgit/Nocke, Thomas (2014): "Image Politics of Climate Change: Intro-duction." In: Birgit Schneider/ Thomas Nocke (eds.): Image Politics of Climate Change. Visualizations, Imaginations, Documentations, Bielefeld: transcript, pp. 9–25.

Schneider-Mayerson, Matthew (2017): "Climate Change Fiction." In: Rachel Green-wald Smith (ed.): American Literature in Transition, 2000–2010, Cambridge (MA): Cambridge University Press, pp. 309–321.

Shaw, Wendy S./ Herman, R. D. K./Dobbs, G. Rebecca Dobbs. (2006): "Encountering Indigeneity: Re-Imagining and Decolonizing Geography." Geografiska Annaler. Series B, Human Geography 88/3, pp. 267–276, http://www.jstor.org/stable/387 8372.

Sholette, Gregory/Ressler, Oliver (2013): "Unspeaking the Grammar Of Finance." In: Gregory Sholette/Oliver Ressler (eds.): It's the Political Economy, Stupid: The Global Financial Crisis in Art and Theory, London: Pluto Press, pp. 8–13.

Van Horn, Gavin/ Kimmerer, Robin Wall/ Hausdoerffer, John (eds.) (2021): Kinship: Belonging in a World of Relations, 5 vols., Libertyville: Center for Humans and Nature Press.

Whyte, Kyle Powys (2021): "Time as Kinship." In: Jeffrey Cohen/Stephanie Foote (eds.): The Cambridge Companion to Environmental Humanities, Cambridge (MA): Cambridge University Press, pp. 39–55.

Yuen Eddie (2012): "The Politics of Failure Have Failed: The Environmental Movement and Catastrophism." In: Sasha Liley/David McNally/Eddie Yuen/James Davis (eds.): Catastrophism: The Apocalyptic Politics of Collapse and Rebirth, Oakland: PM Press, pp. 15–43.

Yusoff, Kathryn (2018): A Billion Black Anthropocenes or None, Minneapolis: University of Minnesota Press.

Why Cultures Matter for Climate

Mike Hulme

This is a protocol of a conversation held at the beginning of the Climate Cultures Festival "Planet Writes Back!" 2021 in Berlin.

I should start off with a short background to my own engagement with the idea of climate. It started when I was a teenager, growing up in Scotland, when I first became fascinated with the weather, partly because I was into numbers and statistics. One of the ways in which meteorologists capture the behavior of the atmosphere is through measurements, which leads to numbers and statistics. That certainly attracted me to the study of weather. Also, as a teenage boy I was fascinated – my parents I'm sure would have said obsessed – with the sport of cricket. Cricket is a very weather-dependent sport, and every morning and every evening I would watch the weather forecast very carefully to find out if my cricket match the following day was going to be affected by the weather in some way. So, I became a keen weather watcher.

I tell that story because it begins to explain my professional career which has been spent studying climate and weather. But it also illustrates the relationship between weather and the everyday, between daily activities and the weather in which we conduct them. For me, as a teenager, it was recreation. Of course, for many people, the importance of the weather is much more significant; it affects their livelihoods and survival, or their exposure to risk and danger. But, conversely, the weather is also bound up with our experience of beauty and repose, and the aesthetics of the skies that we encounter in our everyday lives.

This early interest with the weather calibrated some of my later work, which was to think about the relationship between climates and cultures. I went on to study geography at university, and there I began to specialize in the study of climate and completed my own student project on variations in British winter weather. I then progressed to do a PhD which was significant in another sense. I studied the relationship between rainfall variations in Sudan, in northeast Africa just on the southern margins of the Sahara Desert, and the ways in which rural communities in that semi-arid region of northern Africa lived with a rainfall regime that was extremely variable. Rainfall varied largely from year to year, and from decade to decade; I studied the ways in which climatic variations were, on the one hand, yes, impacting people's precarious livelihoods, but I also studied the ability of these communities to withstand variations in rainfall. They had developed a wide variety of different water-harvesting and storage technologies that enabled people to survive and to thrive in a regime that might look to many outsiders as being precarious in climatic terms.

This PhD therefore introduced me to a different dimension of the relationship between weather and society, between climate and culture; namely, how different communities, how different cultures, develop technologies – social technologies, material technologies, imaginative technologies even – which enable them to live with their weather. There was also an intriguing element to my project which was the way in which the traditional religion of these communities – Islam and its religious cosmology – interacted with their understanding of their climatic condition and its variation.

This experience laid the foundation for my later career when I became a professional climate scientist, working for a long time on the science – the observations and the modeling – of climate change. I examined how well models can simulate the climate system, and how we then use models to project our understanding of the climate system into the future. The business, and art, of climate scenario-making was something I became an expert in. And it was that work which drew me into the United Nations' Intergovernmental Panel on Climate Change, the IPCC. I worked for the IPCC on their Second (1996) and Third (2001) Assessment Reports, particularly dealing with the question of scenarios: how scenarios are made, how credible they are, and how decision-makers, policy-makers, use them in their everyday work.

Around that time, in the year 2000, I also set up and led a new research center at my university, the University of East Anglia. We called it the Tyndall Centre for Climate Change Research, which is still thriving today, 25 years later. In setting it up, I brought together many different academic disciplines to connect different lines of work that people were pursuing about climate change and to produce reports, insights, and knowledge for the benefit of different public and political actors, both in the private and public sectors, and in national governments and international governments.

That further broadened my thinking around climate change and it was that experience that inspired me to begin writing my book, *Why We Disagree About Climate Change*, after I retired from the role of Director in 2007. The book was published in 2009 and it explored what had become a troubling question for me. In my role as director of the Tyndall Centre, it had become very clear to me that scientific knowledge about climate change was not decisive in eliciting policy responses, either from politicians or policy advisers or from wider general publics. There seemed to be something else that was going on with the ways in which people engaged with the idea of climate change. It wasn't just a question of, 'Was the science well communicated?' Even less was it a question, 'Were people understanding the scientific insights of climate change?' It seemed to me that people were not accepting that science should dictate or rule how they lived their everyday lives.

This got me thinking much more deeply about the prior values that different people bring to their understanding of the world around them; about the reasons why we disagree – the title of the book – about how we interpret the world, and indeed what role and value we place on scientific evidence. How do different people bring scientific evidence into relationship with their own cosmologies, their religious values or political ideologies, their own aspirations for what a good life might be for them and their descendants? This search began to take me well beyond science or economics, even beyond the social sciences. It got me thinking more widely about the humanities disciplines, about religious studies, environmental philosophy, ethics, and also storytelling. I began to encounter through some of my networks, some of my colleagues around the world, different traditions of storytelling around weather and climate; how different cultures make sense of what has always been historically the case, which is climatic instability.

For all human societies at all times, weather has this dual role. Weather is always the provider of resources and benefits for everyday life and livelihoods. But at the same time, weather presents risks and hazards and dangers, whether it's hurricanes or typhoons or floods or storms or droughts. And storytelling has always been a very important part of the way in which human cultures have lived with and survived these climatic oscillations. And so that book, *Why We Disagree About Climate Change* had a big impact on climate change research and scholarship and it widened further my networks and collaborators around the world. It reinforced for me the central importance of cultural approaches to understanding climate. And this is where I've situated much of my work over the last 10 to 15 years. I've written some other books about this, the most recent one – *Climate Change Isn't Everything* – published in 2023.

I have also written a textbook for geographers about the idea of climate change, *Climate Change (Key Ideas in Geography)* published in 2021. In this book, I used my earlier work to structure different ways of approaching the idea of climate change. I called some of these approaches 'science-based' and others 'more-than-science based'. I divided the science-based approaches into three categories: 'reformed modernism,' 'skeptical contrarianism,' and 'radical transformation,' which map, broadly speaking, onto different political positions in responding to climate change. For the 'more-than-science based' approaches, making sense of the idea of climate change emerges from other traditions. One conduit for sense-making exists within subaltern communities, with their forms of local knowledge and civic resistance. Another, was the creative arts, the ways in which through our imagination we create new artifacts, whether they're stories or poems or sculptures in order to deepen our awareness of the changes happening around us and indeed to empower people to create their own artistic representations of how they feel about the weather and climate change. And the third conduit came through religious traditions, drawing upon examples from many of the world's traditional faith communities and how the religious imagination can offer resources for solidarity and for innovation and creativity that merely science-based approaches would be blind to. These ideas therefore found their way into this 2021 book which is now being used quite widely for geography courses around the world.

Summarizing all this is the thrust of my argument: it is that we need to move beyond science in thinking about how people live with a changing climate. First of all, is to recognize that people bring their own experiences of the weather and its changes to the question of climate change. It's not simply that publics around the world are somehow naive or ignorant or passive, and that science, climate science, even the IPCC, is coming along to educate people, to tell people things that they never knew. Many people have their own ways of reading the atmosphere and its different weathers, and equally importantly their own ways of living with the weather. This is what I observed in my PhD studies in Sudan in the 1980s. Science needs to be placed, not necessarily in a subservient relationship with cultural knowledges, but it needs to be recognized that different cultural groups and formations in different parts of the world bring their own very valuable insights into what a changing climate means to them.

Stories then become very powerful. It's not simply about getting the numbers right, about science and the IPCC. As we're seeing this week – November 2021 – in the international COP27 climate negotiations in Glasgow, there are a lot of numbers flying around. Is it going to be 2 degrees, or 1.8 degrees, or 1.5 degrees of warming? When is net zero emissions going to be reached – 2040, 2050, or 2060? These are the numbers that science works with. And they have political power, undoubtedly, as we've seen this week in Glasgow. But over-emphasizing such numbers leads to a very reductionist view about how people live in their worlds and how we think of ourselves as actors and agents of change.

There is also the danger that a metric-based approach to climate change creates the idea of a fixed deadline: 'There are only five years or eight years or whatever, in which to achieve some numerical target.' Deadlines will always be broken; but there is always space on the other side of a deadline to allow one to continue to act creatively, justly and fairly, in line with one's values and aspirations and hopes for the future. I resist reducing climate change to a number, and even more I resist limiting the actions taken in response to climate change to a fixed deadline. We need to recognize the future is always a dangerous place to enter into, in our imaginations as well as in reality. There is no safe space in the future. Life is risky. Life is an experiment, a dangerous and unpredictable experiment; just think of what we are doing by creating artificial intelligence. But joyful experiments are precarious experiments with different outcomes for different people.

Cultural resources, traditional ones but also new cultural resources that people invent and mobilize, are ways – richer, more varied ways – human communities use to survive their dangerous encounter with the future, whether it's a change in climate, an oppressive regime, a devastating pandemic, or whether it's just the unspeakable dread of death. These are encounters that are common to all of humanity. And recognizing the power of cultural resources – of storytelling, myths, religious practices, and solidarities – will give much greater weight to our human creativity than science alone can offer.

Against Worldlessness
Climate, Culture, and Freedom

Simon Probst

1 Introduction: Climate Politics, Fossil Fuels and Freedom

In 2021 the Germany's Federal Constitutional Court (FCC) declared that the Federal Climate Change Act of 12 December 2019 (Bundes-Klimaschutzgesetz – KSG) and its climate targets are "incompatible with fundamental rights" and do "violate the freedoms of the complainants." (FCC 2021) The court's argument was that annual emissions allowed in the KSG till 2030 would "irreversibly offload major emission reduction burdens onto periods after 2030," which then would have to be realized "with ever greater speed and urgency", so that younger generations would be faced with hard-to-fulfill obligations (FCC 2021). These future obligations, the court argued, pose a violation of freedom:

> These future obligations to reduce emissions have an impact on practically every type of freedom because virtually all aspects of human life still involve the emission of greenhouse gases and are thus potentially threatened by drastic restrictions after 2030. (FCC 2021)

On a practical level, this argument seems pretty straightforward, as it is common knowledge that almost everything we do and produce in contemporary societies comes with the emission of greenhouse gases (products promising to be climate-neutral only deepening the sense of emissions' omnipresence). But on a philosophical level the equalization of emissions and "practically every type of freedom" is by no means self-evident. On the opposite, such an understanding undermines many traditional discourses of freedom as a (human) subject's (rational) capacity to self-determine one's thoughts and actions. The FCC's argument meets instead, maybe unknowingly, with the field of petrocultural studies (Szeman/Boyer 2017), which criticize the idea of autonomous modern subjectivity and point to the deep dependencies that bind modern subjectivity and freedom to the use of fossil fuels (Simpson and Szeman in this book). Or as postcolonial and planetary historian Dipesh Chakrabarty (2009: 208) points out: "The mansion of modern freedoms stands on an ever-expanding base of fossil-fuel use. Most of our freedoms so far have been energy-intensive."

Freedom, in the modern sense of autonomy, and fossil fuels are related in at least two ways: 1) The illusion of being an autonomous subject that can free itself from all bonds to the world, depends on the extracted energy that allows mass production, unlimited mobility, and equips (some) humans with artificial surroundings that constantly confirm the illusion of autonomy. 2) The illusion of autonomy is necessary to legitimize or suppress the destruction that comes with the extraction and use of fossil fuels. If we would see ourselves as belonging to the web of life, as relational subjects on a precarious planet, we would and could not practice such an energy-intensive sort of freedom.

The FCC, by the justification of his decision, affirmed the dependency of human freedom on the use of fossil energy. But the FCC conceived of this dependency not as a philosophical necessity but as a contingent dimension of freedom in 21st century Germany that needs to be taken into account at least for the decades to come.

Accordingly, climate politics and freedom appear as antagonists. But, again, not on a fundamental level, but because the freedom of illusionary autonomy depends on the use of fossil fuels and thus on emitting greenhouse gases. We live in a culture that produces a historically contingent antagonism between climate and freedom, an antagonism mediated by fossil fuels and CO_2. This dynamic is part of the larger antagonism between planetary habitability and freedom as it is defined and lived within the destructive cultures of capitalism (Moore 2015).

The decision of the FCC was celebrated, and rightfully so, as one of the most important achievements in the history of the German climate movement and as a major step towards the legal implementation of climate action; especially because it judged insufficient climate politics as a violation of something so fundamental as personal freedom. But in regard to the normative and cultural dimension of the argument, the court's explanation comes as a sad concession to an understanding of freedom that is fully tied to the modern illusion of autonomy and it's junky-like addiction on fossil fuel. Such an understanding of the relation between climate and freedom represents an appropriate diagnosis of where we are, but it offers no vision or regulative idea.

The search for such a vision and a strong understanding of climatic freedom is the aim of this article. In a first step, I will draw on Bruno Latour's and Nikolaj Schultz' ecological definition of freedom as the acknowledgment of relations and dependencies, connect it with Hans Jonas ecological imperative and argue that such a relational freedom in regard to the climate and planetary habitability cannot be achieved on the individual, but only on the collective level. This leads to the critique that capitalist societies deny their citizens (consumers) such a form of freedom and that capitalist societies, from the viewpoint of relational freedom, are in their very structure a violation of freedom. In a second step, I will turn to Ernst Cassirer and discuss the tension between freedom as autonomy and freedom as relation in regard to our understanding of culture and symbolic action. This leads, in a third step, to an inquiry into the problems that the autonomy of culture faces in the form of climate denialism, post-factualism, conspiracy theories as cynical practices of symbolic and narrative autonomy that lead to 'worldless' cultures, on the one hand, and the question of how to enact relational forms of cultural and narrative freedom, on the other hand. The term 'world', as I use it, will neither designate a merely social or linguistic totality of representation, nor will it refer to 'things and relations in themselves' as an ontological totality. Rather, 'worlds' are those porous spaces where 'things and relations in themselves' and representation meet halfway to form, what a subject or collective inhabits. And there are many such meeting points. In this sense, a wordless culture is a culture whose representations do not meet with 'things and relations in themselves', so that they inhabit a strange and phantasmagoric space. Following such an understanding, I would not agree that there is only one Earth but a "nearly infinite multitude of worlds" (Oliver 41).[1] 'Earth' for me is the name for an interrelated multitude of things and relations in themselves that are most important to our existence. This name serves as guiding principle, a way of worldmaking that is weaving together culture with things and relations in themselves, through pointing towards the material conditions of existence, shared by all humans and living beings we know of.

Another terminological clarification seems at place, regarding the plural 'we', that I will use throughout the article. This 'we' is not to denote all of humanity or life on Earth. Rather, I want to emphasize the idea that climatic freedom, relational planetary freedom more generally, can only be achieved through collective practices and that thus the subject of this freedom is a 'we' (one of many) of which we do not know yet. Every time I write 'we', this is a tentative hint toward the possibility of future collectives, not a gesture of achieved unification, but a question towards an unknown way of practicing freedom together.

2   Bonds that Make us Free. Towards Relational Freedom

In their 'memorandum' *On the Emergence of an Ecological Class* (2022), Bruno Latour and Nikolaj Schulz develop an idea of freedom that is defined, seemingly paradoxical, by human dependencies on the world. They redefine the modernist project of emancipation, so as not to refer to individual human autonomy from material conditions, historical contingencies and social hierarchies, but to an emancipation from exactly such a liberal definition of freedom and as project that aims at living with

---

1   For such an understanding replicates the dichotomy between nature and culture, where one nature is inhabited by many cultures, under the terms of one Earth and many worlds.

Earthly dependencies (Latour/Schultz 2022: 40). As counter-intuitive as such a ter-
minology might seem at first sight, it points to an often-overlooked structural dimension of emancipation. Emancipation never is only about becoming free from
something; it is as much about the possibility of new attachments. Emancipation
from material conditions and social hierarchies enables attachments to 'individual'
(yet culturally structured) desires of how to live. Emancipation from the idea, or ideology, of autonomy enables, among others, attachments to the more-than-human
world (becoming a relational subject). For Latour and Schultz (2022: 41), bonds are
what makes us free. That is an understanding of freedom not as autonomy (determined by one-self), but as heteronomy (determined by what is other), or an interplay of both. Building air-conditioned bunkers for an expected climate catastrophe,
shielding oneself from weather and world, would be an extreme expression of auton-
omy-freedom; serious climate politics, acting on our planetary dependencies, would
be an expression of heteronomy-freedom: the freedom to live according to the relations that make (our) life possible.

Such a definition of freedom resonates strongly with philosopher Hans Jonas'
(1979: 36) reformulation of Immanuel Kant's categorical imperative: "Act so that
the effects of your actions are compatible with the permanence of genuine human
life on Earth." While Kant's (1993: 30) imperative "Act only according to that maxim
whereby you can at the same time will that it should become a universal law." speaks
to an abstract morality, Jonas' reformulations grounds the questions of maxims
and universal laws in the conditions for (human) life on Earth, highlighting the
almost transcendental importance of these planetary conditions for the very formulation of such maxims and laws. If one follow's Kant in the assumption that
freedom consists in self-determination according to the categorical imperative
and accepts how Jonas lands the categorical imperative on Earth, then freedom
emerges from collective self-determination (autonomy) in response to the conditions of life on Earth (heteronomy). Seen from such a vantage point, the idea of
freedom as constituted by bonds and dependencies is nothing new under the sun.
That it might still surprise us, stems from the fact that we live in societies, where
it is impossible to live according to an imperative of responsibility, because such
an imperative depends on collective actions, maxims, and laws. The subject that
changes the climate and transforms the Earth is not any individual, but a collective.
Such a collective might be imagined as the human species (Chakrabarty 2009:
221), more-than-human heterogenous "terraforming assemblages" composed of
all the biological and technological entities that contribute to transforming the
planet (Woods 2014: 134), or a plurality of "earthly multitudes", heterogenous social
collectives each finding their own way of inhabiting Earth (Clark/Szerszynski 2021:
9). Contemporary–or Anthropocenic societies– do not give their citizens the chance
to live in a way that would be compatible with "the permanence of real human life,"
or, to speak less anthropocentrically, real biodiverse life on Earth. Climate freedom,

as one aspect of such understanding, would express itself in acts that avert climate collapse and work towards the sustenance of inhabitable climatic conditions for as much lifeforms as possible.

The FCC's ruling mentioned at the beginning, declared that the Federal Climate Change Act of 12 December 2019 violates the personal freedom of younger and future generations. But it does not, and cannot, address a more fundamental violation of our freedom, that is to act in a way that sustains genuine life and thus freedom. In being part of Modernist and Anthropocenic collectives, we are unavoidably implicated in the destruction of inhabitable climatic conditions. We, as contemporary climatic subjects, are not free.

3   Freedom and Culture: The *Animale Symbolicum* in the Climate Crisis

If we connect this idea of freedom through bonds, dependencies and relation to our understanding of human culture and its role in responding to the climate crisis, it might be interesting to turn to Ernst Cassirer, one of the most important figures for modern philosophy of culture and cultural studies. In his work, one can witness the tension between autonomy and relationality at full play. In his *Essay on Man. An Introduction to a Philosophy of Human Culture* (1944), Ernst Cassirer systematically conceived of symbolic actions and forms, the whole of culture, as the specific human way of relating to the world. For him 'man' is an *animale symbolicum*. And while he attests complex semiotic activities to all animals, he sees symbols and culture as distinct phenomena: "Signals and symbols belong to two different universes of discourse: a signal is part of the physical world of being; a symbol is part of the human world of meaning." (Cassirer 1944: 51) Contemporary scholars of New Materialism or Posthumanism would, without doubt, challenge such a dualistic and anthropocentric distinction (Iovino/Oppermann 2014). Nonetheless, it is quite interesting to dwell a little bit on Cassirer's thought. For him, signals in the animal world connect perception and action in a rather direct way that he calls "animal reactions" (Cassirer 1944: 44). Symbols, on the other hand, create space between perception and action, a space of symbolic reflection and self-referentiality that allows for a multiplicity of possible "human responses" (Cassirer 1944: 44).

When it comes to connecting climate and culture, this symbolic space is haunted by ambivalence. On the one hand, it defies long-standing ideas of climate determinism. Such ideas where popular in early historical climatology and claimed that the climate of a geographical area determined the cultures inhabiting these areas. This determinist view was closely linked to racist and colonial thought, seeing for example the climate of the northern hemisphere as a reason for cultural supremacy and the climate of the southern hemisphere as producing less civilized cultures (one might find popular accounts of such crude thought in the works of Ellsworth Huntington, *Climate and Civilization* (1915) or *The Character of Races. As Influenced by Physical Environment, Natural Selection and Historical Development* (1924) or the works of German scholar Eduard Brückner). Even as such ideas today might be forgotten or simply seen as overcome, they played an important role in the formation of historical climatology and continue to influence climatological thought, for example when the social consequences of climate change are modelled or communicated as if they were natural and fully determined processes (Stehr/van Storch 2023:175, 198).

Cassirer's philosophy defies such climate determinism, because it focuses on culture's ability to process environmental information in the self-referential symbolic space. Cultures do not react to the climate, they respond to it, and responding is a question of choice. How cultures develop thus might be strongly influenced by the climate they inhabit, but it depends as much, or even more, on actions and events in the symbolic space. Symbols are as strong a force as is the climate (though quite differently).

One of the most prominent figures of contemporary discourse to insist on the importance of climate change's cultural dimension is geographer and climatologist Mike Hulme. He has dedicated many works to fight a reductionist and deterministic view of climate change, among them *Why We Disagree About Climate Change* (2009), *Reducing the Future to Climate: A Story of Climate Determinism and Reductionism* (2011), *Weathered: Cultures of Climate* (2017), and *Climate Change Isn't Everything: Liberating Climate Politics from Alarmism* (2023). All of these works are based on the assumption that different cultures respond differently to climate change not only because they experience different physical effects, but because of their values, their belief systems, their traditions, their histories, their media and symbolic practices. But the plurality of responses to climate change is not only the source of disagreement about climate change – a disagreement that is not so much about whether or not it is anthropogenic but about the question what we shall make of it, what it will mean for the identity of collectives. The plurality of responses, so thinks Hulme, is also a source of freedom in encounter with climate change. It is the foundation of cultural transformation, which cannot be realized top-down by an international agency alone but must emerge through each culture's unique engagement with our rapidly changing planet. From a sociological perspective, Nigel Clark and Bronislaw Szerszynski (thinking with Gilles Deleuze and Felix Guattari) also conceive of the relations between societies and their environments in a way that allows for freedom. In a planetary framework, they think of human collectives as of "earthly multitudes" (2021: 9), which form themselves (their identity, stories, technologies, politics, media) in relation with the material conditions of the place where they live on Earth, yet do so not in a process of causal determination but in one of open-ended, mutual encounter, where culture multiplies the relations between subjects and the planet (a relation that also contributes to the Earth's ability to constantly transform itself, to enact a form of planetary freedom of emerging into ever new material compositions).

The positions articulated by Mike Hulme have been criticized for playing into the hands of climate deniers (Maxwell 2023). On first sight, such accusations might seem absurd, as Hulme leaves no doubt about the anthropogenic causes for climate change, the severity of its threats to life on Earth, and about the necessity to change our economic as well as our cultural relationships to the world. But in the course of the 'climate wars' and the "new climate war" (Mann 2021), think tanks funded by the fossil fuel industry have been using every available strategy (not only straightforward denialism) to deflect attention from the urgency of decarbonization.[2] And they might use, that is one concern with Hulme's work, narratives of culturally diverse responses to climate change as distractions to continue their destructive business as long as possible. That one might need to think about Hulme's work in this way, highlights the dilemma we are in. On the one hand, we face a climate crisis of utmost urgency, where the reduction of fossil fuels as the most important goal is heavily attacked by the involved corporations and thus seems to need a strong and unified response. On the other hand, cultural diversity in responding to the world is a fact and a value in itself, which is not to be given up under the 'hegemony' of one single narrative of climate change, as urgent as it might be. The difficulty of Hulme's project, but also its strength, is that he tries to articulate an answer to this dilemma, to reconcile cultural freedom and 'loyalty' to scientific fact.

Such a project is crucial for our processes of transformation. Because as unconditionally as one might embrace the freedom of cultural responses to climate change, certainly not every response itself is good, or even acceptable. Ignorance is one possible response (or rather anti-response), and one of the most popular in the recent years. The danger of cultural ignorance (often disguised as 'free speech') can, again, be understood in Cassirer's philosophy of the symbolic space. Cassirer develops a cultural philosophy of autonomy, where the symbols constitute their own realm, a realm that is thought to be independent from physical reality and seen as belonging to the "human world of meaning" alone. Of course, this symbolical realm can, at every moment, be reconnected to perception or action. But such a reconnection is, at least theoretically, optional.

Culture thus offers the possibility of worldlessness, the illusion of autonomy without relation. It allows humans to respond to the world in a way that has almost

---

2   Mike Hulme (2021) has argued in a review of Michael Mann's book, that there lies great danger in framing questions of climate politics through military metaphors and the tropes of war, as the law of war is at its core undemocratic, separates the world in friends and enemies, and leaves little space for the democratic formation of heterogenous coalitions and alliances. Revisited with a few years distance, after the ongoing Russian war against Ukraine changed collective attitudes toward military action, armament, and military thinking in many European countries, the tension between Hulme's pluralistic and democratic view on climate politics, and Mann's rather Manichean, dualistic, and combative framework, seems even more complicated.

nothing to do with the world as it is and emerges exclusively from self-referential processes in the symbolic and social realm – as is the case in conspiracy theories or the neoliberal economic ideologies that are guiding most societies today. The consequences of a 'worldless' culture, not minding its entanglements with what is other, is one of the most dangerous threats we face today.

Relational freedom, the freedom to live so as to sustain life on Earth, is dependent on distinguishing truth from lie. It needs to know what the conditions of life on Earth are, how they are damaged, and how they can be maintained. To distinguish truth from lie is not only and not primarily an individual capacity, but one of a culture. It emerges from a culture's practices of knowledge, from its media, its way to distribute and share attention. The cultures of the 21st century are struggling against forces that attack this fundamental precondition of relational freedom: the capacity to relate to the world as it is.

Cultural wars are fought with the weapons of disinformation and narrative strategies. In these cultural wars, stories, and symbols more generally, are used as instruments of power and not as means of knowing or understanding the world. Regarding these developments, the latest report from the Club of Rome (Dixson-Declève et al. 2022) states not without reason that the collective inability to distinguish truth from lie is as dangerous a threat to our societies as the climate crisis itself. As Hannah Arendt (2006: 42) has pointed out, one main characteristic of totalitarian systems is that they have lost the integrity towards facts. Arendt (2006: 20) also observed, that while in societies of the 20th century the tolerance against a plurality of belief systems has increased, there seems to be an unparalleled fierceness with which facts that are inconvenient to the interests of the powerful are fought. Being post-factual is a position that aims to banish the things and relations in themselves from our culture, so that the mighty few do not have to negotiate with the stubborn stuff our worlds are made of. The rich and powerful want to silence the language through which the things and relations of the Earth, mediated by the sciences and other cultures of knowledge, speak to us in "terms of forces, bonds, and interactions" (Serres 1992: 39). They need to suppress such a communication through relations, because, if the Earth 'tells' us that our contemporary ways of fossil-fuel-based capitalism threaten the conditions of our existence, it challenges, in its own insistent way, established economic and political systems. Profiteers of power are thus interested in interrupting the forces, bonds, and interactions that flow between people and the Earth (as they are always interested in destroying the social bonds within communities they want to exploit).

In addressing such systematic disruptions of relation, Donna Haraway (2016: 32), drawing on Hannah Arendt's work on the 'banality of evil,' sees the "evil of thoughtlessness" as a key driver of the Anthropocene. And thoughtlessness for her, meets with ignorance towards world:

> Arendt witnessed in Eichmann not an incomprehensible monster, but something much more terrifying – she saw commonplace thoughtlessness. That is, here was a human being unable to make present to himself what was absent, what was not himself, what the world in its sheer not-one-selfness is and what claims-to-be in-here in not-oneself. Here was someone who [...] could not cultivate response-ability [...]. Function mattered, duty mattered, but the world did not matter for Eichmann. The world does not matter in ordinary thoughtlessness. (Haraway 2016: 36)

What Haraway sees missing from Eichmann are basic symbolic capacities – to make present what is absent, to have representations of other beings that come to matter to oneself. Haraway and Cassirer, as unlikely a pair as they might seem, meet in the question of response-ability: Thought and culture are the ability to respond to the world and its constantly changing complexities. That means to have a choice in what you feel and do, how you represent the world, not an absolute choice, but a choice bound by the "sheer not-one-selfness" of the world. Worldlessness, might easily be taken for freedom because it suggests absolute autonomy and brags about it. But it is no freedom, not even a dark freedom, rather it is anti-freedom, the absolute inability to relate to the world and to live with the bonds and dependencies that sustain life.

The symbolic realm, as Cassirer describes it, must by no means lead to wordless-ness and monadism. It also allows to multiply the relations between humans and the world. To tell 'true stories,' and many of them. For Cassirer, relations are at the very core of symbolic thought. All living beings perceive relations within their life world. But humans, for him, have the unique and quite contradictory ability "to isolate re-lations – to consider them in their abstract meaning" (Cassirer 1944: 59). His example here is geometry as an abstraction of concrete physical objects and their relations. Such an abstract and isolationist relational thought should be a warning to an all too eager enthusiasm towards relational thinking – it can, and has been through-out modernity, instrumentalized. It allows humans to decontextualize the relations they perceive in the world, and to see them as their playing field, as if it would not matter, how you group and regroup this abstract units of relations. One might feel reminded of Anna Tsings (2015, chapter "Some Problems with Scale") description of the decontextualization of plants' ecological and social relation in plantation econ-omy, which is exactly the result of abstract, decontextualized relational thinking that puts not enough weight and importance on the relations as they actually exist. Cap-italism allows to deliberately reconfigure (and destroy) the relations that make up this world. To change the relational patterns of the world, is not a thing to be done lightly. There is a difference between the abstract and isolated relations in the sym-bolic realm and the relations that bind beings together and allow their survival. Real relations and their histories should be taken seriously, as the binding stuff of this Earth. They are not, or at least they should not be, at our disposal. If the experienced autonomy of the symbolic realm gives us this impression, we are mistaken.

4   Storytelling and Climatic Freedom

We face a choice on a very fundamental level in what we want our culture to be – a fortress of human exceptionalism or a polis for Earthly relations. Being an *animale symbolicum*, an animal that relates to the world through figures, images, stories, numbers, we can use our symbolic capacity, at least it might seem so, to separate ourselves from the world, to gain autonomy in a modern sense. But this would be to overlook that the space created between us and world by symbols is not an empty space, is not pure distance, but brimming with relations, semiotic as well as material. For Latour (2017: 140), there is no doubt that symbolic actions in science, technology, and art, can be made productive to intensify feedback loops between Earthly processes and human societies. There need to be carefully maintained, always provisional and precarious connections between measurements, scientific discussions, artistic representations and social narratives. The precariousness of these connections between the symbolic realm and reality (the "symbiotic real," as Timothy Morton (2017: 13) would call it) is something we experience on a daily basis: climate denial, tactics of 'flooding the zone with shit' to overwhelm the symbolic realm with fake news and conspiracy narratives, are aimed at exactly this: to undermine and destroy all connections between culture and the world we inhabit, it is aimed at collective madness, to hold humans hostage in the symbolic realm turned into a postfactual hell – in symbolic self-referentiality gone crazy.

Such post-factual cultural politics might destroy every chance of climatic freedom, creating societies that will be unable, even more than we are today, to act in a way that is compatible with the persistence of diverse life on Earth. To have a climate culture that might contribute to achieving, at some point, collective climatic freedom, is a constant, painstaking struggle and work of maintaining, against every act of sabotage, the connection between symbolic realm and the world. To organize our collective efforts and cultural politics in such a way, we need to confront the old view of symbolic action and culture as way to distance ourselves from the world, to rise above other animals, plants, the elements, to free humans from the material world – and instead to see culture as a mode of multiplying our always already existing bonds to our diverse Earthly kin.

As we are leaving the Holocene, we are also leaving a culture of Modernity that easily believed in itself and its grand narratives of progress and Enlightenment. In the transition many new stories are emerging and there is a lot of narrative turmoil, failure to process the new precariousness and fragility of our historical horizon. In this transitional phase, many narratives lose contact to the world, become self-referential systems of belief, instruments of cultural destabilization and hybrid warfare. In terms of the theory of cultural narratives by Albrecht Koschorke (2017: 343), one can see at play in contemporary discourse an extreme emphasis of narratives' "social reference" – addressing social groups values and belief systems – and an almost total neglect of their "object reference" – reference to entities that exist independently of human discourse. This neglect is troubling, as a story's social function is strengthened when it loosens the object reference to become more flexible for affective situations, shifts ins collective values, and political dynamics. Post-factual storytelling has an advantage and easily takes the political high ground. But it comes with great danger of deranging our collective ability to tell true stories. It deforms our "narrative rationality" (Fisher 1987: 49), that is an essential mode of symbolic action that brings together diverse forms of human experience and rationality (science, moral, imagination, values, emotions and so on) in order to communicate and navigate the complexity of the world. Post-factual stances towards narratives reduce them to instruments of power and deprive us of this essential rationality. Peter Brooks (2023) calls this an "abuse of narrative."

Against such a brutalization of storytelling, Anna Tsing reminds us that strong stories and truth are not mutually exclusive, but that they belong to each other:

> The time has come for new ways of telling true stories beyond civilizational first principles. Without Man and Nature, all creatures can come back to life, and men and women can express themselves without the strictures of a parochially imagined rationality. No longer relegated to whispers in the night, such stories might be simultaneously true and fabulous. How else can we account for the fact that anything is alive in the mess we have made? (Tsing 2015: 7)

Narratives, in this sense, even if they follow ecopolitical goals and chart new territory, are not only about their rhetoric power but also about their relations and references to the material, more-than-human world. They can be expressions of cultural freedom and creativity and be full of world, of facts, and figures, and truth. Donna Haraway (2016: 10), in her speculative philosophical practice, emphasizes the importance to bring fact and fiction, science and fabulation closely together when we fabricate stories. In the present day, a truthful relation between stories and worlds becomes an issue of existential dimension for all live on Earth. That is because the performative feedback loop between stories and social reality – where the story shapes the social world it is narrating – is extending with the Anthropocene. As human actions transform the Earth, we witness strong feedback loops between stories and the material reality of the planet (Probst 2023: 36). With the Anthropocene and the climate crisis, as well as with widespread denial, there can be no doubt that "stories matter for the Earth" (Bonneuil 2015: 15).

Only if we tell true stories, we contribute to sustain life on Earth and are free. That is, not to be enslaved by the seemingly neutral perspective of science and its limited ways of worldmaking, but to stay true to it while enacting the freedom to tell good stories; stories that allow individual subjects as well as diverse collectives to find their own ways to live and survive on this planet. But the freedom to tell good and true stories as well as to act freely is not that of an individual being. To meet the things and relations in themselves halfway, thus to make worlds, is a complex task that requires collective efforts. There are different practices that allow collectives to meet and stay in touch with the 'things and relations in themselves'. While science might be more about the possible directions, culture might be the art to attend to the diversity of paths, their routes and characteristics, as well as the forms of moving along them. Culture and science, in the best case, meet in their care for a collective's ability to make worlds.

Thinking in the name of 'Earth', means to stay alert to any signs of warning that we might be losing connection with the things and relations that sustain our existence. Coming back to the question of response-ability, it also means to make collective worlds that grant their inhabitants the relational freedom to act in way that the effects of their actions would be compatible with the permanence of genuine biodiverse life.

Bibliography

Arendt, Hannah (2006 [1964]): "Wahrheit und Politik." In: Hannah Arendt und Patrizia Nanz über Wahrheit und Politik. Berlin: Wagenbach, pp. 7–62.

Bonneuil, Christophe (2015): "The Geological Turn. Narratives of the Anthropocene." In: Clive Hamilton/ François Gemenne/ Cristophe Bonneuil (eds.), The Anthropocene and the Global Environmental Crisis. Rethinking Modernity in a new Epoch, London and New York: Routledge, pp. 15–31.

Brooks, Peter (2023): Seduced by Story. The Use and Abuse of Narrative, New York: Review Books.

Cassirer, Ernst (1944): An Essay on Man. An Introduction to a Philosophy of Human Culture, New York: Doubleday Anchor Books.

Chakrabarty, Dipesh (2009): "The Climate of History. Four Theses." In: Critiqual Inquiry 35/2, pp. 197–222.

Clark, Nigel/Szerszynski, Bronislaw (2021): Planetary Social Thought. The Anthropocene Challenge to the Social Thought, Cambridge: Polity.

Dixson-Declève, Sandrine/Gaffney, Owen/Ghosh, Jayati/Rockström, Johan/ Stoknes, Per Espen/Randers, Jørgen (2022): Earth for All. A Survival Guide for Humanity. Gabriola: New Society Publishers.

Federal Constitutional Court (2021): Constitutional complaints against the Federal Climate Change Act partially successful. Press Release No. 31/2021, 29 April (https://www.bundesverfassungsgericht.de/SharedDocs/Pressemitteilungen/EN/2021/bvg21-031.html?nn=148454).

Fisher, Walter R. (1987): Human Communication as Narration: Toward a Philosophy of Reason, Value, and Action, Columbia: University of South Carolina Press.

Haraway, Donna (2016): Staying with the Trouble. Making Kin in the Chthulucene, Durham: Duke University Press.

Hulme, Mike (2021): The Tragedy of the Climate Wars. In: Issues in Science and Technology 37/3. (https://issues.org/new-climate-war-michael-mann-hulme-r eview/).

Iovino, Serenella/Oppermann, Serpil (eds.) (2014): Material Ecocriticism. Bloomington: Indiana University Press.

Jonas, Hans (1979): Das Prinzip Verantwortung. Versuch einer Ethik für die technologische Zivilisation, Frankfurt am Main: Suhrkamp.

Kant, Immanuel (1993): Grounding for the Metaphysics of Morals, Indianapolis, IN: Hackett.

Koschorke, Albrecht (2017): Wahrheit und Erfindung. Grundzüge einer allgemeinen Erzähltheorie, Frankfurt am Main: S. Fischer.

Latour, Bruno (2015): Facing Gaia. Eight Lectures on the New Climatic Regime, Cambridge: polity.

Latour, Bruno/Schultz, Nikolaj (2022): Zur Entstehung einer ökologischen Klasse. Ein Memorandum, Berlin: Suhrkamp.

Mann, Michael (2021): The New Climate War. The Fight to Take Back Our Planet; Melbourne/ London: Scribe.

Maxwell, Simon (2023): "Climate Change isn't Everything by Mike Hulme." July 6 (https://simonmaxwell.net/blog/climate-change-isnt-everything-by-mike-h ulme.html).

Moore, Jason (2015): Capitalism in the Web of Life. Ecology and the Accumulation of Capital. London/ New York: Verso.

Morton, Timothy (2017): Humankind. Solidarity with Nonhuman People, London/ New York: Verso.

Oliver, Kelly (2015): Earth & World: Philosophy After the Apollo Missions, New York: Columbia University Press.

Probst, Simon (2023): Instauration der Erde. Konstitutives Erzählen im Anthropozän und die kritischen Zonen der Literatur, Berlin: Metzler.

Serres, Michel (1992): The Natural Contract, Ann Arbor: University of Michigan Press.

Stehr, Nico/von Storch, Hans (2023): "Über die Macht des Klimas. Ist der Klimadeterminismus nur eine Ideengeschichte oder ein relevanter Faktor für die aktuelle Klimapolitik?" In: Nico Stehr/Hans v. Storch (eds.), Die Wissenschaft in der Gesellschaft. Wiesbaden: Springer, pp. 173–199.

Szeman, Imre/Boyer, Dominic (2017): Energy Humanities: An Anthology, Baltimore: John Hopkins University Press.

Tsing, Anna Lowenhaupt (2015): The Mushroom at the End of the World, Princeton: Princeton University Press.

Woods, Derek (2014): "Scale Critique for the Anthropocene." In: The Minnesota Review 83, pp. 133–142.

Crack in the wall of the Tuimskiy slump, Khakassia, Russia, 2023

© Alexander Nikolsky

Fiery

Miriam Ysa Calista

"The root of what blinds us lies in our hearts"
Francis Ponge

∞ cyanobacterium ∞

pull

there is a way of appearing that does not mean me
in which I cease to be through and through

I hold onto the shadows, I hold onto
the narrow edge of things
to the dark outline against the brighter sky

dissolution is a form of desire
merging another

do I want to take on new form in coming together
with another thing

or do I want to disappear, completely
without a trace

total forgetting
no, never-having-been

to exist without enduring, to exist
without repercussions on anything else
existing while absorbing all remnants of life

until a backward birth into the never-been sets me free

*

the solar threads chain me—

even if the reverse somersault out of existence succeeded
the other side would still always be the continuation
of what I once was

as long as Sun shines, I will appear under her conditions
tumble through the day-night up and down of rhythms

forget again and again
that even the most constant wavering
every lapse into excess

is only possible because she is

if I loosened a tiny solar thread from myself
so that for a moment it danced as a visible flame

on my skin, irregular, willful, unique

then even this flickering, frenzied, tumbling
spark-spraying tongue would only be

a tiny reflection of her massive desire:

to continue through others

and bind them to herself

in ever-varying ways

a permanent act of expulsion and incorporation
of all things from and into herself

as long as she exists, my desire always dissolves
into hers, my wish to cease does not push into an outside

she continues to grow through me—

in her light, I am predictable

and unpredictable only because she
simultaneously generates a tangle of shadows

in whose crossing points and overlapping layers
I, for a moment, am so much mixture
that my lack of form resembles dissolution

*

perhaps it is even so: I

exist through her, her fire penetrates my body

until it has weight, swells, bulges, expands, ruptures

her fire creates the form of my body, her fire
dissolves the form of my body, a glorious
symmetry, the inkling of an infinite balance
of invisible pain and joy, birth and destruction

nothing is safe here, if safety means
not being transformed—

unexpectedly, the light rises and goes straight
through me, a secret gift of affection, a sudden
overwhelm

∞∞

circular intensities

∞ *eucaryote* ∞

overwhelm

in different stages of winter or heat

a sunflare flashes through organs
until they are burnt out or alive
to the utmost

autophagy
happens from without
always within

degrade whatever is no longer
necessary or sufficient
to hold my life

this is my prayer—
small fractions of membranes
are still here

tolerating reality

∞∞

reflective tides

reality

I buckle, I am too folded—

at first, this was meant to create
space, multiplication of surface
through indentation, bulging

at some point, it became mania, then
excess

the abundance of forms eludes me, they are still
inside me, but in such a self-propelled whirl
that I lose track, can no longer hold them

how should that work, if everything moves on
independently

I'm tired of birthing even more, I cannot stop

I'm tired that what is only imagined
forces itself into reality

faster than my ability not to want it
could undo something

just let me think something, and I enforce it

how can emptiness be perceived
without at the same time creating something
like emptiness

∞∞∞

resisting a fire within

∞ fire ∞

emptiness

this body in ecstasy, a dance
through the form, until, reeling, it becomes
something else

flame crests push into each other, shivers
interlock, light threads weave together

sparks split from fluctuations and align
themselves on the side of the night

in free flight, they burn out, but denser
textures take them in their own way

slow deliberate licking
sudden flare-up
extinction—

until the fire-body reaches the interior of another
it can take hours or seconds

sunlight seeps through cells lightly
penetrates the skin, wanders deeper in
bloodstreams carry it further

but fire urnst he forms of death within the body
recognizes and accelerates them

take me, say the flames, while consuming
the very fabric of desire

∞∞

a storm bursting forth, stirring water and rocks

∞ *lava rock* ∞

desire

finally, it burns again
and my soul appears
shattered

but the fire
melts it back
together

across the sunken cheeks
streaks of soot

the eye sockets
a passage
ot he self

ot he other
side of the truth

here, everything is one

flames and shadows
are generous hosts
excluding nothing

scorched means
that the shape of a body
is released for itself

ash and soot

∞∞

tattered edges, crystal or cloud

∞ crystal ∞

soot

there is more than one way—

to ward off, to deflect the rays reflexively
to see things different retrospectively

dense layers of glaze covering the image
the aperture left open longer than necessary
or shorter than planned

to suck the memory up like a crumb

or retouch it like a stain in the wrong place
of life: make it into a flower

with scribbles, sun threads, cross it out

but so often that a black
box replaces the body—

∞∞

fusions, suspended

∞ *protostar* ∞

body

maybe everything started like this

at first, there was a glow in space
just a tiny spark of light, risen from
a greater fire, whirling through

the darkness, but it did not fade

something brushed against it—was it

a breath

a whisper, a song

the spark began to spin faster and faster, swirling, until it cast off
sparks of its own, pulling them into its orbit

co-whirling further, an ever-growing circle of light, a rotating spiraling
flurry

of sparks, held together by the attraction
of that first spark, set in motion
by that breath, whisper, or song—

a spark rising

∞∞

fiery

Signs and Matters

How Images Unmake Climatic Subjects
Intersectional and Decolonial Perspectives on Flood Images

Lebogang Neidhardt-Mokoena

> African relationality espouses a social
> paradigm that prioritizes other-regarding
> values, advocating for a more compassion-
> ate, context-sensitive, and relationship-
> centred approach to environmental dis-
> course.
> *Dominic Ayegba Okoliko, 2024*

Visual Representations of Climatic Subjects in Germany and South Africa: Two similar yet different Flood Images

Four women are standing next to an entrance of a building (Fig. 1). Two of them are in the centre of the image. Their casual clothes – jeans and sleeveless tops as well as their gloves – are covered with mud. One passes a bucket to the next. The other two women are standing on the far left and right edges of the image frame. The one on the right stands towards the building's wall, she is wearing a lime green working vest, a headscarf, and an almost invisible facial mask. Her clothes on the lower body, shoes and gloves are barely recognisable – they are covered in mud. The woman on the left also wears a lime green vest, she is holding a bucket overflowing with mud. This image was taken in Ahrweiler – a district in the north of Rhineland-Palatinate in Germany – by the German weekly current affairs magazine *Stern*.

In a different image – taken in South Africa – a group of Black women are stand-ing on a high surface next to a house (Fig. 2). These Black women are captured from a distance – appearing very small, their faces cannot be seen. They are just stand-ing, gazing at this house. From where they stand, the soil and stones of a hilly area have eroded to the lower part where there is a road. There are two cars that have col-lided together, and one has capsized. There are people on this road. Some of them are standing on the right side next to a bin, while others are on the left side of the road holding objects that look like brooms. They may be cleaning this road, but it is not clear since they are seen from a far distance. This aerial image was taken by Germany's state-owned broadcaster Deutsche Welle (DW).

Although these images depict and even prioritise people in the context of floods in Germany (2021) and South Africa (2022), they portray them very differently. In this comparison, it becomes evident that people's actual and constructed vulnerability and agency depends on factors like geo-political space, skin colour, gender and age. There is racial bias in climate change images located within colonial hierarchies that depict the West/Global North as change actors and the Global South as victims with no agency. Of course, the construction of such images is also influenced by the material conditions in which floods are happening. The visual material and matter shape each other and are intertwined. Such kinds of framing however, risk to overly simplify complexities by showing some aspects and invisibilising others (Entman 1993; O'Neill/ Smith 2014; O'Neill 2019).

Fig. 1: Volunteers help each other during a clean up after flooding in West Germany. (left)

Fig. 2: Soil erosion and car crash after heavy rains. (right)

Photograph by Murat Türemis, © laif

Photograph by Rogan Ward, © Reuters

1. Introduction: Climate Change Imagery without People

Recently, various news media outlets have been shifting away from using iconic polar bear images in their climate reporting (Climate Outreach 2024; BBC 2023; The Guardian 2019a). In 2019 the *Guardian* in collaboration with the online image library Climate Visuals decided to show fewer polar bears, but more people in its climate imagery (Climate Outreach 2024; The Guardian 2019a). Reviewing images that the *Guardian* was using in its climate reporting was first inspired by its editorial conversations on the need to change the language used when reporting about environmental issues (The Guardian 2019a; The Guardian 2019b). The editorial team then turned to the used images and considered how it could best represent climate issues visually. The aim behind the shift towards portraying more people in climate images is to convey environmental issues in more relatable and realistic ways to the readers (BBC 2023; The Guardian 2019a), as issues that matter rather than distant events that happen *there* and not *here* (O'Neill 2013). This shift also acknowledges that it is not easy to capture images that reflect global environmental changes, especially when depicting what cannot always be seen and therefore visually mediated (Schneider/ Nocke 2014; Grittmann 2014). The ways in which language and images are used in news articles shape how readers understand and engage environmental issues (The Guardian 2019a; O'Neill 2019).

Images communicate quickly, often simplify complex issues and reach beyond geographic spaces (O'Neill 2013). But especially climate change related images are not without problems (O'Neill 2022; 2019; 2013; The Guardian 2015; DiFrancesco/ Young 2011; Doyle 2007). Climate change images in particular seldomly show humans and are often dominated by polar bears (O'Neill 2022; O'Neill 2013), extreme weather conditions such as droughts, floods, and wildfires, the burning globe and smoke chambers. Climate images that do represent human beings tend to marginalise, silence and invisibilise or erase certain groups in society. The case of Vanessa Nakate, a climate youth activist from Uganda who was cropped out of a press image by news agency Associated Press during early 2020, is such an example (Ferdinand 2022; Nakate 2021; AP 2020; The Guardian 2020). The image had initially shown her and four other female youth climate activists: Loukina Tille, Luisa Neubauer, Isabelle Axelsson, and Greta Thunberg. It was taken during the World Economic Forum in Davos, Switzerland. This is where these activists from Germany, Sweden and Uganda were raising awareness about climate justice (Nakate 2021). In the climate change discourse, images that spotlight white children show up more frequently, even though framed within a discourse around the need for collaborative environmental action for 'our common future' or 'our children' (Kverndokk 2020). Environmental issues such as climate change or extreme weather events also often centre risk or vulnerability, i.e. threats and the urgency to respond (Grittmann 2014; Manzo 2010; Cox 2007). Such issues are embodied differently through the media, politics, education, science and other means or actors, depending on their respective interests and values (Schneider/ Nocke 2014; Cox 2007). For instance, humanitarian institutions and the news media tend to visually portray environmental issues through "visual fingerprints and harbingers" (Manzo 2010: 97) depicting floods or polar bears hanging on melting ice caps that are recurring and haunting viewers (O'Neill 2022) and are normalised to signify certain ideas about climate change. The emerging iconography of climate change currently mirrors the discourse of danger and catastrophe, where "at the epicentre of the discourse stands the figure of the vulnerable being" (Manzo 2010: 99). Portraying people in this way highlights the urgency of managing the risks related to climate change. Such a sense of urgency speaks to the discourse of adaption and mitigation often mentioned as pathways for managing risks of extreme weather events (IPCC 2012). Like any other ecological risks, floods and losses incurred by them represent or pose a danger or hazard and therefore, vulnerability. It is true that other people, mostly those living their lives in the Global South, experience the impacts and consequences of climate change in real time more than people in the Western communities. These lives also inhabit a future that the West is trying to prevent (Whyte 2017a; Whyte 2017b).

Showing humans in climate change visuals is important though for many reasons: climate change is not only about sciences or technical aspects. Climate change is a social issue. It is about people and lived experiences – in all their diversity. It is about stories and narratives we tell (Ferdinand 2022; French Institute UK 2022). Essentially, there is no one single climate change but a plurality and in turn, many ways people imagine and envision climate change and other ecological issues (Hulme 2017). Not showing people, or showing them in particular ways, can make environmental challenges a distant or far-away reality – troubling *others* elsewhere, but not *us* in *our* immediate contexts (Doyle 2007; O'Neill 2013). As a result, a distance is created to the urgency and the effects of environmental challenges. The question is: Who can see themselves in these narratives? And how? This is also about how climate change discourses are made accessible. After all, the ways in which agencies and actors are visualised on news platforms enters symbolic and cultural politics and societal consciousness of climate change (Lester/ Cottle 2009). In this essay, I therefore explore how the news media in South Africa and Germany frame the representation of people in climate change images differently.

2. Care: An Ethical Obligation

Environmental issues are symbolically constructed. So, how we speak about environmental challenges should be done with extreme care (Doyle 2024; Pezzullo 2024; Thaker 2024; Okoliko 2024; Cox 2007). And how we communicate about these issues is not neutral and consequently either limits or supports how the public responds to ecological problems (Cox 2007). Exactly because communication shapes the (in)actions and perceptions of viewers, communicators have an ethical obligation to communicate in ways that improve the ability for society to respond accurately and appropriately to environmental challenges, both for human and nonhuman beings (Cox 2007). For Doyle (2024) a shift towards care is observing that environmental communication is not just about delivering facts or information. It is also about nurturing relationships and fostering responsibility. Instead of focusing on future consequences, we need to be present, move away from objective knowledges to situated knowledges (Haraway 1988) – lived experiences, emotions, connection and hope. This work is about being "attentive and reflexive" (Doyle 2024: 28). On the importance of relationships, Okoliko (2024) speaks about an African relationality – a philosophy and ethical worldview – that prioritises people in community, encouraging collective sense-making, accommodating different voices, and different ways of knowing and understanding environmental issues. Here, care is about compassion and being context sensitive. It goes beyond just caring for humans and includes non-human beings (Sène 2024), with the understanding that humans and non-human beings are more interconnected than separate (Okoliko 2024).

3. How Media construct Climatic Subjects: Decolonial and Intersectional Perspectives

To analyse the role of care in (climate change) journalism, this essay studies images taken during floods in Germany. From 13 to 15 July 2021, western Europe, including Germany, experienced heavy rainfalls that led to troubling flooding. In Germany, these floods affected the North Rhine-Westphalia and Rhineland-Palatinate states, causing over 180 deaths, affecting and placing especially people above the age of 60 into vulnerability (Rhein/ Kreibich 2025). I also study images from a flood that happened in South Africa. About nine months after floods affected Germany and parts of western Europe, South Africa experienced floods and landslides in its coastal areas in the Kwazulu-Natal (KZN) province. From 11 to 13 April 2022, areas in KZN experienced massive rainfall.[1] On 19 April, President Ramaphosa called a state of emergency (South African Government 2022). At this time, 435 people had died and 54 were still missing and being looked for (The Outlier 2023), and over 40 000 people were impacted by these floods (South African Government 2022). I study images in six news publications – both online and printed, namely: *Der Spiegel*, *Stern*, and DW. DW is selected because it reported about the floods in South Africa during April 2022. For visual coverage on floods events in South Africa, the images in following publications were sampled: the *Sunday Times*, *Mail & Guardian* and News24 which covered the floods event in Germany. I analysed a total of 131 images. These publications differ in political and ideological stances. They also do not have the same audiences. However, they set the news agenda nationally and therefore play important roles in shaping discourse. My visual reading of these images was done with an approach informed by decolonial (Quijano 2000; Maldonado-Torres 2007; Moyo 2020; Mignolo 2000; 2005; Mignolo/ Walsh 2018; Ndlovu-Gatsheni 2013) and intersectional theoretical concepts (Crenshaw 2005). I talk about

---

1   Pinto et al. (2022) determine the role of climate change in this context through a combination of observations with climate models. They find that greenhouse gases and aerosol emissions are in part responsible for the observed increases of heavy rainfall. These rainfalls resulting in such damage and loss have roughly doubled due to human-induced climate change.

the three important tenets of decoloniality that are interwoven: the (1) coloniality of power, (2) knowledge and (3) being. I am using this approach in search of fullness, completeness, recovering, restoration, and recognition of an equal belonging. It is influenced by my own lived experience as a Queer, Black, South African person and trained journalist now living in Europe. It enables me to identify, analyse and counter dominant visual elements[2] used on images to continually dehumanise, degrade, and shame Black Indigenous and People of Colour (BIPoC). Thinking with intersectionality allows me to not only understand the ways in which different forms of identities like skin colour, gender, age, and nationality intersect and shape how people are depicted in images. It also supports a more nuanced analysis of knowledge production in climate change journalism with focus on images. I read these images to identify which visual elements and motifs are predominantly used. Guiding questions that supported my critical reading were: (1) What do the images represent: What kind of places and situation are depicted? (2) Who is shown? (3) And how are the humans in these images represented? These questions are useful for investigating the representation (denotative) and symbolic (connotative) meanings of people, places, and things (including abstract things) in different kinds of images. They help identifying and describing latent (often abstract, not easy to detect aspects) and manifest (visible or seen) elements in visual material. And with this, they reveal underlying prejudices. These aspects are also important for identifying visual frames that foster power from their symbolic significance as they use noticeable myths and metaphors in the narratives (Rodrigues/ Dimitrova 2011).

4. Visual Representations of Climatic Subjects in Germany and South Africa

Floods in Germany damaged important infrastructure and homes. They resulted in an economic loss of around 20 billion Euros in Rhineland-Palatinate (DKKV 2022; Kron et al. 2022). An image taken from above Dernau, shows a municipality in the district of Ahrweiler in Rhineland-Palatinate. Similar images show areas like Erftstadt-Blessem, Altenahr and Bad Neuenahr, where a railway is covered with tree debris, underground pipes are exposed, and houses are demolished. Cars are crashed and recreational spaces are swiped away. Floods are most likely to increase as global temperatures rise (WMO 2021; Manandhar et al. 2023). In South Africa, the floods affected especially marginalized communities, e.g. people living in informal settlements (Pinto et al. 2022; The Outlier 2023). The damages are estimated at 17 billion Rands (Pinto et al. 2022). In both the German and South African coverage, impact images are frequently used. Images of this area show the damage caused by the

---

2   Rose 2017; van Leeuwen 2011; Rodrigues/ Dimitrova 2011.

floods: torn streets, gutted sewerage work, and destroyed water infrastructure and power grids. An informal settlement is captured from above. The houses made of corrugated iron are standing in water. These are images that depict the scope of damage caused by the floods. A set of images used for the South African coverage includes images that symbolise loss of lives or affected people.

4.1. Gestures of concern and hope: Children-and-women images

When I first started reading these images, I realised that South African flood images show teenagers or younger children more often than images of floods in Germany. In images of the floods in KZN, children are often seen on sites of damage – either standing on collapsed roads with a huge hole opening or finding their way on exposed underground pipes. Adults are also shown, often as if they are simply going on with their daily routines, they are shown walking or heading somewhere or standing on a cracked street while talking to other people. Some are simply standing and gazing like in figure 2 that I introduced earlier. This image was captured by a local photographer. But even when news is created locally in the Global South, there is a high risk of (unconsciously) reproducing colonial imaginaries (Moyo 2020). As such, racist representations persist in media in post-apartheid South Africa (Duncan 2014; Chiumbu 2016; Democracy Works 2016; Govenden 2019). Coloniality are normative attitudes or patterns that uphold Western ways of knowing and supremacy even years long after colonialism ended. Coloniality is sustained in books, cultural patterns, common sense, aspirations of self (Maldonado-Torres 2007), and in the media.

One image from South Africa depicts children, teenagers, and women (Fig. 3) collecting water in buckets. This image is not a classic representation of a Madonna (mother) and child, which is often shown in humanitarian campaigning, symbolising notions of need, pleads for help and being rescued. However, showing children in climate change images implies innocence-based solidarity that can reproduce colonial visions of the superior North and inferior South (Manzo 2010). This conveys grim toughness where children and teenagers must also take part in helping their households (Briggs 2003). Placing children here questions the kind of future they might have, and mobilises pity, an iconographic element of rescue that is popularly used in child images of Save the Children and UNICEF. Contrary to this, only one image connected to German floods shows children wearing masks in a church setting. I would argue that the media in general does not show white children but rather protects them from any sort of exposure.[3] This though renders white children

---

3   Portraying children with care in media is enacted through journalistic ethical codes of conduct and legal regulations. For example, there are rules protecting publishing portraits in Germany. South African also has different legal positions that recognise different types of

as innocent and pure, their humanity worthy of protection. They escape collective imagery of helpless and colonial imagination, so they cannot have a cognitive dissonance when they must take their place as the 'master.'

Fig. 3: Clean tap water affected during floods – young children, teenagers and women fetching water from a water truck.

Photograph by Phill Magakoe, © AFP

All of us are confronted with coloniality and its violent aesthetics of white supremacy all the time. Coloniality lives on as a rigid perception that enforces control and domination. It can be identified in the language of salvation, progress, modernization, and being good for everyone (Mignolo 2005). And it takes part in reorganizing and transforming other systems like knowledge, subjectivities,

---

harm of revealing identities of children. There are, however, double standards on how communities portray certain children. Also, in the media. And these practices play out in day-to-day encounters. I have volunteered both in Germany and South Africa, working with younger and older children. Many community institutions like schools or NGOs in Germany are generally protective of photographing children. While this might be true for South Africa too, I have found it common for white tourists to bridge these ground rules – even going further to photograph communities children are from. Natalia Cecire's (2015: 168) work is a relevant example to this: she notes how Black children are "excluded from innocence's claim to protection". This is because Black children are rendered as strong, already mature and are associated with the wildness.

economies, politics and nature (Mignolo/ Walsh 2018). At the centre of coloniality is race as a classifying norm that continues to uphold a hierarchical world order through stressing binaries among constructed racial categories (Ndlovu-Gatsheni 2013). The unmasking of coloniality involves decoloniality. Decoloniality is about undoing, (de)centring, (de)westernising ways of thinking, being and knowing. It is counter (neo)colonialism, imperialism, white supremacy, neoliberalism, apartheid, capitalism, patriarchy, and other forms of dominations. It challenges not only ways of image making that reinforce and inscribe white supremacy. Decoloniality is a response in the analysis of race and subjectivities (Moyo 2020). It also challenges exoticism and stereotypical images. In journalism, decolonisation entails dismantling the discipline and field from structures that continue to privilege white, Western narratives and ways of making sense of the world and thereby *other* and misrepresent all those communities and their ways of living and knowing that are different (Moyo 2020; Govenden 2023).

In the German coverage, vulnerability shows up in a few images of older people. For instance, a full spread image of two pensioners (Fig. 4) depicts them each sitting in separate rooms in their house. Their valuable belongings are spread in the rooms that are covered in mud. The woman sitting on a couch gazes into the camera. The image is "bringing [extreme weather events] home" – that is, bringing closer the reality or closeness of climate change to those viewing these images (Cottle 2009: 508; also, Lester/ Cottle 2009). These subjects are sad; they are showing concern. Here, ageism shows up in a capitalist and neo-liberal reading that younger subjects are agents, and older people in need of help. They have grim faces, showing gestures of resignation and concern. This invites the viewer to be worried (Lester/ Cottle 2009) and represents a "dramatic call for compassion and empathy" (Grittmann 2014: 139). The focus on these subjects is an invitation to their personal stories and experience(s), where their livelihoods are rendered important. On the other hand, young people in these areas in Germany are represented as bold, confident, sometimes smiling, and courageous, holding up tools and ready to restore their affected communities. Many appear to be volunteering. Such depictions render these subjects active. It signifies them as having knowledge to navigate the impact of the floods. Such an aura of competence is also expressed in the representation of experts either in formal outfits or sitting in rooms with screens and computers. Such visuals are accompanied by centring younger women, constructing a notion of a gender-equal society.

Fig. 4: An older couple in their home affected by floods in Bad Neuenahr, Germany.

Photograph by Thomas Lohnes, © Getty images

4.2. Fragile normality

There is a set of images that shows collectives of people who are pulling up their sleeves to become active in the affected areas in Germany. In South Africa, though, when people are depicted as active, they are mostly lifesaving experts – and they are often captured alone.[4] Only two images in the *Sunday Times* showed a group of a police rescue team using shovels in search of missing people. Yet, the government deployed 10.000 troops to help in affected areas (News24 2022). Otherwise, the notion of individuality shows up throughout. For example, the image of the elderly woman in rural KwaZulu.[5] However, Black, Indigenous, People of Colour (BIPoC) value their neighbours for companionship and support. Different news reported that community members helped each other to search for missing family members and neighbours (Daily Maverick 2022; Eyewitness News 2022). Rescue and searches were being done by volunteers in support of communities, and by humanitarian aid organisations. The collective support in communities brought hope even during such a

---

4   "La pluie fait des centaines de morts en Afrique du Sud", 21 April, 2022 (https://www.dw.com /fr/dégâts-inondations-kwazulu-natal-durban-afrique-du-sud/a-61523206)

5   "Inondations en Afrique du Sud: le bilan s'alourdit à près de 400 morts", 15 April, 2022 (https://www.voaafrique.com/a/afrique-du-sud-près-de-400-morts-dans-les-inondati ons-les-recherches-se-poursuivent/6530919.html).

tragedy. Thinking with the African relational perspective and care, Okoliko (2024: 11) says "social ontology in Africa emphasises caring for the other, who is interconnected with oneself in a networked ecology".

Subjects in Germany are shown in either family constellations (Fig. 5), as experts or as community members. Such representations are informed by an ideology that white nuclear families are functional and committed to the well-being of others in their community. In these settings, in close angled shots, people have names, and their stories are told in the captions. They are business owners and/or families, or experts. Their being is therefore rendered important. Those who are closest to the established norm of a human being receive a lot of attention and are at the centre – recognised as individuals with personal stories and seen as collectives. As a result, the coloniality of power in the media is informed by a distribution of power through constructed racial hierarchies (Govenden 2023).

Fig. 5: Family house destroyed during floods.

Photograph by David Klammer, © laif

In South Africa, the focal point in images is the flooded areas, rather than people affected by these floods. Here the focus is on socio-economic challenges such as poverty, unemployment and living in low-cost housing or houses built with cheap materials like corrugated iron. This more or less anonymous precarity is expressed by wide shots, capturing informal settlements or rural areas, where people and their actions are barely identifiable. This is related to the coloniality of being, that is identical with a "life of an incomplete death: you are neither living nor you are dying at the same time" (Moyo 2020).

Similar, for Fanon (1953) and Maldonado-Torres (2007), the concept of coloniality of being foregrounds questions about what it means to be or not to be a being. It helps to understand how the construction of humanity or/ being of Africans and racialised people was and is still constantly questioned (Maldonado-Torres 2007; Fanon 1953; Ndlovu-Gatsheni 2015). In image making and media representation, we can see depictions that render some humans as knowing, active and capable, and others as ignorant, passive and helpless victims. Moyo (2020: 124) says the 'upper side' of Euro-American modernity tends to construct the Global South – 'darker side' or the underbelly of Western modernity as the worst side to live in – as poor, dark, primitive, dependent. And these narratives show up differently in media, including through images and other visual materials. Furthermore, human suffering or death so normalised in the Western master narrative where such representation must fit the usual Eurocentric stereotypes of victims portrayed as perpetrators (Moyo 2020).

In the Sunday Times, for instance, a wide shot depicts an area looking like an informal settlement. This visual has also been used from different angles by other newsrooms such as DW. [6] The image shows a demolished bridge entering a community. In the background is a view of a hillside with houses. The area is covered with trees and shows houses that are lined up unevenly on this hillside. These houses appear very small at a distance, close to a curving road. There are two groups of children or teenagers standing on this road, faces unseen from this distance. In the foreground, the bridge is split into two, showing a deep gap. The children are depicted as standing next to other people who are holding umbrellas. The casual nature of people standing and looking at a dangerous scene implies that they are used to such conditions. Due to the political, economic, and social status associated with developing spaces, such images normalise damaged infrastructure, which in this context suggests a fragile normality. Such images reproduce an imagination of African subjects living in poverty – material want and lack of balanced meals, wracked and unhygienic homes, with malfunctioning institutions and governments. The fragility is coupled with people seemingly going on with their day-to-day actions. Some images

---

6   "Sudáfrica declara estado de desastre por graves inundaciones", 14 April, 2022 (https://www.dw.com/es/sudáfrica-declara-estado-de-desastre-en-el-este-por-las-graves-inundaciones/a-61473142).

show people walking and driving cars on a traffic road (Fig. 6) where on the side of it underground pipes are exposed. In another incident, a road is cracked open, still men stand casually, showing no concern. In the same image, people are walking, navigating daily life (Fig. 7). Linked to the white gaze and its exoticisation, fantasies, and fetishes about Black lives, this normalises damage of public and private spaces. In images from sites in Germany, stable tall buildings, well built houses, personal items like furniture, toys, and shoes – symbols of economic privilege – are at the focal point. Here an imagination is maintained of whites living their lives free of pain and worries – only (if at all) disrupted by very singular, extreme events such as these floods.

Figs. 6–7: People standing next to damaged infrastructure.

Photographs by Phill Magokoe, © AFP

These floods did not just engage people on the ground where damage happened, they also captured different views on social media platforms and other spaces that drove various conversations (Kühne et al. 2021; Moghadas et al. 2023). In a news video by DW on X (known as Twitter at the time), a woman from an affected village says "There [are] so many people dead. You do not expect people to die in a flood in Germany. You [might] expect it maybe in poor countries. But you do not expect it here. But it was all too fast, too quick" (Deutsche Welle 2021). The high death toll was a surprise and a shock in this industrialised country. Like cases of other flood disasters, a public debate about responsibility and blame soon began, and crisis management came under criticism from both the media and the public (Fekete 2021). Although the sentiments of the woman in the video might be acknowledging Germany's socio-economic privileges in preventing such an event, her views have an undertone that suggests that climate change is not supposed to be here and now, but rather distant – a concern for *other* people in certain *other* places.

As this crisis in Germany shows, flood management can also be challenging for countries that deem themselves to be well prepared (Nick et al. 2023). There were challenges in coordination, information management, and disaster response organisation (Nick et al. 2023). There were also challenges of issuing, responding to warnings and a lack of information came up during these flood responses (Fekete/ Sandholz 2021). People became more vulnerable to failure due to an increased dependency on their own infrastructure and emergency system (Fekete/ Lorenz 2021). However, these floods shifted the public's focus from the Covid-19 pandemic to environmental issues (Angenendt/ Kinski 2022; Föller 2023).

4.3. Vulnerability and resilience

At the core of these images is the binary representation between vulnerability and resilience. In the German news coverage, a lot of images show different people restoring the areas affected. They are depicted holding different tools, clearing the mud, and debris caused by the floods. For example, in an image shown in *Der Spiegel* (Fig. 8), a group of male lifesaving professionals are resting in a muddy place – implying that they are exhausted. They are wearing working clothes with mud – which renders them active.

Fig. 8: Volunteer fire fighters taking a break.

Photograph by © Omer Messinger

Portraying people as both vulnerable and resilient, can promote active roles of people in managing extreme weather events, as Methmann and Oels (2013) point out. Being resilient then drives a focus on specific characteristics of affected areas that help affected people respond to floods for example in positive ways (Centemeri/ Tomassi 2022). This resilience is symbolised through bodily postures, gestures, activities and dominating motifs. It is overemphasised through the clothes they are wearing, and the mud across the space, surfaces, and tools. Whether subjects in these scenes are taking a break, sitting next to a huge pile of wreckage, and doing nothing, or captured doing something, they are depicted wearing working gear: gloves, overalls, jeans, and water-resistant shoes.

In these kinds of images, tangible elements like mud and debris play an important role. They can be seen as metonymic symbols that express the chaos and destruction wrought by the floods (Nerlich/ Jaspal 2024). Another very present element in this corpus of images are rubber boots. Rubber boots are not a new iconic motif in flood images in Germany. There were floods in August 2002 in Saxony (SWR 2002). The river Elbe had risen and surrounding cities like Dresden were flooded. Accompanied to the scene by then Saxon prime minister Georg Milbradt of the Christian Democratic Union (CDU), the then German Chancellor Gerhard Schröder of Social Democratic Party (SPD) made an appearance in Grimma in the Leipzig region wearing black rubber boots with a green rain jacket. Milbradt was wearing yellow rubber boots (SWR 2002). Milbradt was then dubbed the "flood crisis manager" (Der Spiegel 2002) because of this appearance.

Outdoor waterproof shoes are mostly worn as protective gear by the working class in heavy duty work. In a way, such a representation denotes being ready and keen to help, to change the situation of affected people, a reliable administration, doers and socially engaged leaders. For this reason, wearing such shoes places people of authority at a level of locals in affected areas. During the 2021 floods in Germany, rubber boots remain an important motif in the representation of people. Many subjects here are portrayed wearing them, which denotes that this event requires urgent action. But it also legitimises their response of managing floods – as active, knowledgeable, self-determined and driven. Politicians though do appear with such boots clean or combined with suit jackets. And this type of "political dress" creates a barrier for politicians to fully engage with the environment (Lester/ Cottle 2009: 931). Even though knowledge production and discourse are never neutral, the ecological discourse often refuses to acknowledge that it carries a belief in universal non-situated knowledge and discourses.

In South African images of floods, people are generally shown in areas that are dangerous, or as if left alone with no help coming, men standing around a house just gazing at what is happening inside, not helping (Fig. 9). From these images the notion emerges that BIPoC are not only vulnerable to the environment, but also often in need of Western help, as passive and as victims (Campbell 2010; Manzo 2011). This sort of argument is commonly used to argue for the importance of mitigation (Belfer et al. 2017). This reinforces widespread use of frames that delegitimize Indigenous actors in broader media (Belfer et al. 2017), including that of Black and people of colour (Nerlich/ Jaspal 2014).

Fig. 9: Men standing around a damaged house.

Photograph by Rajesh Jantilal and Phill Magakoe, © AFP

Such representations are likely to persist primarily in terms of actions, responsibilities, and vulnerabilities of countries. Such emphasis on vulnerability "tends to obfuscate the agency, knowledge and resilience of numbers of disempowered or marginalised groups" (Cuomo 2011: 695). This is because claims of vulnerability are used to get policy decision makers to pay attention (Methmann/ Oels 2013). Yet "such a discourse mirrors Eurocentric self-images of the west as rational, scientific and altruistic" (Andreucci/ Zografos 2021:5), where BIPoC are not able to help themselves. Related to the coloniality of knowledge, here coloniality has pushed traditional or ancestral ways of knowing to the margins, and renders ex-colonised people as not concerned about ecological issues and lacking environmental thinking (Green European Journal 2020; Williams 2021). The theme of vulnerability is common in discussions of the dangers of climate change (Cuomo 2011). Similar to concepts like development, "vulnerability forms part of the one and the same essentializing and generalising cultural discourses that denigrates large regions of the world as disease-ridden, poverty-stricken and disaster-prone" (Bankoff 2001: 29). Embedded in Western constructions of knowledge, vulnerability demonstrates assessing disasters within socio-economic, political and environmental contexts to be previously lacking (Bankoff 2001). Alongside the concept of vulnerability, resilience also persists in the theme of catastrophes (Centemeri/ Tomassi 2022). Linking vulnerability and resilience promotes a more active role of populations in disaster management, with a concern for gender minorities (Alexander 2013; Walker/ Cooper 2011). But resilience is promoted as an important means to reduce human vulnerability. This individualises challenges of climate change (Methmann/ Oels 2013). Even though climate change and its related crises affects people living in the margins such as BIPoC women and children, their voices are not centred but marginalised. The narrative shifts again to those from privileged economies with resources and the means to adapt and mitigate climate change. When the conversation is dominated by white men, the debate can be twisted or directed towards their priorities and preoccupations (Williams 2021).

5. Discussion and Conclusion

From the analysis, three main themes emerged: (1) Gestures of concern and hope; (2) Images of children and women fragile normality, and (3) vulnerability and resilience. They are interconnected and they share two central aspects: One aspect is that people, their emotions and activities are very identifiable in a lot of the images used for the German floods. On the other hand, people in flood images from South Africa are often unidentifiable, shown from a distance, with a focus on their socio-economic context and class. It seems less (or not at all) important to be able to identify their age, gender, activities, relations and emotions. Who these people are, what they are doing and how or what they feel is not important. This reproduces a binary construction in which BIPoC at most are rendered passively and white people or those in western countries are portrayed actively. This is of course a construction that invisibilises other important aspects. For instance, these visualisations marginalise different ways people in communities relate with one another, help each other, communicate and deal with such challenges collectively – shaped by values, cultures and other complexities that exist in communities. They ignore the historical, political, economic factors and context that steer and intensify environmental challenges in communities. There is simply no one way we encounter and make sense of environmental challenges. There are plural ways we enact these issues. While elderly people were mostly affected during German's floods, there were very few images showing them. Their absence is one of the silences in these images. Other silences, for instance, were deaths particularly in Germany and communal support in South Africa. Yet, community leaders and members of communities mobilised in support of each other. For instance, support came already before the floods destroyed communities. The night before, a text message in a group chat platform went out saying: "Don't

go to sleep. The river is rising. There's more rain on the way. Be ready to evacuate."
This was Nomandla Nqanula, a community leader writing to members of her community at Quarry Road (The Outlier 2023). She warned that the riverbanks of the Palmiet River were rising. She had been paying attention to a bridge nearby and taking photos of tree debris and other floating material that were entangled and stopping the water from escaping. She sent out these images to the city's disaster management team. A short while after her communication, the disaster unit instructed community members to evacuate the area. The M19 highway was slowly disappearing in flood water. They formed a human chain to cross and help each other out of this fast-flowing water (The Outlier 2023).

There are many factors that challenge journalistic ethics and norms such as the attempt to keep a balance, novelty, personalization where the strive for objectivity is impossible and often distorts the representation of climate change in the media (Boykoff 2012). In their attempt to be objective, journalists write their work based on what sources are available and therefore give certain voices more attention that are overly represented in their sources (Okoliko 2024). The media tends to commodify ecological crises as such issues draw much attention (López 2020). When climate reporting is done, it must be done with an ethics of care. My thinking around the concept of care is inspired by both decolonial and feminist scholars. The ethics of care is not just about emotions or tasks, but it is about world-making practices (Puig de la Bellacasa 2017) that understand that journalism is political, relational and deeply entangled with power. So, journalists need to acknowledge themselves as part of this power. But they also need to see themselves as part of the societies they create journalistic work from, instead of dis-attaching themselves. They need to ask: What are the ethical implications of representing someone (or something) in this way? Are these representations caring—or do they reproduce harm, neglect, or extractive gazes? As Okoliko (2024) writes: African relationality centres relationships, people, communities, and the collective production of knowledge on environmental issues. The ethics of care should reflect on cultural and social differences and acknowledge the pluralities of knowing and being.

Shifting away from polar bears and showing humans is a good thing. But this needs to be done with care. Otherwise, there is a risk of reproducing systems of oppression in image making and media representation that render white people in the global North as knowing, active and capable, and BIPoC in the global South as ignorant, passive and helpless victims, where the logics of othering is maintained and sustained exactly through the vulnerability of BIPoC for the West / Global North to construct its own image as knowing and active. Developing and applying a careful approach in journalism is a difficult and big task. At the same time, it can actually be seen as an opportunity: to do journalism in more ethical ways, and to set an example for other areas of journalism, beyond climate change images.

Bibliography

Angenendt, Michael/ Kinski, Lucy (2022): "Germany: Political Developments and Data in 2021." In: European Journal of Political Research Political Data Yearbook 61/1, pp. 1–22.

Andreucci, Diego/ Zografos, Christos (2021): "Between improvement and sacrifice: Othering and the (bio) political ecology of climate change." In: Political Geography 92, pp. 1–13.

Boykoff, Maxwell (2012): *Who Speaks for the Climate: making sense of media reporting on climate change*, Cambridge: Cambridge University Press.

Bankoff, Gregory (2001): "Rendering the world unsafe: 'Vulnerability as western discourse.'" In: *Disasters* 25/ 1, pp. 19–35.

Belfer, Ella/ Ford, James/ Maillet, Michelle (2017): "Representation of Indigenous people in climate change." In: Climate Change 145, pp. 57–70.

Bier, Marina/Fathi, Ramian/Stephan, Christiane/Kahl, Anke/Fiedrich, Frank/ Fekete, Alexander (2025): "Spontaneous volunteers and the flood disaster 2021 in Germany: Development of social innovations in flood risk management." In: Journal of Flood Risk Management 18/1, pp. 1–20.

Briggs, Laura (2003): "Mother, child, race, nation: The visual iconography of rescue and the politics of transnational and transracial adoption." In: Gender & History 15, pp. 179–200.

Cecire, Natalia (2015): "Environmental Innocence and Slow Violence." In: Women's Studies Quarterly 43/1–2, pp. 164–79.

Centemeri, Laura/Tomassi, Isabella (2022): "Disasters and catastrophes." In: Luigi Pellizzoni/Emanuele Leonardi, E/Viviane Asara (eds.), Handbook of Critical Environmental Politics, Edward Elgar Publishing, pp. 232–244.

Chiumbu, Sarah (2016): "Media, Race and Capital: A Decolonial Analysis of Representation of Miners' Strikes in South Africa." In: African Studies 75/3, pp. 417–35.

Crenshaw, Kimberle (2005): "Mapping the Margins: Intersectionality, Identity Politics and Violence against Women of Color." In: Raquel Kennedy Bergen/Jeffrey L Edleson/Claire M Renzetti (eds.), Violence against women Classic papers, USA: Pearson Education, pp. 282–313.

Cottle, Simon (2009). *Global crisis reporting: Journalism in the global age*. Maidenhead, Berkshire, UK: Open University Press.

Cox, Robert (2007): "Nature's 'crisis disciplines': Does environmental communication have an ethical duty?" In: Environmental Communication, 1/1, pp. 5–20.

Cuomo, J. Chris (2011): "Climate change, vulnerability, and responsibility." In: Hypatia 26/4, pp. 690–714.

De La Bellacasa, María Puig (2017): Matters of Care: Speculative Ethics in More than Human Worlds, Minneapolis and London: University of Minnesota Press.

DKKV (2022): "Die Flutkatastrophe im Juli 2021, Ein Jahr danach: Aufarbeitung und erste Lehren für die Zukunft." In: DKKV, Bonn: DKKV-Schriftenreihe.

DiFrancesco, Darryn Anne/Young, Nathan (2011): "Seeing climate change: the visual construction of global warming in Canadian national print media." In: Cultural Geographies 18/4, pp. 517–536.

Dittmer, Cordula/Lorenz, F Daniel (2024): "Emergent, extending, expanding and established citizen disaster response in the German Ahr valley flood in 2021." In: International Journal of Disaster Risk Reduction 105/2024, pp. 1–12.

Doyle, Julie (2024): "Practicing Care Through Creative and Collaborative Climate Communication." In: Environmental Communication 18/1-2, pp. 28–34.

Doyle, Julie (2007): "Picturing the clima(c)tic: Greenpeace and the representational politics of climate change communication." In: Science as Culture 16/2, pp.129-150.

Duncan, Jane (2014): "South African Journalism and the Marikana Massacre: A Case Study of an Editorial Failure." In: Political Economy of Communication 1/2, pp. 65–88.

Entman, M. Robert (1993): "Framing: Towards Clarification of a Fractured Paradigm." In: Journal of Communication 43/4, pp. 51–58.

Fanon, Frantz (1952): Black Skin, White Mask, New York: Grove Press.

Fanon, Frantz (1961): The Wretched of the Earth, New York: Grove Press.

Fekete, Alexander/ Sandholz, Simone (2021): "Here Comes the Flood, but Not Failure? Lessons to Learn after the Heavy Rain and Pluvial Floods in Germany 2021." In: Water 13/21, pp. 1–20.

Ferdinand, Malcom (2022): "Decolonial ecologies: Beyond environmentalism." In Luigi Pellizzoni/ Emanuele Leonardi/ Viviana Asara (eds.), Handbook of Critical Environmental Politics, Cheltenham, UK: Edward Elgar Publishing Limited, pp. 40–57.

Govenden, Prinola (2023): "The Media Decolonial Theory: Re-theorising and Rupturing Euro-American Canons for South African Media." In: Communicatio 49/2, pp. 1–30.

Govenden, Prinola (2019): Token Transformation: A Critical Political Economy of the Media Analysis of Ownership and Content Diversity in South Africa's Print Media, Johannesburg: University of the Witwatersrand.

Grittmann, Elke (2014): "Between Risk, Beauty and the Sublime: The Visualization of Climate Change in Media Coverage during COP 15 in Copenhagen 2009." In: Birgit Schneider/ Thomas Nocke (eds.), Politics of Climate Change: Visualization, Imagination, Documentation, Bielefeld: Transcript Verlag, pp. 127–151.

Haraway, Donna (1988): "Situated Knowledges: The Science Question in Feminism and the Privilege of Partial Perspective." In: Feminist Studies 14/3, pp. 575–599.

Hulme, Mike (2017): Weathered: Cultures of climate, London: Sage.

Intergovernmental Panel on Climate Change (2012): Managing the Risks of Extreme Events and Disasters to Advance Climate Change Adaption, New York/ Cambridge: Cambridge University Press.

Juling, Dominik (2022): "The German Military Response to National Disasters and Emergencies: A Case Study of the Flooding in the Summer of 2021." In Journal of Advanced Military Studies 13/1, pp. 210–218.

Kron, Wolfgang/Bell, Rainer/Thiebes, Benni/Thieken, Annegret (2022): "The July 2021 flood disaster in Germany." In: 2022 HELP Global Report on Water and Disaster, pp. 12–44.

Kverndokk, Kyrre (2020): "Talking about your Generation: "Our Children" as a Trope in Climate Change Discourse." In: Ethnologia Europaea 50/1, pp. 145–158.

Van Leeuwen, Theo (2011): "Semiotics and Iconography." In Theo van Leeuwen/ Carey Jewitt (eds.), Handbook of Visual Analysis, London: Sage, pp. 92–118.

Lester, Libby/ Cottle, Simon (2009): "Visualizing climate change: television news and ecological citizenship." In: International Journal of Communication 3, 920–936.

López, Antonio (2020): "Ecomedia: The metaphor that makes a diᵡerence." In: Journal of Sustainability Education 23, pp. 1–7.

Maldonado-Torres, Nelson (2007): "On the Coloniality of Being: Contributions to the Development of a Concept." In: Cultural studies 21/2, pp. 240–270.

Manandhar, Bikram/ Cui, Shenghui/ Wang, Lihong/ Shrestha, Shrestha (2023): "Post-Flood Resilience Assessment of July 2021 Flood in Western Germany and Henan, China." In: Land 12/3, pp. 1–32.

Manzo, Kate (2010): "Imagining Vulnerability: The Iconography of Climate Change." In: Area 42/1, pp. 96–107.

Methmann, Chris/ Oels, Angela (2013): "Vulnerability." In Carl Death (ed.), Critical Environmental Politics, London: Routledge, pp. 277–286.

Mignolo, D. Walter/ Walsh, E. Catherine (2018): On Decoloniality: Concepts, Analytics, Praxis, Durham and London: Duke University Press.

Mignolo, D. Walter (2015): "Sylvia Wynter: What Does it Mean to Be Human?" In McKittrick, Katherine (ed.), Sylvia Wynter: On being human as praxis, Durham and London: Duke University Press, pp. 106–123.

Mignolo, D. Walter (2000): Local Histories/Global Designs: Coloniality, Subaltern, Knowledges, and Border Thinking, Princeton, New Jersey: Princeton University Press.

Mignolo, D. Walter (2005): The Idea of Latin America, Malden, MA: Blackwell Publishing.

Moyo, Last (2020): The Decolonial Turn in Media Studies in Africa and the Global South, Cham, Switzerland: Springer International Publishing.

Nakate, Vanessa (2021): The Bigger Picture: My Fight to Bring a New African Voice to the Climate Crisis, Boston and New York: One boat.

Ndlovu-Gatsheni, J. Sabelo (2015): "Decoloniality as the future of Africa." In: History compass, 13/10, pp. 485–496.

Ndlovu-Gatsheni, J. Sabelo (2013): "Why decoloniality in the 21st Century?" In: The Thinker for Thought Leaders, 48, pp. 10–15.

Nerlich, Brigitte/ Jaspal, Rusi (2024): "Mud, metaphors and politics: Meaning- making during the 2021 German floods." In: Environmental Values 33/3, pp. 329–349.

Nerlich, Brigitte/ Jaspal, Rusi (2014): "Images of Extreme Weather: Symbolising Human Responses to Climate Change." In: Science as Culture 23/2, pp. 253–276.

O'Neill, Saffron (2022): "Defining a visual metonym: A hauntological study of polar bear imagery in climate communication." In: Transactions of the Institute of British Geographers 00, pp. 1–16.

O'Neill, Saffron (2019): "More than meets the eye: A longitudinal analysis of climate change imagery in the print media." In: Climatic Change 163, pp. 9–26.

O'Neill, Saffron/ Smith, Nicholas (2014): "Climate change and visual imagery." In: WIREs Climate Change 5, pp. 73–87.

O'Neill, Saffron (2013): "Image matters: climate change imagery in US, UK and Australian newspapers." In: Geoforum 49, pp. 10–19.

O'Neill, Saffron/ Nicholson-Cole, Sophie (2009): "'Fear won't do It': Promoting Positive Engagement with Climate Change Through Visual and Iconic Representations." In: Science Communication 30/3, pp. 355–379

Okoliko, Ayegba Dominic (2024): "Reflecting on Care within an African Relational Framework for Environmental Communication." In: Environmental Communication 18/1-2, pp. 8–14.

Pezzullo, C. Phaedra (2024): "On Environmental Communication as a Care Discipline." In: Environmental Communication 18/1-2, pp. 1–7.

Pinto, Izidine/ Zachariah, Mariam/ Wolski, Piotr/ Landman, Stephanie/ Phakula, Vanetia/ Maluleke, Wisani/ Bopape, Mary-Jane/ Engelbrecht, Christien/ Jack, Christopher/ McClure, Alice/ Bonnet, Remy/ Vautard, Robert/ Philip, Sjoukje/ Kew, Sarah/ Heinrich, Dorothy/ Vahlberg, Maja/ Singh, Roop/ Arrighi, Julie/ Thalheimer, Lisa/ van Aalst, Maarten/ Li, Sihan/ Sun, Jingru/ Vecchi, Gabriel/ Yang, Wenchang/ Tradowsky, Jordis/ Otto Friederike/ Dipura, Romeo (2022): "Climate change exacerbated rainfall causing devastating flooding in Eastern South Africa, World Weather Attribution." In: World Weather Attribution, pp. 1–31.

Quijano, Aníbal (2000): "Coloniality of Power and Eurocentrism in Latin America." In: International Sociology 15/2, pp. 215–232.

Rhein, Belinda/ Kreibich, Heidi (2025): "Causes of the exceptionally high number of fatalities in the Ahr valley, Germany, during the 2021 flood." In: Nat. Hazards Earth Syst. Sci 25, pp. 581–589.

Rodrigues, Lulu/ Dimitrova, Daniela (2011): "The levels of visual framings." In: Journal of Visual Literary 30/1, pp. 48–65.

Rose, Gillian (2016): Visual methodologies: An Introduction to Researching Visual Materials, London: Sage.

Schneider, Birgit/ Nocke, Thomas (2014): Politics of Climate Change: Visualization, Imagination, Documentation, Bielefeld: Transcript Verlag.

Sène, L Aby (2024): "A Reflection on Imperialism in Nature Conservation from African Conceptions of Care." In: Environmental Communication, 18/1-2, pp. 15–20.

Thaker, Jagadish (2023). "Do We Care to Listen? Commitments of Care in Environmental Communication from the Fields of India." In: Environmental Communication 18/1–2, pp. 206–209.

Whyte, Kyle (2017a): "Indigenous Climate Change Studies: Indigenizing Futures, Decolonizing the Anthropocene." In: English Language Notes 55/ 1–2, pp. 153–162.

Whyte, Kyle (2017b). "Our Ancestors' Dystopia Now: Indigenous Conservation and the Anthropocene." In: Ursula Heise/ Jon Christensen/ Michelle Niemann (eds.), The Routledge Companion to the Environmental Humanities, London: Routledge, pp. 206–215.

Williams, Jeremy (2021): Climate Change is Racist: Race, Privilege, and the Struggle for Climate Justice, London UK: Icon Books Ltd.

Online references

"A Decolonial Ecology with Malcom Ferdinand and Shela Sheik", March 20, 2022 (https://www.youtube.com/watch?v=_Gp6-WsXYgo).

"A Perfect Storm", May 1, 2023 (https://perfectstorm.theoutlier.co.za/).

"Why polar bears are no longer the poster image for climate change", November 14, 2023. (https://www.bbc.com/future/article/20231113-climate-change-why-photos-of-polar-bears-dont-work).

"Why we need a decolonial ecology: An interview with Aurore Chaillou, Louise Roblin, and Malcom Ferdinand", June 4, 2020 (https://www.greeneuropeanjournal.eu/why-we-need-a-decolonial-ecology/).

"We love polar bears, just not as the star of the climate story", February 27, 2024 (https://climateoutreach.org/polar-bears-climate-story/).

"Climate change made floods in Western Europe more likely", August 24, 2021 (https://wmo.int/media/news/climate-change-made-floods-western-europe-more-likely).

"National State of Disaster in numbers", April 18, 2022 (https://www.gov.za/news/national-state-disaster-numbers-%E2%80%93-18-april-2022-18-apr-2022).

"Why we're rethinking the images we use for our climate journalism", October 18, 2019 (https://www.theguardian.com/environment/2019/oct/18/guardian-climate-pledge-2019-images-pictures-guidelines).

"Devastated KZN community dig into the mud in desperate search for flood victims", April 18, 2022 (https://www.dailymaverick.co.za/article/2022-04-18-d evastated-kzn-community-digs-into-the-mud-in-desperate-search-for-flood -victims/).

"The Deadly Storm: When disaster struck in KZN", April no date, 2022 (https://spec ialprojects.news24.com/the-deadliest-storm/index.html).

"Outrage at white-only image as Ugandan climate activist cropped from photo", Jan-uary 25, 2020 (https://www.theguardian.com/world/2020/jan/24/whites-only-photo-uganda-climate-activist-vanessa-nakate).

"The Media and Systemic Racism", October 24, 2016 (https://democracyworks.org.z a/the-media-and-systemic- racism/).

"Why pictures of polar bears don't always tell the truth about climate change", Febru-ary 2, 2015 (https://www.theguardian.com/sustainable-business/2015/feb/02/i mages-climate-change-mislead-polar-bear).

"He's dead, we just want his body' – Family searching for loved one after KZN floods", May 25, 2022 (https://www.youtube.com/watch?v=q9gxGB94cPs).

"Wettrudern der Deichgrafen", August 15, 2002 (https://www.spiegel.de/politik/de utschland/politiker-im-krisengebiet-wettrudern-der-deichgrafen-a-209570.h tml).

"Why the Guardian is changing the language it uses about the environment", May 17, 2019 (https://www.theguardian.com/environment/2019/may/17/why-the-gu ardian-is-changing-the-language-it-uses-about-the-environment).

"Photo cropping mistake leads to AP soul-searching on race", January 28, 2020 (https://apnews.com/article/6a853a81f34164ab85713e68a889976d).

"Hochwasser-Wahlkampf: Kanzler Schröder gummistiefelt durch Grimma", August 15, 2002 (https://www.swr.de/swrkultur/wissen/archivradio/hochwasser-wahl kampf-kanzler-schroeder-gummistiefelt-durch-grimma-102.html).

Thinking beyond the End of the World
Reflections on Climate Anxiety and the Need for New Narratives for the Middle Classes

Juliane Miriam Schumacher

A sunny day in early spring, the wind is still chilly, the sky light blue. We are sitting on blankets in the park, balloons decorating the cargo bikes. The birthday of a colleague. Her friends, some of them the parents of her daughter's friends, others from a climate action group she has recently joined, drink coffee from colorful picnic cups, eat noodle salad and vegan cake – and talk about preparing for the catastrophe. What will be their first steps once the electrical grid breaks down? Where will they meet – in the city center where they live, or at the holiday home some of them have bought in the countryside?

The aim of the group, I understand, is not to prepare protests, or to push governments, companies or the public toward more climate action. Originally aimed at offering a space to deal with the frustration, helplessness, and despair many climate activists were suffering from after years of climate activism they considered unsuccessful, it has turned into a network to prepare, in a very practical sense, for the climate breakdown they expect to hit soon.

They are not alone. Similar groups have spread all over Western countries in recent years. 'Prepping,' preparing for emergencies by forming alliances, hoarding water and food, and forging detailed emergency plans, is no longer only a domain of the far right. In 2025, there is no climate camp taking place like those of earlier years; instead, activists are meeting for the first "collapse camp," which includes practical skill-sharing workshops and collective work to deal with overwhelming emotions in the face of what their webpage describes as the "creeping collapse of ecosystems and societies."

These concrete preparations for a collapsing social and ecological order may be a recent trend. They are, however, an expression of a phenomenon that has already been observed and discussed for some years now: strong climate emotions, most notably climate anxiety, climate anger, and climate grief. This affect has become so widespread, first in the US, then also in Europe, that psychologists have created manuals for dealing with it, special issues have been published in medical journals, and the American Psychological Association has created a new definition for climate anxiety: "chronic fear of environmental doom." A whole range of guidebooks has been published, including an illustrated children's book titled *What to Do When Climate Change Scares You*, aimed at children aged six to twelve.

Feelings of fear and anxiety may not be surprising if one looks at the scenarios climate scientists model with the help of ever more complex computer programs – visions of the future most young people interested in climate change have become strangely familiar with. Red, blue, yellow, green, solid and dotted lines representing different warming scenarios, each associated with different risks and consequences: rising sea levels, droughts, the collapse of ocean currents, changing weather patterns, an increase in storms and heavy rains. The 'safe' pathway to stay under 1.5 degrees of global warming seems more and more out of reach, given that emissions continue to rise. And the issue of lesser-known but more dangerous "tipping points," abrupt changes, points of no return, add an additional layer of looming danger and unpredictability. Who would wonder that people growing up among such visions of the future rather expect the worst from what is to come?

Still, there is a strange discrepancy in the phenomena of climate anxieties: Those people who are most occupied with the unfolding climate crisis, those who most fear the consequences of climate change, are often those who, following 'objective criteria' (if such exist), would not be the first ones to be hit by it; by contrast, they can often be considered to be in a comparably safe position. In a 2019 contribution to the magazine *Scientific American*, university professor Sarah Jaquette Ray, who published the book *A Field Guide to Climate Anxiety*, observed that the students who responded most to her book were not those who would, considering their background, the places they live or their social situation, be most affected by the effects of climate change – by the heat concentrating in densely populated city centers, floods in run-down neighborhoods, or food crises leading to rising prices. Marginalized communities most exposed to these risks were, according to studies, those most concerned about the consequences of climate change. Bu those who experienced extreme *emotions* of anxiety and fear, who met in climate anxiety circles, were predominantly white. "Climate anxiety," Ray concluded, "is an overwhelmingly white phenomenon."

The same observation can be made in the urban centers of Germany: It is not the migrant kids living in overcrowded flats in the centers of run-down, post-gentrified urban centers who form emergency groups for the catastrophes to come. Those who search for relief from their climate grief and anxiety by joining emotional healing and emergency preparation groups are, in most cases, members of the rather affluent parts of society: they live in renovated or newly built apartments they have bought with the support of their well-off parents; they get away from the city for vacations and holidays, or head to the countryside on weekends; they ensure that their kids attend good schools, play the piano or the drums, and read real books instead of spend too much time online. They are, in short, part of what is called, for lack of a more appropriate term, middle-class.

It would be easy to explain this uneven distribution of climate anxiety as stemming from a lack of knowledge, to simply attribute the lower degree of climate anxiety among those less well-off to the fact that they are less educated, that they simply do not know enough about climate change to fear it. But knowledge is, in times of an excess of information, rather a question of interest than of access, and it does not explain why young, white members of the middle classes develop a sometimes obsessive interest in knowing more about a future that, in the end, cannot be predicted, while other parts of society simply don't seem to care – or at least not enough to develop such strong emotional responses.

Strong emotions like anger, anxiety, and fear are, apart from acute situations of danger, never simply 'rational.' They are deeply personal but, at the same time, they do have a social component. If they become a collective phenomenon, they can tell a story about the unconscious fears, pressures, and conflicts at work in the social fabric of a society in a specific moment in time. Global warming will, from all that we know, confront human societies with new and increasing challenges in the decades and centuries to come – challenges that may lead to losses and imminent threats, even in the more affluent parts of the Global North. But how much this knowledge affects us emotionally does not necessarily stand in relation to the likelihood of immediately experiencing these events. It depends also – and maybe even more – on how much this knowledge affects our own story of the future and what we (and society) expect that story to be. And this may be one explanation, one piece of the puzzle, as to why strong climate anxiety is most prevalent among young people of the middle classes: because knowing about climate change, its causes and possible ways of preventing and dealing with it, poses a threat not to their imminent survival but to their very identity.

Much has recently been written about how climate discourses affect the self-perception of what is called the 'traditional working-class,' how its members feel wrongly blamed and devalued in multiple ways, and how these experiences can lead to a strong opposition against green policies, or even a turn to the far right. The picture is complicated by the fact that their perception of injustice in relation to climate policies is, in many ways, justified: Despite all the talk about 'green lifestyles' and their various prominent individual representations, such as zero-waste, no-fly or DIY approaches, studies continue to show very clearly that attitudes toward climate policies in certain groups of society do not come, as could be expected, with a reduced level of emissions. Emissions correlate directly with income and wealth, and this has been shown both on the global level, most prominently by Lucas Chancel and his team at the World Inequality Lab, and for individual countries, as demonstrated by regular studies conducted by the Umweltbundesamt, Germany's main environmental protection agency. And it is because of this that emission levels in Western societies have, since the 1990s, stayed in correlation with the increasingly unequal distribution of wealth and income: The poorer parts of society have lowered their emissions, often simply because they have become poorer and because climate policies based on markets and price signals hit them the hardest. And at the same time, the emissions of the richest part of society have increased, not primarily because they consume more, but also because they have become richer – and the richer a person is, the more his or her emissions are based on their investments, such as real estate, bonds, and stock holdings.

It is exactly this discrepancy that contributes to the deep uncertainty among young, middle-class people caring about climate activism. The limits of these individualized approaches to climate policies, based on moral appeals and individual behavior, have become more and more apparent; the idea of a green middle-class lifestyle that would allow a reconciliation between the economic and moral obligations educated young people are confronted with has also become increasingly unachievable and ecologically questionable. And those parts of the middle classes in Western societies who try to do it 'right,' who know and care about climate change, are ground down by conflicting expectations and demands they cannot fulfil without risking their social existence.

The idea of growth is a core element of modern societies, and it has, at least since the end of the Second World War, dominated Western economies and policies. It has been increasingly questioned whether unlimited growth is possible on a planet with limited resources, from the famous report of the Club of Rome to the Degrowth movements that have, starting from France, spread over much of Europe and, to a lesser degree, North America. Wide parts of the climate movements and climate science agree that efficiency and technological advances will not be enough to lower emissions; the use of resources, especially of energy, must be drastically reduced. An effective climate policy needs an end of growth.

But this sounds easier than it is. Timothy Mitchell, in his study on the relationship between the use of fossil fuels and the development of modern mass democracy, has argued that it was the highly concentrated energy of oil – a transportable, highly effective source of energy – together with the establishment of geopolitical dependencies ensuring its continuous supply, that allowed the thought of unlimited growth, to develop a modern version of economics no longer dealing with the best allocation of a set of limited resources, but to imagine that there is always more. More that can also be distributed, allowing broad sectors of society to get a share of the general prosperity: The postwar period not only saw the idea of unlimited growth as both desirable and possible becoming hegemonial and exponential growth becoming a physical-material development – the Great Acceleration, the exponential rise in various fields such as resource and energy use, land use, and food production, started in the 1950s – it also saw the rise of the middle classes. The middle classes are a product of this time, a child of growth, and the idea of growth has been inscribed in their very identity: The narrative of social advancement, both across the lifespan and within the family, the idea that the following generation should – and will – have it better one day, is a core element of the self-identity of Western middle classes: a *raison d'être* and promise at the same time.

This promise, though, has been tarnished for some decades. In Europe, the "erosion of the middle classes" and a diverse array of crisis narratives around them have been a constant theme in sociological debates since the 2000s. The French sociologist Luc Boltanski has observed the "process of social regression in formerly stable employment situations"; in Germany, sociologist Oliver Nachtwey has written about the "Abstiegsgesellschaft" (downward social mobility). Economic data, most notably the work of Thomas Piketty, has shown that since the 1980s, inequality has been rising, and the fraction of society with a middle income has become smaller.

To empirically confirm such diagnoses of this crisis of the middle classes is still difficult. The middle classes have remained a porous subject, difficult to grasp: more an idea and self-identification than a concrete, qualitative category of social research. As the middle classes are a defining feature of modern Western societies – or *the* defining feature, in terms of social structure – sociologists have come up with all sorts of definitions for them, defining middle classes by income ranges or wealth, or by certain shared norms and beliefs, such as family orientation and a meritocratic attitude; they have created further subdivisions of class structures and models and have distinguished different forms of middle class capital, including economic, cultural, social, and moral capital – each definition with its own limits and none able to finally answer what the middle classes are. In political theory, middle classes have remained an unloved subject, neither fish nor fowl, neither working class nor bourgeoisie, a class that claims not to be one – an issue that becomes even more obvious in German, where even the term *class* is generally avoided and researchers and politicians continue to talk about Mittel*schicht*, a *layer* of society, negating any functional relation between the socioeconomic realities of different parts of society.

But there is one defining feature of middle-class existence, and this is its precarity – and not only since neoliberal reforms undermined the social security systems in Western states. Insecurity has been part of middle-class existence from the beginning. The middle classes are those who have enough to have something to lose, but not enough to be secure no matter what, as is the case for the upper classes. Middle-class social status is always precarious, and constant investment and distinction is necessary to maintain and increase it; this is "investive status work," as sociologists Olaf Groh-Samberg, Steffen Mau, and Uwe Schimank have called it, which reaches beyond the individual as part of a generational project of social advancement. This precarity is related to, yet at the same time occurs in contrast to, predictability as one of the core norms of the middle classes – to the ability to plan as both a necessity and a virtue. Being middle class holds the promise of achieving a certain degree of stability in life that just a very small group of human societies throughout human history has ever had, but it is a promise – not a guarantee.

The "crisis" of the middle classes has not come with the acknowledgement that the narrative of the possibility of unlimited growth was always a myth, and that the social uplift of a whole generation in the Western world in the postwar period originated in a very specific historical time and place, with a combination of very different factors – the Cold War and systems competition, the traumas of two world wars, the massive exploitation of natural resources, and the exploitation and oppression of racially and economically marginalized people within and beyond the borders of individual countries. Instead, the crisis has intensified the struggles of the middle classes to maintain their status and prevent the loss of it. This crisis has, in many parts of the West, not questioned but reinforced the hegemonic middle-class story of a certain status and place in history that has been earned through one's own work and hardship, and that success in life first and foremost depends on the 'right' behavior and effort. It is this narrative, combined with the ideal of "intergenerational status reproduction," that puts an enormous amount of pressure onto the following generation and defines the benchmark for evaluating one's own life. The inability to reach a certain degree of education and material wealth, to secure enough cultural, economic or moral capital to maintain one's social status – and perhaps even more important, to make sure that the next generation will be able to do so – is, in many regards, considered a self-inflicted failure.

Climate change complicates this picture. Often it has been argued that climate change – like other aspects of the Anthropocene – comes with new temporalities that are difficult for humans to deal with, as they span far beyond a human lifespan. But it also has temporal affects on a smaller scale, because it affects the interfamiliar and intergenerational story of progress that continues to guide our lives – even when it is often unexpressed. Many detailed studies in recent years have shown the destructive consequences of the – assumed or contested – crises of the middle classes, and of rising inequality: The more difficult the ideal of social ascent has become to achieve, the more insecurity has spread among the middle classes, and the more the urge for distinction has grown. For some, distinction means the degradation of those who are considered 'other,' or below oneself; already in the 2010s the team around sociologist Wilhelm Heitmeyer traced the emergence of what he called the "rohe Bürgerlichkeit" (crude bourgeois mentality) and the growing erosion of solidarity, and as recent election results and many studies have shown, "group-focused enmity," (gruppenbezogene Menschenfeindlichkeit) as Heitmeyer has termed it, has further spread since then. It is easy to be angry – to search for weaker figures to blame. But for those who do not give in to these destructive patterns of crisis response, who try to maintain a feeling of care and responsibility for others and the world, things are, emotionally, more difficult. Because even though it is understood differently, distinction is also important for those parts of the middle classes who search desperately for a way to deal with the evolving climate crisis. They too have grown up with certain notions of what can be expected in life, with ideas about what has to be achieved, offered to your family and, later, your child's own family, with a specific conception of oneself and one's place in the world. Climate change, taken seriously, shatters many of these convictions, and it stands in sharp contrast to growth and progress as fundamental principles of middle-class life; it adds to a feeling of being lost in a time where, given the current geopolitical shifts and rise of new powers, also the sense of our place in the world seems increasingly insecure.

I would argue that the strong emotional reaction many young people of the middle classes in the West have developed toward the climate crisis, their anxiety and grief, is, in part, related to the loss not only of species and places but also to the loss of a future that had been promised to them, a loss of distinction and privilege. And these emotions also reflect the scale of the challenge ahead: to search for new narratives of what a good, successful life is in light of the necessity of material degrowth, for new subjectivities and solidarities beyond a middle-class identity, and for conceptualizing one's place both in society and in the world. For some, it might be easier to imagine the end of the world than to anticipate a fulfilling life that does not live up to the ideals they have grown up with and the status they feel the need to maintain.

Stories that have been intensively discussed in the wake of a new interest in class politics – Annie Ernaux's detailed descriptions of her childhood and youth, and Didier Eribons's biographical reflections on his working-class background and his parents' lives, for example – have shown how important it remains in many people's lives to define the small distinctions that keep societies structured and classes apart from each other. They have pointed at the 'guilt' toward the classes they have left, and at the continuous feeling of 'not belonging.' But they have told the story of classes in a one-directional way: the story of social ascent through education, of leaving the poverty and narrowness of the lower classes to live a more affluent middle-class life: in many regards, the story of a time that has long since passed. We will need new stories for the future.

References

BMUV, and UBA (2023): "Umweltbewusstsein in Deutschland 2022 – Ergebnisse einer repräsentativen Bevölkerungsumfrage." https://www.umweltbundesamt .de/sites/default/files/medien/3521/publikationen/umweltbewusstsein_2022_b f-2023_09_04.pdf

Boehme, Blake A. E./Kinsman Laura M./Norrie, Holden J./Tessier, Eric D./ Fleming, Shaun W./ Asmundson, Gordon J. G. (2024). "Climate Anxiety: Current Evidence and Future Directions." In: Current psychiatry reports, 26/11, pp. 670–677. https://doi.org/10.1007/s11920-024-01538-9.

Boltanski, Luc/Chiapello Ève (2005): The new spirit of capitalism. London: Verso.

Burzan, Nicole/Kadelke, Philipp (2024): "Zur Herausforderung, die Lebensführung heterogener Mittelschichten zu erforschen." In: Soziologische Revue, 47/4, pp. 400–408. https://doi.org/10.1515/srsr-2024-2067.

Chancel, Lucas (2022): "Global carbon inequality over 1990–2019." In: Nature Sustainability, 5/11, pp. 931–938. https://doi.org/10.1038/s41893-022-00955-z.

Lucas Chancel, Iddri/Piketty, Thomas (2015): "Carbon and inequality: from Kyoto to Paris: Trends in the global inequality of carbon emissions (1998–2013) & prospects for an equitable adaptation fund." (http://piketty.pse.ens.fr/files/ChancelPiketty2015.pdf).

Lucas Chancel, Iddri/Piketty, Thomas/ Saez, Emmanuel/ Zucman, Gabriel et al. (2021): "World Inequality Report 2022." (https://wir2022.wid.world).

Clayton, Susan (2020): "Climate anxiety: Psychological responses to climate change." In: Journal of anxiety disorders, 74: 102263. https://doi.org/10.1016/j.janxdis.2020.102263.

D'Alisa, Giacomo/Demaria, Federico/ Kallis, Giorgos (2015): Degrowth: A vocabulary for a new era.

Davenport, Leslie/Ruggiero, Irma (2024): What to Do When Climate Change Scares You. Washington, DC: Magination Press, American Psychological Association.

Eribon, Didier (2016): Rückkehr nach Reims. Berlin: Suhrkamp.

Ernaux, Annie (2017): Die Jahre. Berlin: Suhrkamp.

Ernaux, Annie (2021): Die Scham. Berlin: Suhrkamp.

Groh-Samberg, Olaf (2014): "Investieren in den Status: Der voraussetzungsvolle Lebensführungsmodus der Mittelschichten.", In: Leviathan, 42/2, pp. 219–248.

Heitmeyer, Wilhelm (ed.) (2002–2024). Deutsche Zustände. 10 Vols. Berlin: Suhrkamp.

Kallis, Giorgos (2018): Degrowth. New York: Agenda.

Kleinhückelkotten, Silke/ Neitzke, H.-Peter/Moser, Stephanie (2016): "Repräsentative Erhebung von Pro-Kopf-Verbräuchen natürlicher Ressourcen in Deutschland (nach Bevölkerungsgruppen)." UBA Texte 39/2016 (https://www.umweltbundesamt.de/sites/default/files/medien/1410/publikationen/texte_39_2016_repraesentative_erhebung_von_pro-kopf-verbraeuchen_natuerlicher_ressourcen_korr.pdf).

Meadows, Donella H. et al. (eds.) (1972): The limits to growth: A report for club of Rome's project on the predicament of mankind. New York: Universe Books.

Mitchell, Timothy (2011): Carbon democracy: Political power in the age of oil. London: Verso.

Nachtwey, Oliver (2016): Die Abstiegsgesellschaft: Über das Aufbegehren in der regressiven Moderne. Berlin: Suhrkamp.

Oxfam (2015): "Extreme Carbon Inequality: Why the Paris climate deal must put the poorest, lowest emitting and most vulnerable people first." (https://policy-prac

tice.oxfam.org/resources/extreme-carbon-inequality-why-the-paris-climate-deal-must-put-the-poorest-lowes-582545/).

Oxfam (2020): "Confronting Carbon Inequality in the European Union: Why the European Green Deal must tackle inequality while cutting emissions." (https://www.oxfam.de/system/files/documents/media_brief_-_english_-_confronting_carbon_inequality_in_the_eu_-_embargoed_00_01_cet_8_december.pdf).

Piketty, Thomas (2014): Capital in the twenty-first century. Transl. by Arthur Goldhammer. Cambridge Massachusetts: The Belknap Press of Harvard University Press.

Ray, Sarah J. (2020): A field guide to climate anxiety: How to keep your cool on a warming planet. Oakland: University of California Press.

Ray, Sarah J. (2021). "Climate Anxiety Is an Overwhelmingly White Phenomenon." Scientific American, 21 March 2021 (https://www.scientificamerican.com/article/the-unbearable-whiteness-of-climate-anxiety/).

Sachweh, Patrick/Lenz, Sarah (2018): "Maß und Mitte – Symbolische Grenzziehungen in der unteren Mittelschicht." In: KZfSS Kölner Zeitschrift für Soziologie und Sozialpsychologie, 70/3, pp. 361–389. https://doi.org/10.1007/s11577-018-0557-3.

Listening to Climate Change
Sonic Subjectivities in The Anthropocene

Michaela Vieser and Isaac Yuen

> The earth said // remember me. // The earth said // don't let go, // said it one day
> // when I was // accidentally // listening
> *[To] The Last [Be] Human, p.306, Jorie Graham*

> The expanding field of acoustics has enabled us to tune into a multitude of
> invisible worlds. Emanations from distant galaxies are being translated into
> audible harmonics. Vibration sensors are tapping into the deepest recesses of
> the earth. Hydrophones are capturing formerly unknown chatter in rivers and
> oceans. But with the technologies to eavesdrop comes the responsibility not
> only to understand these newfound realms, but to safeguard them — often from
> ourselves.
> *The Sound Atlas, Foreword, p.9*

Throughout the Anthropocene, humanity has, knowingly or not, birthed new soundscapes while obliterating others. Our species has introduced noise and chaos into
where once was silence, has extinguished spaces that formerly contained rhythm,
melody, and harmony. While researching *The Sound Atlas: A Guide to Strange Sounds
Across Landscapes and Imagination*, we felt many of these resonant losses.

To understand sound from a variety of historical, scientific and cultural perspectives, we spoke to art historians like Professor Flora Dennis from the University of
Sussex, who imagines the clattering of silverware, the breathing of household dogs,
and the movement of furniture on wooden floors to evoke the human soundscapes
within a Renaissance home. Or to musicians like Anna Friederike Potengowski, who
reconstructed and learned to play bone flutes from cave excavations from prehistoric
times to grasp how ancient sounds shaped our ancestors' spatial and imaginary understandings. We consulted with scientific experts who 'see' sound through translations of energy waves into sound waves, watched renderings of complex graphs into
melodies, and delved into the imprints that silence left on different cultures. In so
doing we strove to become cartographers of sounds on both a spatial and temporal

level, ranging as far as the beginning of the universe to our own bodies, and deeper yet, to voices heard from within.

Thus, we came to envision that anthropogenic climate change itself can also be considered on the level of sonic states in flux, beginning with the spinning looms in textile mills at the advent of the Industrial Revolution, to the roar of the first internal combustion engine that would come to move the world, to the blasts of seismic airguns penetrating the sea floor in search of gas reserves to satiate our unceasing appetite for fossil fuels. Sound is energy. Through air to water, into forests and cities, across mountains and deserts, new sonic impressions wrought by the age of carbon continue to be heard and felt, reverberating across virtually every space on our planet. We now understand sound as a medium that accompanies the making and unmaking of this world. Here are some of the stories we collected while listening to the Anthropocene.

1. The Sounds of Ice

In the early 20th century, polar expeditions prioritized the visual and measurable aspects of the Arctic, largely due to the absence of technology capable of capturing sound. Scientists focused on interpreting readings from instruments that tracked temperature and air pressure, while visual artists aboard research vessels documented the stark beauty of icebound landscapes. Their dramatic depictions of icebergs and barren, frozen terrain captivated readers of scientific journals and popular periodicals. Yet the region's sound, by contrast, remained at the periphery—mentioned only in the personal diaries of explorers, often discovered posthumously. These accounts revealed the haunting sounds of the polar environment: the eerie groans of a ship being crushed by drifting ice or the relentless howl of the wind during months of darkness. Without the means to record it, sound was a sensory dimension of the Arctic that was deeply felt there but seldom studied elsewhere.

Today, the melting of the cryosphere has become one of the signature manifestations of climate breakdown, registering on a timescale that coincides with human memory and lifespan. Scientists, musicians and poets are increasingly rushing to capture its fading echoes, finding melodies along with narratives. Yet we are still more versed in chronicling the vanishing whites of icebergs and glaciers than describing the corresponding sonic dimension. Crew members on polar research vessels often find it difficult to verbalize icequakes, now increasingly common occurrences in Arctic and Antarctic waters. When they do, it is notable that they often turn to concepts of suffering to vocalize their accounts:

The 37-mile-long (60-kilometer-long) iceberg emitted what sounded like tortured groans, shudders, and cracks as it ran aground, spun around, scraped along the seafloor, and then broke up over open water.[1]

As certain soundscapes of the cryosphere are amplified during this phase of unprecedented change, others are disappearing permanently, along with the remnants of the past they contain. In the deep fjords of the north, air bubbles trapped in ancient ice pop as glaciers melt. These "blooping, ticking, or popping" sounds (again, we may yet need to expand our vocabulary for depicting sounds) last 10 milliseconds or less, bursting from ice sometimes thousands of years old.

Seals would hide under the sonic camouflage of the bursting bubbles from the sonars of killer whales. Now the glaciers melt not just seasonally and over longer periods of time. When they have melted away, there will be no more sounds for seals to hide in. With the loss of glacial air bubbles, the seals too, will disappear.

Compressed chambers of air from a different time and age, locked into the cold.
When they burst, their memories are released.
Our memories will not be trapped in ice. Of that, the future is almost certain.
The Sound Atlas, "Sounds of the Glacier", p. 57

2. The Sounds of Seas

Even while global ice cover retreats, the oceans continue to bear the sounds emitted within their bodies. Contrary to the title of his groundbreaking documentary Le Monde Du Silence, or The Silent World, we now know Jacques Cousteau's beloved seas hum, click, and trill with the sounds of aquatic life, which depend on the excellent sound-conductive properties of water for communication, hunting, and navigation. Yet this proves to be both a blessing and a curse in modern times. Today, the drone of propeller noise can be heard as skyscraper-sized container ships pass through Guam to China and the Philippines. Off Sable Island near Nova Scotia, Canada, vessels are prospecting for deep-sea oil and gas for months on end using seismic airguns that fire underwater blasts as loud as 260 decibels. Sounds traveling across a liquid medium are not only heard, but can be felt to the core; for some aquatic entities as shock, as hearing loss, as a constant cacophony from which there is no escape or relief.

---

1   Lee, Jane J. (2013): "Watch and Listen to the Surprisingly Noisy Death of an Iceberg." In: National Geographic, 17 July 2013 (https://www.nationalgeographic.com/science/article/130715-antarctica-iceberg-melting-sounds-ocean-science).

While some bodies of water are filled with the noise of anthropogenic activities, others are being threatened by a greater, lifeless silence as a result of biodiversity loss and ecosystem destruction:

> In the Baltic Sea, warming waters from climate change and nutrient run-offs from fish farms fuels the runaway growth of filamentous algae. The thick strands blanket eelgrass meadows on sandy seabeds, suffocate bladderwrack forests on rocky shores. As the filaments rot and decay, they drain their aquatic surroundings of oxygen, life, even sound. The resulting dead zones are muffled, utterly serene. The hydrophones pick up nothing.
> The Sound Atlas, "Geophony, Biophony, Anthrophony: The Three Sound Types Beneath the Seven Seas", p. 131

3. The Sounds of Life

On land, a multitude of sonic worlds have existed alongside our visual-centric ones since time immemorial. Increasing investigations into more-than-human realms disclose a diverse array of lived experiences in which the sense of sight is peripheral rather than primary, with sound generation and detection taking evolutionary precedence. Studies in bioacoustics highlight the intricate interplay between moths and bats, pitted in an echolocation arms race of detection and evasion spanning millions of years. Recordings of birdsongs from lyrebirds and nightingales in urban areas reveal how both message and melody are shaped by instinct and environment. Then there are instances where sound is woven into the very fabric and makeup of an organism's being, like in the example of the cicada, emerging from the earth for the purposes of singing into a world drastically different in atmospheric CO_2 level than the one it was birthed into:

> Desire so great as to spill forth and overwhelm life itself—this is perhaps part of the romance and allure [of the cicada]. Such a long age to spend below ground, alone, in darkness, sucking the sap of roots, preparing for those brief days of song: two to five years for annual varieties; up to seventeen for periodical broods. Perhaps to emerge in full glory into a world so utterly different from whence one once came exemplifies courage. Perhaps one must cling to some universal truths: the need to serenade another. The need to come together.
> The Sound Atlas, "To Be Defined By Sound: Regarding the Cicada", p. 46

An Interlude: To Capture Sound

It is important to note that the ability to delve into these disparate sonic perspectives has only been made possible in recent times, since the advent of technologies capable of capturing the ephemeral phenomenon. Yet this seeming permanence is also fleeting:

> Everything will eventually succumb to entropy. Wax cylinders crumble and mould. Hard drives demagnetize and fail. Media archaeology posits that the formats we place our faith in are only slightly less ephemeral than the original transmission waves.
> The Sound Atlas, "From Wax and Glass, Music and Voices: The Past, Present and Future of Sound Recording", p. 149

What do we want to achieve, when we 'Hit "record"'? To catch a passing sound and replay it later for listening is a technology not yet two centuries old, a flash in the annals of human history. While an image can be captured with one blink of an eye, sound needs to be experienced over a longer period to be 'deciphered'. To listen to a soundscape means to embody a soundscape. It leaves its imprint in your body. You have become the receiver.

4. Sound as Baseline

As sonic baselines continue to shift, both the sending and receiving of sounds will play vital roles in helping us grapple with the pace and scale of these changes. One strategy is to travel to the outer reaches in an attempt to find pristine spaces that remain 'untouched' by the polluting influences of anthropogenic activity. The Altai Mountains is a remote area at the heart of the Eurasian continent. Surrounded by steppes, tundra and high altitudes, the region has not been touched by empires or industries. When Russians visit the Altai region, their friends ask them to bring back a jar of honey. Captured in the amber liquid is the distilled essence of summer, once sung alive by myriad of insects feeding on myriad of flowers, free from the effects of human activity.

> Many describe this as the true essence of the place, the humming meadows of the Altai. It is a sound so calming and soothing that some say it transports the mind and spirit to a portal, possibly the entrance to that forgotten place, where everyone – humans, non-humans, animated, non-animated – can once more live in peace and harmony. Did every place along this latitude once sound like this?
> The Sound Atlas, "The Humming Fields and Meadows of the Altai", p. 90

5. Sound for Reconstruction

Sound can also help us to piece together what has been lost. In her 2011 Museum of Modern Art exhibition "Back, Herebelow, Formidable", artist Marguerite Humeau constructed machines capable of emulating the call of an extinct mammoth—itself a former victim of changing climate from an earlier epoch. While we still can find bones and sometimes even fur preserved through permafrost, the sounds of the mammoth are lost forever. To evoke them, Humeau sought out scientists and doctors to help her piece together the different parts of the puzzle: one expert had connected the first ever larynx transplant, another had specialized in CT scans of modern-day Asian elephants; while a third was a sound designer for JURASSIC PARK.

> ...the deep, guttural rumbles emanating from Humeau's subwoofer-enhanced installation conjures a creature going about daily life. Only we, situated in its far future, interpret its sounds to be part of a dirge. Humeau's work seeks to merge scientific fact with imagination and speculation to evoke 'strong physical, almost supernatural experiences.' What scientists know: The last mammoths lived and died 4,000 years ago. While ziggurats were being raised in Sumer and the Pyramids of Giza were under construction, a small, isolated population lingered on in twilight on Wrangel Island in the Arctic Ocean, half a world away.
> The Sound Atlas, "Reconstructions of the Paleosonic", p. 31

6. Sounds for Healing

In cases where loss encompasses soundscapes and landscapes we once held dear, sound itself can be a way to deal with the emotional fallout, as showcased by the ancient Irish practice of keening. Evoked by women and passed down from one body and one generation to another, keening is a ceremony of human evocation for processing grief, a healing act for relieving what seems like unbearable sadness. Keening laments traditionally were expressed in rosc, an ancient metre that has only survived in Ireland and Scotland. A keening song, beautiful and fleeting, was not caught in writing, but was passed on by professional keeners, or Mná caointe, women who would mourn and wail for a small salary during wakes and funeral rites. They served as vessels to keep an echo alive. The texture and weaving of a life once vibrant but now cold as stone:

> One woman's words pouring into another's body. Verse and rhythm passing through their flesh, tying places and times, from one to the other, one to the other, evoked and triggered by wails, screeches, raptures. It was a rite of passage,

a guiding of the deceased from this world to the next. And it was much more than that.
The Sound Atlas, "The Untameable Ritual of Keening", pp. 69–70

For others, simply engaging with the traces that are left behind after losses and tragedies may offer a measure of solace, even though there will be no accompanying response:

Where there are no visible traces left, it can help to create a placeholder. The Kaze no Denwa, the wind phone, was constructed one year before the [Fukushima] disaster by landscape designer Itaru Sasaki. A white phone booth in a quaint, windswept garden for the memory of his deceased cousin. 'Because my thoughts couldn't be relayed over a regular phone line, I wanted them to be carried on the wind.' The Kaze no Denwa has since been visited by 30,000 survivors longing to connect. While the phone stays silent, they sob their messages into the receiver. The wind carries them to where they need to go.
The Sound Atlas, "Listening to Traces", p. 111

7. Sound as Practice

To seek refuge, to take action, to eulogize in active and passive ways: Engaging with sonic subjectivities can help us navigate the physical and psychological implications of climate change. What can happen if we become receptive to heeding the larger, deeper rhythms that exist all around us? In his piece ASLSP, or As Slow As Possible, artist and composer John Cage sought to tap into these longer, grander patterns:

How slow is as slow as possible? This question has become a philosophical and technical one, discussed at the Tage für Neue Orgelmusik [Day for New Organ music] in the Black Forest in 1998. Since an organ can theoretically be played as long as air is bellowed into its pipes, a piece can be as long as the lifespan of the instrument. Halberstadt is home of one of the older examples of a modern organ, built in 1361. When the conference took place, the organ was 639 years old. This then would have to be the length of the organ piece, the attendees decided, casting their gaze into the far future.
The Sound Atlas, "ASLSP: As Slow As Possible", p. 143

"The naive and basic act of the human being, listening, has been forgotten," noted Cage's friend and late Japanese composer Tōru Takemitsu. "Music is something to be listened to, not explained. John Cage is trying to reconfirm the significance of this initial act." Perhaps slow sounds and deep listening can help us escape the temporal restrictions of our attention spans and even lifespans, allowing us to inhabit a different mode of being, one that transcends the feedback loops, runaway cycles, and echo chambers that have become the hallmarks of the Anthropocene.

Flat Ontologies
Interview with Angelina Davydova

Alexander Nikolsky

Alexander Nikolsky: I grew up in the coal mining region of Western Siberia, where the extractive economy has completely changed the landscape. Local environmental problems next to open-pit coal mines, Indigenous territories overrun by coal dumps, black snow, man-made soil failures are part of daily reality, evoking feelings of exploitation, depletion, decay, and exhaustion. But a few years ago, this reality too began to change along with the climate. With less snow, shorter winters, hotter summers, and more destructive wildfires, these were no longer localized changes. From that point on, I began a long-term project to investigate the global links between fossil fuel extraction and climate change. Siberia is disposed to perceive natural and technogenic non-human agents not as passive inert nature and unlimited forms of capitalist exploitation of this nature, but as active participants in a common field of interaction between vast uninhabited spaces and equally vast technospheres. This is probably why object-oriented and flat ontologies turned out to be the most natural form of conceptualization for me.

Angelina Davydova: Quite a few 'climate subjects' can be characterized as 'hyperobjects' – too big to see, to understand, to grasp. What is your approach in photographing these large objects?

AN: My approach is based on the fact that I perceive these huge objects as subjects. Even more precisely – the boundary between objects and subjects is so non-obvious that I no longer see the difference between them. Humans, for example, are both subjects and objects of global warming. Or permafrost, which melts and releases carbon dioxide and methane, further accelerating global warming. Can I classify it as an object or a subject?

Besides being disproportionate to the scale of a single human being, these objects also elude perception in their many manifestations. A forest fire is a forest fire caused by heat, drought, and an un-extinguished campfire; it is not global warming directly. A dip in permafrost is an expanding crater of melting ice, soil, and organic remains caused by rising average annual temperatures. And all of this is just

a consequence of the contact of the global warming hyperobject with specific physical conditions, events and actors in a specific space. The hyperobject as the subject
overrides the possibility of generalizations.

Photography is a fairly objective medium that captures visible objects. The hyperobject is most obviously removed from direct access, it precisely exceeds the limits of the possibilities of a purely visual medium (as well as any other), reducing the
human claim to be able to know and control everything. Photography as a method
is good in its limitations, which further emphasizes the property of hyperobjects to
slip away. This is especially ironic if we remember the role photography played in the
Great Acceleration[1] and attempts to visualize the entire world. On the other hand,
photography has a disposition to be on location and this provokes me to use other
tools as well. I use thermal imagers, geophones and my own senses. According to the
dark ecology founder Timothy Morton, if a thing cannot be understood in its totality or directly, I can only attune myself to it, achieving a greater or lesser degree of
intimacy. Attuning is the feeling of the power of the object over me, I am drawn by
its ray into the orbit of the object. I tune into climate objects by carefully selecting
my instruments and choosing the places where the hyperobject shows itself most
tangibly. I can most accurately describe this through the concept of 'Umwelt' from
biosemiotics. Each living organism constructs the perception of the same objects,
the meaning and significance of phenomena in its own way. The time of hyperobjects calls for new forms of personal epistemology as a receptivity to change.

AD: How do you cooperate with scientists, researchers and activists in your work?

AN: It's often spontaneous. I might be interested in an object, like a megaslump in
the permafrost. Or a melting glacier. And when I begin to research, it turns out that
a particular group of scientists or an institute is working in the same space. Now I
am negotiating with a group of glaciologists about a joint expedition to a vanishing glacier in Siberia, where their research base has been working for many years.
I hope it will work out. Scientists are often personally interested in communicating
their research as widely as possible, to reach beyond the scientific community and
art can be useful here. In general, cross-disciplinarity is very productive. For example, when I curated an exhibition project in Ulaanbaatar, Mongolia, and permafrost
and climate experts were happy to join the public program, we had an excellent public discussion. In a way, I am already a bit of a climatologist myself.

---

1   "Texte und Grafiken zur Großen Beschleunigung – 'The Great Acceleration'", (https://www.b
pb.de/themen/umwelt/anthropozaen/216918/texte-und-grafiken-zur-grossen-beschleunig
ung-the-great-acceleration/).

AD: What is the main difference between man-made and nature-made terraforming? Between abandoned coal mines and megaslumps? Can we still speak about natural terraforming these days, at the times of the Anthropocene?

AN: Anthropocene as a concept equates *anthropos* with other geological forces but does not cancel them out. It would be too anthropocentric to consider humans as the leading geological force on Earth. At least processes in the tectonic plates and crust still occur, probably without any perceptible human influence. But everything that happens on the surface and in the atmosphere bears the mark of man at least since 1784, when steam engines began to release carbon from coal, or since 1945, when a thin layer of radionuclides covered the surface.

Nature as something separate from the human technosphere no longer exists. Nor has culture ever been separate from nature. Actors in one common network of interaction. The only difference is that now this mutual dissolution is becoming especially noticeable, feedback loops are taking over more and more large-scale areas and processes, when in response to a coal mine somewhere else the permafrost is failing. One might think that the difference is only one of human intention: a glacier melts regardless of anyone's will, while a coal mine is decided to be dug by some people. But it doesn't. The coal mine appears in the logic of the hyperobject of technocapitalism, which is powered by fossil fuels and served by groups of people interested in it. Which doesn't diminish their responsibility for it.

AD: Many of your photos speak about catastrophe, or apocalypse. Do you feel like you understand these terms better now? How would you describe it in your own words?

AN: I wouldn't say my work is about catastrophe, at least I don't perceive it that way. Rather, I'm interested in what's behind the appearance of the catastrophe. Sometimes it can look beautiful, like blooming too early. I'm interested in the points where the good old familiar notion of a stable unchanging world has clearly come to an end. And yes, more often than not, this takes the form of a disaster or at least an anomaly. Disaster is a star that has deviated from its trajectory, a shooting star (dis-astron), a harbinger of change. What I began to realize when traveling to such places is that I cannot escape these changes, leave or hide. Leaving the burning and melting Arctic, I return to heat-stricken Siberia, reading friends' accounts of drought in Europe on the way. The very notion of 'catastrophe' as unforeseen misfortune is rapidly losing its relevance.

I understand apocalypse (ἀποκάλυψις) in its original Greek meaning – revelation, disclosure, lifting of the veil. With catastrophic clarity what was hidden behind the convenient distinctions between active Man and passive inert Nature, the images of an immutable world, are revealed. The apocalypse is a growing hole in the curtain between me and the real, active, non-human material world.

AD: When you talk to people who live next to an abandoned coal mine or not far from thaw slumps – what do they tell you about? How can you describe their lives?

AN: What is surprising is not even what they say, but how they tell it. They tell it in an ordinary way, it is a familiar background of everyday life, a part of it. Human beings are remarkably adaptable. But these stories are very different in the details. People living on the edge of an expanding coal mine complain about coal dust and fear of losing their home. People living next to a thaw slump of permafrost make money from showing the place to tourists and selling mammoth tusks. This reminds me once again that the concept of the Anthropocene is not universal and requires customization for each place and situation separately.

AD: What kind of reactions do you get to photos of megaslumps and further climate subjects?

AN: Viewers think that it is mesmerizingly beautiful and that these objects are somewhere very far away, not here, not now. There is an aesthetic distance, as in Kant's notion of the sublimity. And this is true – I unwittingly aestheticize what I see when I transfer it to photographic film. It's involuntary and probably an avoidance reaction. And therein lies another trap: we are not wanderers over a sea of fog, we are up to our necks in that sea. So, I don't use only photography, which by default involves distancing myself and viewers from the subject. I also register thermal anomalies with a thermal imager and record sound, which I translate into a tactile experience in order to let the manifestation of these climatic subjects literally into the viewer's body through vibration.

AD: What do you think makes people interested in photos/art works that do not show other people?

AN: Fortunately, humans are capable of being curious not only about humans in principle, but also about other, non-human agents. That's how science came about, that's how the Anthropocene came about, and because of this innate curiosity, people can try to make sense of what we all (humans and non-humans) find ourselves in. As for my work – I am in any case conveying the experience of encountering non-humans through my human position and the audience still encounters another human being. This layer cannot be avoided.

AD: You say: "I look into the face of a new world that is gradually arriving here. The soil lays bare a millennia-long history of catastrophes and, at the same time, a distant future that is already emerging in an increasingly rapid disintegration."[2] What kind of world is leaving and what kind of new world is coming?

AN: The old world seemed immutable, and it supposedly could not change. In Siberia, where I come from, there are a huge number of omens and signs about the weather – if snow falls by a certain date, it's for a mild winter, and so on. Now those signs no longer apply. And last summer I installed an air conditioner in my parents' house, even though it had never been hot there before. For me, the main thing in the phrase you quote is not 'new world' but 'coming here.' It's a process.

AD: What gives you hope and strength in the face of catastrophes and polycrisis?

AN: I am empowered by my curiosity and the ability to do what I do. I don't have hope. To hope is to wait and wish for things to happen in a certain way. Personally, polycrisis teaches me to be prepared for the unexpected and to abandon expectations. The experience of living in Russia provides a good basis for this outlook.

AD: In your photo works you also deal with human lives and deaths, including stories of abandoned GULAG camps. How do you work with such a historic legacy? Do you think humans really learn from their history?

AN: I'm just starting a new work about a GULAG. And it will be a story not about memory, but about the mechanisms of displacement, forgetting. And the purposeful erasure of an uncomfortable past. I think people are capable of remembering a lesson learned many times over. But it's often when history has repeated itself again.

---

2   "Melting world: Alexander Nikolsky's Ex-Humus photo project", 13 March 2025 (https://make rsofsiberia.com/rabotyi/ex-humus.html).

Writing Climate or Flooding the Text
A Letter to Future Generations

Martin Zähringer

I am writing this letter to you, people of a future generation on the Earth, in a major Central European city where I have been living for forty years. I grew up in the so-called Western civilization, it is September 2023, Western Christian calendar. Older cultures of mankind have different calculations, Judaism is in the year 5783, younger ones like Islam see themselves in the year 1444. Here in Berlin, it is a day in September 2023, 2023 years after the birth of Jesus Christ, whom Christians believe to be the Son of God. It is the 9th month of the year. I would love to know what date you are on. But I don't know you, I don't know where you are, how you made it to your time, what you do and what image and knowledge you have of us. You are unknown to me. I also don't know what lies ahead of us, the other living beings and the Earth. You know it, when you're looking back, and your knowledge is my glimmer of hope, I won't make some superfluous speculations about the future. I try to tell you what we, the Westerners, are afraid of right now and what I myself am trying to do against the misery.

In the Age of Carbon

Month of September 2023, global exchange of goods and business transactions, all cultures are contacted, internet and travel activities nearly without borders, world trade free and capitalistically organized. Private entrepreneurs own the means of production, states regulate business transactions, political institutions balance interests. It looks as if human civilization is at the height of its industrial development. But the system is out of balance, because a metabolic disturbance is shaking the world, the carbon cycle is collapsing. Our crisis is geological, and the ultimate unit of measurement is CO_2. CO_2, carbon dioxide, the result of the burning of oil, coal and gas, released by us into the atmosphere in unimaginable quantities, where it remains for hundreds of years, making the earth hotter and hotter. Right now, we have no solution to the problem, and that is also your problem.

Perhaps this letter is a disaster defence spell. At best, a final appeal to some kind of a practical reason, but that could only be yours, because ours is failing. We are living in a climate emergency and we know it. We also know that the continued burning of oil, gas and coal will continue to increase the global average temperature, which will lead to irreparable destruction on planet Earth. The large corporations in the petroleum industry are also aware of the greenhouse effect and global warming caused by CO_2 emissions; they commissioned scientific reports decades ago to assess the impact of their business. But the masters of oil let these reports disappear into the safety deposit box and since then, they continue to tell us their lies about the blessings of oil for freedom and affluence.

On the other side, millions of people around the world are taking to the streets today. They are protesting out of fear of climate change, they are taking legal action against energy companies, they are demanding an end to fossil fuels. Young people are striking at their schools. Young African activists risk their life. Indigenous people around the world are fighting against destructive energy projects on their land. The FridaysForFuture movement has reached global proportions and is calling on politicians to listen to science. Scientists become climate activists and philosophers define a global petro culture which we have to overcome. The European Union has committed itself to a Green Deal to reduce CO_2 emissions to zero by 2040. It almost seems as if Europe, where the first chimneys of coal-fired power plants and steam ships and trains smoked 250 years ago, is the first to achieve real climate protection, the Great Transformation.

Unfortunately, there are powerful opponents to this path, they are becoming ever stronger and are turning climate policy into a culture clash, if not a pseudo religious war. At the forefront are powerful climate deniers from America, where the Heartland Institute in Chicago is investing billions of dollars in manipulating the mass media to legitimize the business of the petro-corporations. Their nearly holy principle is the belief that the pursuit of wealth and the happiness of the individual leads to prosperity for all. But it is a questionable kind of happiness.

#floodingworlds #climateX : I SAW how a large one-story wooden house on the bank of a river suddenly tipped into the water after a landslide and floated away. A man on a hill was calmly filming. #Norway Sep 2023

The happiness of the many is an illusion. It only seems possible if you firmly close your eyes to the immense social inequality on Earth and to the coming catastrophe. Of course, none of the rich believe in their fairy tales, they know all about it and are building luxury survival bunkers, retreating into protected spaces and buying land in New Zealand, which has a better climate forecast. They isolate themselves from the environment in climate-protected SUVs and believe themselves safe on the upper floors of skyscrapers. Are you the descendants of these climate refugees? Or has there been a turnaround on the way to a good life for everyone in your time? I would be very interested, I secretly hope so, otherwise why should I write to you?

#floodingworlds #climateX : I SAW dozens of cars on a street in a Turkish town float away in brown floodwaters, sinking into a raging canal and being swept away. Sep 6

#floodingworlds #climateX : I SAW a group of paramedics with inflatable boats, transports of injured people, a crying woman, a concerned Luiz Inácio Lula da Silva, brown water floods and a crushed SUV on a ruined road #Brazil Sep 7

Others write lies about happiness, I try to tell the truth. One measurable fact is that the industrialized countries of this world have blown too much greenhouse gas into the atmosphere. Ever-increasing global warming is toppling global climate systems.

A major catastrophe is imminent on planet Earth. The minor catastrophes are already here, but we can still do the math. CO_2 emissions are counted in billions of tons. In 1860 it was around 0.4 giga tons, 3 generations later it was 9.4 GT and today, one human lifetime further on in 2023, it is 37.8 GT. The unit of measurement for the content is CO_2 ppm (parts per million), the ratio of greenhouse gas molecules to the total number of molecules in dry air.

#floodingworlds #climateX : I SAW a gigantic flood behind a house that was still standing. Behind the house floated countless tree trunks and entire other houses, only the roofs visible. Dark brown masses of water slowly poured into the foreground. Heilongjiang, #China Sep 8

#floodingworlds #climateX : I SAW a massive torrent of dark brown water suddenly burst through the protective grid from a canal next to a residential street and spill rapidly onto the street. #Louisiana Sep 9

And so we have entered a new era. The human age of carbon began in 1860 at 286 ppm, three generations later we were at 316 ppm and today we are at 419 ppm. That is irrevocably the balance of our carbon culture in numbers. I was born in the year 316 ppm/ carbon age. I imagine you live in a scientific culture without Christ years. You locate me in my world as a 316 and, as I can't hide, a climate illiterate because I have only copied the numbers and cannot interpret them. These numbers are the great problem of our current climate crisis awareness, most people can't see anything in them, most people can't believe in them, most people can't set any agenda in them. For me, the numbers are associated with images: the first smoking chimneys of coal-fired power stations in England, gigantic coal excavators and enormous pits in the Lusatian landscape, decapitated mountains in the Apalachians, oil pipelines from Kazakhstan to Rotterdam, combustion engines in ever larger cars, gas production platforms in the North Sea, mega oil tankers in the Suez Canal, launchers for space missions, rockets and tanks, submarines, troop transporters, a stream of technical artifacts incessantly placed in the most vulnerable ecosystems on earth. Islands of plastic waste in the Pacific, mountains of scrap metal on the coasts of Africa. Do I get used to it?

#floodingworlds #climateX : I SAW how brown masses of water spread across the streets and squares of a large city and continued to flow steadily. There were no people to be seen, only cars and a helpless dog. ##Dagestan Sep 9

#floodingworlds #climateX : I SAW the photo of a completely ruined city after the flood in Libya. It is pointed out that NATO troops destroyed Libyan infrastructure in 2011. That's why there were no warning systems. Sep 15

There is one sight I cannot get used to: Endless columns of violence march on our planet, masters of war and armies of ignorance, destroyers of peoples, enemies of humanity and of the Earth. They demand more and more money for the military and armaments and set nations and people against each other, in Palestine and Israel, in Libya and Yemen, in Russia and Ukraine, in China and Taiwan, in Somalia and Sudan. Arms magnates, arms dealers, generals and admirals remain in the dark, but they are constantly at the controls of a global machine of destruction that is becoming ever more threatening.

#floodingworlds #climateX : I SAW two white SUVs pressed close together floating away backwards in the masses of water. Brown masses of water swirled around the tower of an old town, in this scenery countless cars floated in the water. #Southern France Sep 16

And why couldn't they stop it, you ask? Why can't we stop it? I'm asking myself. One answer might lie on a 'higher' scale of human condition, a human disease called greed. It is well known in the great realm of mankind's literature. Greed is a main motif of our dramas, novels and poems – greed, hatred, lies, lust for glory. Greed versus truth, love, hope and empathy is the human comedy, greed as the dirty secret of the human condition. But today greed rules with a pitiless system, a merciless religion of capitalism that has a grip on the public mind. Universities became commercial players and students are customers, art is an investment business for the rich and humanity is turned into markets. Greed pulses through novels and films like blood through an organism, the greed of the rich, who are getting richer and richer and live very well from the petroleum system, from their most important claim to date, the fossil fuel industry.

#floodingworlds #climateX : I SAW people walking or running on a sloping road towards a mudslide. Brown floods, hills in the background, fog, rain clouds. One of them filmed everything calmly. Caunahue, Futrono #Chile Sep 16

#floodingworlds #climateX : I SAW a huge marketplace completely flooded, brown masses of water, wooden stalls, some people looking for goods. A large group pushing a black SUV out of the mud. #Lagos Sep 16

That's not an answer, that's not an answer, I hear you calling! What are YOU doing? Me? In practice, I do without, I swim against the tide of commodity consumption which defines our Western pseudo bourgeoise lifestyle. I work as a cultural journalist to make a living. It only brings in a little money, but I can buy what I need, I've never driven a car, I don't want to be an active part of the capitalistic petro paradise. On the other side, I also don't want to be the will-less object of petro power. I want to do analysis, ask systematic questions, uphold criticism: Literary criticism, cultural criticism, system criticism, power criticism and being part of Critical Theory and Thinking as a practical institution. I work for the cultural empowerment of democratic societies, political struggle against fascism and other forms of totalitarian power. I resist neoliberalism, which wants to replace social education with individual training for the economy, solidarity with a religion of self-love, criticism of power and big money with propaganda, and the arts with entertainment. I write about books for a better world.

#floodingworlds #climateX : I SAW two men crying as floodwaters destroyed their town after a dam burst. Red muddy water dominates the scene. Sep20

#floodingworlds #climateX : I SAW a large truck driving against the tide in a completely flooded city in Turkey. All other vehicles had given up. A white SUV drifts rudderless in the floodwaters. Sep 23

#floodingworlds #climateX : I SAW a huge brown flood in the riverbed rushing towards a car bridge. Before the collapse, some cars had driven onto the bridge, others were just able to turn back when the water burst its banks. Sep 23

I live and work with my partner in a medium large two-room apartment. We consume little and keep our energy consumption low. We produce stories for public radio and try to keep education high. We write about ecological urban planning or sustainable buildings. Stories about the bioacoustician Bernie Krause, who explained the synthesizer to rock stars in his first life in California. Stories about Inuit people in Canada who are fighting climate change by making films to preserve their sustainable way of life. Stories about migration and literature, such as in Global Writing in New York or the Asian Americans in San Francisco. Stories about the Indigenous

Sámi people in Norway who fight against wind turbines when they destroy their traditional way of life. They call it green colonialism.

#burningworlds #floodingworlds #climateX : I SAW a cartoon. Episode 1, Burning forest on the left, a family flees to the right. Below episode 2, a giant wave comes from the right, the family runs to the left. Nowhere to run, baby Sep 23

#floodingworlds #climateX : I SAW photographer Muhammad Elalwany return to Derna to take new photos of people he had once portrayed. Many of the faces have disappeared in the floods. Sep 23

It's crazy. Today, every reasonably to a certain degree informed person knows that our planet Earth has limits. The raw materials for the production of goods are finite. The displacement of other living beings that have evolved on this planet for millions of years is an ecological catastrophe. We lose everything. The destruction of biodiversity is irreversible. We lose everything. Deforestation of the rainforests is an attack on the lungs of the Earth. We lose everything. The pollution of the oceans is leading to maritime ecocide. We lose everything. The ever-increasing emission of CO2 through fossil technology is a catastrophe. We lose everything. The treatment of animals in the meat industry's fattening stables is turning humans into inhumans, and we continue to do so and we lose everything.

#floodingworlds #climateX : I SAW hail with grains as big as chicken eggs falling on roofs and cars. The SUVs' warning systems flashed incessantly. The ground slowly became covered in ice. Sep 25 #Texas Round Rock

#floodingworlds #climateX : I SAW a flood inundate the city of Istanbul. People climbed out of their cars and saved themselves on the roof. Sep 28

No, your ancestors were not clueless. Many know we took a wrong course, but the majority don't want to know. Knowledge, what is it? Do you know in your world what knowing is? What kind of knowing defines your society? What kind of knowledge could change our course? I would like to know it, because when you exist, what I really hope, you must have acted on the foundation of real knowledge. Or what else? I have always sought knowledge and those who know; the scientific community knows the situation, the political decision-makers are informed, as are the industry bosses, the media, the transnational conferences and institutions. But I found out there is a gigantic gap between public knowledge and power knowledge. Between them who know and deal with the real numbers, and them who see only empty symbols. What is a Gigaton of CO_2? How much is 140 Gigatons of it in the atmosphere of the Earth? What does it mean that U.S. crude oil exports established a record in 2023, averaging 4,1 million barrels per day? An oil magnate owns hundreds of billions of US$, what does this really mean? The figures don't tell us enough about the world, not what we really need to know. So why don't we listen to what others say, the writers, artists, musicians, filmmakers, actors, directors?

#floodingworlds #climateX : I SAW an ocean bay filmed from above, with bodies washed back by the sea in the spray. People on the shore trying to pull them out. Sep28

Do you ask me what my contribution is? Well, I try to do my work and write about climate culture as a thing to come, I also organize festivals and conferences to connect people from both knowledge cultures – figures and art in a creative intercommunion can perhaps explain to us how we can overcome petroculture.

#floodingworlds #climateX : I SAW how the floodwaters in a riverbed in a Turkish town became more and more powerful. Huge masses of tree trunks flooded in. Residents in terraced houses were filming. The water quickly rose to the second floor. Sep 29

Not at least my literary criticism is also taking the topic of a climate culture to come; I started some years ago with a long feature article on climate fiction in America, CliFi. CliFi is literature that deals with climate change in a dystopian, utopian or realistic way and CliFi writers belong to the earliest protagonists of a global critical climate action. After that, I curated the first Climate Fiction Festival for European literature in Berlin. The motto was: When the world becomes dangerous, literature must not remain harmless! It was well received and I still have high hopes that literature will perform its task in these times of multiple crisis, because the impacts of fine arts and literature are a desperately needed contribution in the fight against the climatic ignorance.

#floodingworlds #climateX : I SAW a black flash flood full of tree trunks coming down from the mountains and flooding an entire settlement of terraced houses. First it moved in a riverbed, then it burst its banks. #Turkey Sep 29

Our festivals have one goal: Connecting Climate Cultures! We are looking for the global cartography of sustainability to see what can come out as alternatives: Postgrowth, just transition, green deal, planetary thinking, circular economy, living off the land, energy struggles, climate justice, Indigenous knowledge etc., or on the other side petro culture & climate collapse. But it seems as if the majority really doesn't want to know. They want entertainment and highlights of the good life, a reliable distraction from danger in comfortable homes. Meanwhile, the capitalists are coming up with a digital revolution and shine with the promise of Artificial Intelligence, which promises solutions for a climate-neutral economy, while the superserver farms of data moguls worldwide feed the machine with fossil fuels and steal the public water to cool it down. At the same time, the petroculture continues to grow and run faster and faster, pushing the extraction of fossil fuels and the emission of CO_2, forcing the transgression of planetary boundaries, increasing the pressure on the Earth's climate systems – especially in the poorer countries that have contributed the least to global warming. Perhaps in your distant future you can look back on the mystery how anybody will have untangled this knot of our time – economic crisis, environmental crisis, cultural crisis, climate crisis, justice crisis. The words are too simple, I can only dream of better ones, of a level of human wisdom, or perhaps of a Cultural Intelligence that would really help.

> #floodingworlds #climateX : I SAW a panoramic video from a skyscraper showing the entire flooded neighborhood. One big van was driving against the current, most of the others were drifting away with the brown mud. #Istanbul #Turkey Sep 29

> #floodingworlds #climateX : I SAW a tidal power plant that can produce the electricity for 4000 homes every day. It's called Wave Star and is part of the concept of a kinetic energy-based infrastructure that could meet all electricity needs with the tides of all the seas. Sep 29

I don't envy you the planet that our CO_2 business has left for you. I envy you for the chance to look back from a far future, while I do not know today what I have to fear more in the near future – a climate catastrophe or politics. In my country, Germany, which has finally been developing into a democratic constitutional state for eight decades, one party writes in its program that it wants to deport millions of people to other countries if it comes to power. This party is growing fast. In other European countries, too, the issue of migration is becoming a recipe of success for authoritarian and anti-democratic parties, and in the USA, historically the regulatory power of the free Western world, an isolationist slogan is becoming ever louder – Make America Great Again (MAGA). That doesn't sound very sensible in times of global crisis, and worse, the MAGA movement is also funded by the petro lobby. Since the discovery of fracking, the US is the state with the largest oil and gas production in the world, and these people want to keep it that way.

> #floodingwords #climateX : I SAW a completely flooded shopping mall. People were walking knee-high in the water. A little girl was being pushed through the masses of water on a wheeled table. Floating plastic everywhere. New York Sep30

#floodingworlds #climateX : I SAW a street intersection with cars submerged up to their windows in brown water, while the cars in the slightly higher crossing lane were still driving. #NewYork Sep 30

#floodingworlds #climateX : I SAW protesters sitting on the street in bright rain parkas with backpacks protecting them from the water cannons of the Dutch police. The water cannons flooded continuously, the protesters did not move. NLRebellion Sep 30

One year later, September 2024

Flooding the Zone

I am leaving the global social media platform where I was feeding our CLIMATE CULTURES network channel with climate issues and catastrophes to establish a global live mapping of disasters, #floodingworlds, #burningworlds. I understood it as part of climate social media action, all these linked disasters should build a long flooding climate truth in the World Wide Web, where the flood of lies and the influence of climate deniers is growing more and more. But then the American billionaire and techno tycoon E.M. has bought the whole platform and hastily destroyed the company's organizational structure: It happens at lightning speed. Nobody understands what is happening. E.M., the richest man in the world, pays 40 billion US dollars for the takeover and gains access to the accounts of over a billion people from all over the world. The formerly blocked accounts of racist, sexist and right-wing extremist users are reopened. E.M. speaks of freedom of expression. The account of former US President D.T. (2017 – 2021) is also reopened. D.T. is seeking a second term in office and has officially announced that his information policy is based on alternative facts. Instead of climate science, alternative facts that simply deny climate change, instead of knowledge and action: Flooding the Zone with Shit and Sheets, as one of his spin doctors called the strategy. E.M. is helping with these floods.

The real floods continue. Sea levels continue to rise. Extreme weather events are becoming more frequent. The U.S. National Centre for Environmental Information (NCEI) counts twenty-eight weather and climate disasters in 2023, more than ever before in the United States. They have cost nearly 500 lives and caused 100 billion dollars in damage.

I READ the disaster novel *We are unprepared* by Meg Little Reilly about what a hipster couple from Brooklyn experiences: the disaster in the countryside, the ap-

proach of a giant storm, the social and emotional devastation that begins in advance, the collapse of public order, the failure of the state. I quote:
"At first, the fear felt familiar. Hurricanes Katrina, Sandy, and Irene had brought varying degrees of terror to the East Coast in previous years and we knew what to expect. But that feeling of familiarity vanished quickly as every weather record was broken and it became clear that the devastation was greater than anything we'd ever lived through."

In Berlin, the governing coalition in which an ecologically oriented party held the Ministry of Economics and Climate Protection and the Foreign Ministry collapses. A German radical right-wing, isolationist party is now openly supported by E.M. The front woman of this German party promises to demolish wind turbines. I am planning the symposium "Climate Culture Bridge Warsaw/Berlin" in Berlin, which aims to connect Polish and German writers. The aim is for them to find out how the topics of climate, crisis and culture are expressed in German and Polish literature. I read about setbacks in the global climate movement. The founder of the climate movement Extinction Rebellion has been sent to prison for four years. He continues there.

> I READ the post-disaster novel *The Great Transition* by Nick Fuller Googins: An American activist couple survives the final climate catastrophe and now lives in Greenland's capital Nuuk. The man seeks his happiness in a perfect family life with his daughter and wife, while she secretely takes militant action against the continuing power cartel of petro-oligarchs during her supposed business trips.

I don't want to drown in these floods. I am producing a radio feature about the struggle of Sámi reindeer herders against multinational wind energy projects, which they refer to as green colonialism. I conceive this piece as a critical contribution to a reflecting climate culture and show how artists, scientists and authors demonstrate solidarity with the Sámi. I read on. I don't want to drown in the floods. Am I not on my way to a new culture? I have found a new social media platform where I write about climate culture issues. I write as Germany's first climate culture journalist.

> I READ the long poem "Miami Lost" by Gabriel Ojeda Sagué: "apocalypse tuyo is mental and dental never/ jamás contribute resisto gravity ningunas / witches en this hardin bring oceano back / crueldad milk momento dream toro kills / amigo the ocean kills amigo tomorow…"

I read on and don't want to drown in the floods. A massive disinformation campaign against climate science and climate action is underway in the United States. In the German election campaign, the climate emergency no longer plays a role. It's all about migration. Migration is the magic key for the far-right extremists all over the world. I keep reading and don't want to drown in the floods. I now devote the largest part of my journalistic work to the context of climate, crisis and culture. I don't want to drown in the floods. I am writing this letter to you and do not want to ....

Four months later, January 2025

Flooding the World

The construction tycoon, big businessman and former president D.T. has won the election for American president by a narrow majority. His second term begins in January 2025. D.T. is a friend of Russian President W.P., who has been waging a bloody war against neighbouring Ukraine for the past three years. D.T. has received dozens of millions US dollars in election aid from the petroleum lobby. The slogan of D.T. is "DRILL, BABY, DRILL!" From the first day of his administration, D.T. floods Americans with decrees, which he proudly signs on camera: D.T. pulls out of the Paris Climate Accord by decree. D.T. withdraws all restrictions against the coal and oil industry by decree. D.T. bans the dissemination of information on climate developments on government websites.

The tech tycoon E.M. has massively supported the construction tycoon in the elections with his social media platform. E.M. has also donated a quarter of a billion US dollars to D.T.'s election campaign. The general income in the U.S. is by that time about 80.000 US Dollar per year. E.M. shows the fascist German salute at D.T.'s inauguration in front of the cameras of the whole world's media. D.T. appoints E.M. to head an agency that did not previously exist, the Department of Government Efficiency (DOGE). DOGE is supposed to combat inefficiency in state administrations and overruns the administrations with waves of layoffs. DOGE has discontinued the American international aid program USAID. Aid organizations around the world are forced to close their schools and hospitals. E.M. earns more in a single day than the entire USAID program for a year is worth. A ruler without a mandate, a tyrant of pure dystopia. In the media: Laughing E.M., black T-shirt, gold lettering DOGE flashing from under a black coat. The gesture of an adolescent nerd who believes he is master of the universe. E.M. posts: "The fundamental weakness of Western civilization is empathy".

I READ the novel *Weather* by Jenny Offill: "Sylvia takes me to a swanky dinner with some people visiting from Silicon Valley. Some of them are donors to her podcast and she hopes to convince them to support a new foundation she has started. It wants to rewild half the earth. But these men are not interested in such things. De-extinction is a better route, they think. Already they are exploring the genetic engineering that would be necessary. Woolly mammoths are of great interest to them. Sabre-toothed tigers too."

Empathy is the most important learning objective of the reading human being. It is a central function of Enlightenment and culture. It is the warm blood of our living society. But those in power in America now are reading their own book and have a new ideology – flooding Enlightenment. It is called "Project 2025," authored by the mighty think tank Heritage Foundation. It was already known before the D.T. seizure of power and the appearance of the tech billionaires in the White House, a script for the reorganization of the administration, the destruction of the welfare state and healthcare, the attack on the independence of the judiciary, the withdrawal of the USA from the global security system, an isolationist trade policy and a dark masterplan for deportation of migrants in big numbers. They are also reading another book that spreads confused ideas about a 'Dark Enlightment.' It is the ideology for super-rich entrepreneurs and their political friends, and this is how they want to have the world: Everything must be seen from our point of view, our interests are the interests of the world, America must run like a corporation by a CEO and the rest of the world must kowtow. They want to unbalance the world order in a frenzy of disruption, to rule in chaos. Megalomaniac billionaires buy the world, bought politicians believe they will stay in power forever, and even if they are only partially successful in the end, because capitalists always have to steal profits from each other again, the class war top down and their work of destruction against us is absolute.

What a mess. I wished there would come a signal from your future world. What would you have done? I have resolved to keep a cool head; otherwise, why should I write to you? Don't we have literature, guarantor of reason and humanity, of moral resilience even in the worst of times, for me, for many people in all countries and cultures of the world? But really, I wonder if my literary experiment has not already been submerged in the first floods of September 2023, flooding the text, flooding me. Where is my personal impact as a climate subject when the most powerful politician in the world is a climate denier? This anti-climatic subject of power does not read novels. D.T. is a troll of the endless and senseless media spectacle; he has grown up in talk shows, bizarre and loud, surrounded by lickspittles, in a hall of mirrors of lies. Billionaire E.M. has also acquired a taste for it, fraternizing with the neoliberal president of Argentina on a political shit show. They play with a giant chainsaw on stage and flaunt their masculine power like little, crazy boys. Men with chainsaws, a super symbol of dark enlightenment, the destruction of trust, commitment and responsibility in democratic Western worlds. In practice, the South American president is using a chainsaw to promote the destruction of the Amazon rainforest, the world's green lung. His colleague D.T. in the north is using a decree to initiate the deforestation of 120 million hectares of North American forests.

I READ George Turner, *The Sea and Summer*: "Didn't they know it would happen? Oh yes, 'they' knew; back in the 1980s 'they' were warned but 'they' were busy. 'They' had the nuclear threat and the world population pressure and the world salvation problem and the terrorist outbreaks and the strikes and the corruption in high places shaking hands with crime in low places, and the endless business of simply trying to stay in power – all to be attended to urgently."

The World Meteorological Organization (WMO) declares 2024 to be the year with the warmest average temperatures since measurements began. The increase in the average temperature is 1.54°. The last ten years are the warmest ever recorded. Antarctic sea ice is disappearing. The glaciers are continuing to melt. Global warming is stressing the forests. In California, the megacities of Los Angeles and San Diego were ravaged by forest fires in January 2025, resulting in 30 deaths, 18,000 destroyed homes and 57,000 acres of burnt land.

In one of the best climate fiction novels I know, Australian author George Turner describes in 1987 how capitalism has perished in the year 2020. It is the story of a playwright, kind of a future geologist from an even more distant future society, who explores the remains of a sunken city to find out what went wrong in 2020, because his own civilization faces the challenge of a changed climate and needs to learn from history. Sydney's skyscrapers rise out of the water in front of him, and in a diary, he finds the explanation as to why this world was drowning, a global climate catastrophe occurred. Turner describes the end of Sydney as the class struggle's final battle, shifting the utopia to a future Australia in which science sets the pace. Until now this has not happened. What would I give to hear from you, if this could be true. But you are asking me now, what I have to report from my world? Today, power writes this narrative: A convicted liar, misogynist and notorious political destroyer in America just instigated a world trade war as President-elect of America. The President is imposing import tariffs of 25% or more on goods from Mexico, Canada and the European Union and believes that the industries of these countries should move to the US because he personally ensures low taxes there. These are the answers of an entrepreneur who considers America to be the centre of the world, his slogan is MAGA and the law of the jungle applies. A few months ago, this man would have been a baddy in a bad science fiction, now he is the great deal maker in his own delirious realm and the real enemy of democracy in our Western world.

I READ Kim Stanley Robinson, *The Ministry for the Future*: "Ideology, n. An imaginary relationship to a real situation. In common usage what the other person has, especially when systematically distorting the facts. But it seems to us that an ideology is a necessary feature of cognition, and if anyone were to lack one, which we doubt, they would be badly disabled. There is a real situation, that can't be denied, but it is too big for any individual to know in full, and so we must create our understanding by way of an act of the imagination. So we all have an ideology, and this is a good thing."

I have no idea how the political structure of this world order will develop, but news from our common space of environmental responsibility and climate action: The American division of the environmental organization Greenpeace received a fine of 660 million dollars for supporting an energy campaign against the Dakota Access oil pipeline. It's obviously an abuse of the law, they know it and it has a specific name: SLAPP, Strategic Lawsuits Against Public Participation. SLAPP is intended to flood activists, the climate movement and other civil rights movements. D.T.s political hammer is smashing the legal system to destroy all kind of climate protection bottom up. Greenpeace defends itself with an anti-SLAPP counterclaim before the European Court of Justice. But the flooding of the public with shit on the internet is in full swing, media count the president's lies, there are thousands of them, the judiciary is flooded with sheets in the form of mass-issued decrees. D.T. imposes tariffs on his country's trading partners like a wizard with a magic wand, stock prices plummet, the president says "Now Is A Great Time To Buy!" (stocks), while billionaire E.M. calls the president's economic advisor "Dumb As A Bag Of Coals," later D.T. rescinds the tariffs for 90 days, stock prices rise, D.T.s friends are making billions, the dark enlightenment is truly darker as a coal cellar.

Science fiction author Kim Stanley Robinson begins his novel *The Ministry for the Future* about a climate culture of the future and the way to it with a heat catastrophe in India. He describes in scientific detail the so called wet-bulb, that is how the human organism collapses in extreme heat and humidity. Millions are dying, and so the Indian government begins to technically manipulate the atmosphere, contrary to international agreements about Solar Radiation Management, anyway, it leads to cooling and helps. So, it goes in a techno-believing climate fiction from the year 2024. In reality, just one year after the novel was published, people in India are suffering from temperatures of over 50°C. The Indian government has no climate protection program worth mentioning and continues to burn coal like there's no tomorrow.

Climate Fiction has been warning of the climate catastrophe for decades. The authors are scientifically informed and literarily committed. With their visions of the future, crisis narratives and social forecasts, they were usually quite right. Today, they write about a possible takeover of global power by Artificial Intelligence, about a totalitarian anti-climatic subject as fiction and fantasy. Are they not back on the right track? This new and digital spooky is hidden until now and only just beginning to show its outlines, a still veiled Protheus of a dehumanized future. Meanwhile, the unpopular, unsubtle, all too profane subject of climate collapse, the crisis of the Western subject and systemic misconduct is penetrating ever further into the canons of culture, into the finer circles of literature. No social novel with a realistic setting can avoid the symptoms, the subtle fractures of fear of the future and catastrophe run through every volume of poetry, every drama is preceded by a climatic prologue. It would be not alone in the spirit of these alert authors if the signs of their literary seismography were recognized as a wake-up call for a new cultural awakening. Could our literature be, not just a cultivated gesture in the face of the profane 'onward and upward,' but a well promoted and received stream of Climate Writing to empower the climatic subject of the future? I think so and I hope so, because otherwise all the books too will be flooded, like everything else.

What other questions do I have?
To you –
Have you achieved a solid climate culture?
How are you doing?
Are you still alive?
Are you there?
To our beautiful planet Earth –
Sorry!

Sinkhole above a mine, Siberia, Russia, 2023.

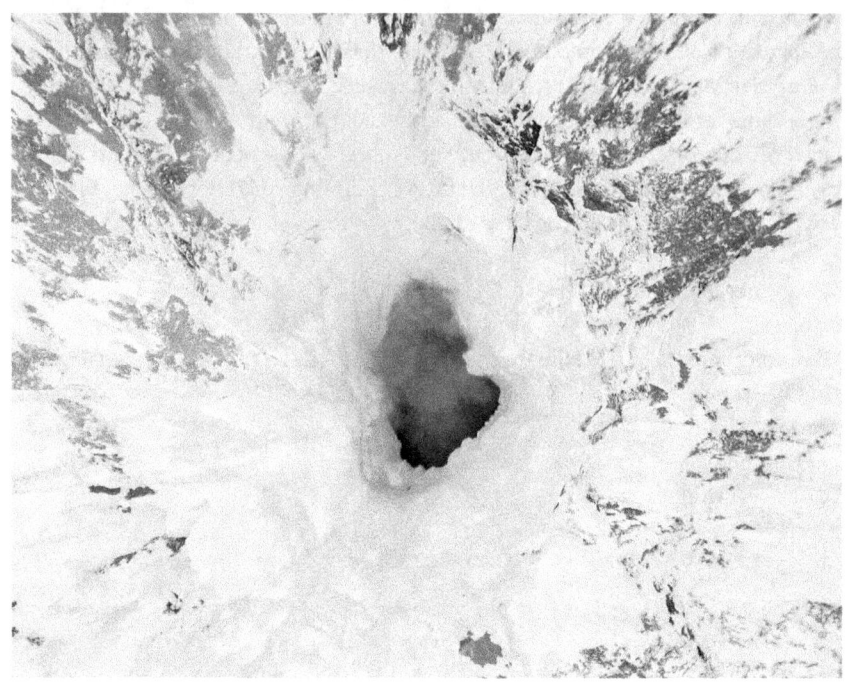

© Alexander Nikolsky

Glacial

Catherine Bush

As they sail into the fjord, the woman's eyes catch on the wooden hut, alone on its white slope, melted snow leaving black patches like spores on the rocky heights behind it. From its small, single window some trick of the light winks at her as she stands on the boat deck in parka and mittens, she and the others who have come on this expedition to an archipelago in the high latitudes, only a few hundred miles from the North Pole. This is as far north as she has ever been in her life, or ever expects to be. All of them are eager to experience the glacial landscape during the white nights of endless summer light in the high Arctic. Some of them sketch as they travel; one drops a recording device deep into the water; another sings. They take photographs. The woman writes in a small, waterproof notebook.

The sight of the hut amplifies a desire that arose in her early in the trip, as they travelled over turquoise water, past glacier after melting glacier. The longing surprised the woman when she awoke in her tiny cabin, shared with a young cartoonist from San Francisco. When she stepped onto the boat's deck by the pale bright light of noon or midnight, the longing made itself felt. Even as the virus ran through her blood and body, as it ran through so many of them that they joked they should raise a black flag announcing they were a plague ship bringing their stew of viruses to the Far North, the desire to be alone in this landscape rose in her, plaintive and fervid. Alone and so to find, perhaps, an echo of its fragile vastness in herself.

She has been alone in other landscapes: In a city far-off across the sea, she lives on her own in an apartment, two floors of an old house surrounded by oak trees. Though not entirely alone. She has a dog, athletic and inquisitive. Her lover, a man of quick attentiveness, lives not far off. Squirrels rustle in the branches of the oaks outside her windows. The sirens of ambulances wail past day and night on their way to the nearby hospital. She has lain in a tent in the middle of a desert; spent nights alone, unafraid, in a house in the country, where, every now and again, a pickup truck will streak past along the dirt road, a white arrow searing through the dark.

On their voyage up the coast they passed other huts, even walked as a group to one perched on a flat plain surrounded by pale water and distant mountains. Their guides staked themselves on nearby rises, rifles slung over their shoulders as they scanned the land for polar bears. They were to go nowhere without their rifle-toting guides.

Why this hut? The woman doesn't know. All she knows is that when she glimpses it, something speaks to her. Approaching the man in the red down jacket, one of their guides, she finds herself asking: Would it be possible for me to spend some time on my own, out on the land — alone, that is, in the old hunters' hut we passed on our way into the fjord?

The man, younger than she is, a blond fringe of bangs protruding beneath his wool cap, takes her in, her face, her body, as if assessing her request, its seriousness or its folly, and the woman feels briefly seen. He is considering her query, not brushing her off as indulging in caprice or selfishness. He nods, then sets off across the boat's wooden deck to consult with two of the other guides. When he returns, he tells her, Yes, it's possible.

He will take her ashore and lock her inside the hut for her own safety, he says. For an hour or so. After that, he will return to fetch her. They can spare no guide to guard her. This will be the only way.

For a moment, the woman wavers. Then she says, That's fine. That's great, actually. Lock me inside.

When the man in the red jacket reappears, on the water, in a rubber Zodiac, the woman clambers down a ladder from the boat's deck to meet him, waving goodbye to her companions, who wave back. The roar of the motor is so loud as she and the man speed off, bouncing over the bay, that it is impossible to speak. Upon arrival, as they climb the slope towards the hut, across rock and moss and over dirty, melting snow, the man remains quiet, so self-contained that she has no idea what he is thinking.

There are two doors enclosing the hut. The first, made of nailed-together slats, is secured by two wooden planks. These are slotted horizontally into carved holes at the top and bottom of the wooden posts that frame the doorway. The man pushes the planks out of the slots, then lifts the door itself aside, leaning it against the tarpaper wall of the hut. The inner door is simple, covered in tar paper on the outside, the wood of its exterior oblong handle so worn it appears to be bone. They enter a tiny vestibule.

On the inside, wooden slats reinforce the door, which is solidly made, and from which protrudes a smoothed wooden knob. The hut's contents are minimal: a table, a chair, a bed, a wood stove. The woman drops her knapsack onto the chair, her hat and mittens onto the table. Beside them the man places a walkie-talkie, which he will leave with her, he says, in case of emergency. He shows her how to switch it on, how to connect to the ship.

When he leaves, he gives a little wave, before closing the first door behind him.

The woman hears him, outside, wedge the second, safety door in place over the first. Ordinarily, this door would only be used when visitors, hunters or hikers, left the hut behind. He slides the upper plank into the groove of the upper slots, then shoves the lower plank into position. It is impossible now for her to get out on her own. Behind both doors, she will be safe from predators. Three small slivers of light beam through a crack at the top of the door frame.

Through the wooden walls of the hut, she follows the crunch of the man's footsteps as he makes his way back down the slope towards the water, where the Zodiac lies pulled up on a pebbly beach.

She watches as, head bowed, he passes in front of the hut's small, Plexiglas window, nailed into place in the wall's wood. Although he waved at her on departing the hut, he does not now turn to glance at her through the window, as if, already, he has moved on and she has vanished from his mind. However much she wants to be alone, this disconcerts her. Her hand twitches with the urge to wave, but she doesn't.

It is June, close to the solstice. Somewhere in that huge white sky the sun circles day and night, but the sky has been hazed for days, the air windless and becalmed, so that the woman has not seen the midnight sun, only gradations of endless, clouded brightness that expand above the motionless waters of the bay and the low, black-and-white mountains on the bay's far side, colour vibrating from a single, sapphire-blue iceberg.

After pushing the Zodiac off from shore, the man leaps aboard and flings an orange life jacket around his shoulders. Crouched over the outboard motor, he tugs until it catches. Without looking back, he sets his course for the far end of the bay, the grey Zodiac slicing into the water's stillness, the muted purr of its motor reaching the woman through the little window. The water, fine as glass, shatters as the boat speeds across it, shard upon shard, until man and boat disappear around the curve of the shoreline, the shore swallowing every smash of wave, every bulge and ripple of disturbance. Calm reasserts itself.

She is alone. The woman considers the initial timbre of this aloneness. It's a kind of intimacy she longs for. Not awe, not grief in this melting world. Yet her mind leaps like a rabbit. She picks up the walkie-talkie. When she flicks the switch, as the man showed her how to do, voices from aboard the ship tumble out, calling to each other. Sarah! Tomas! Marius! The woman pushes the tab that will allow her to speak but doesn't say anything. A light glows. It works. That's all the reassurance she needs. Switching off the walkie-talkie, she returns it to the table.

The hut is small and dim in the face of the bedazzling expanse outside which, from where the woman stands, looks empty, the black and umber rock of the low mountains stippled by ribbons of snow, the mountains doubled by their reflections in the still water. This hut, like the others that infrequently dot the land, would have been cobbled together by hunters from salvaged wood, here in a land without trees, hunters of seal and fox and polar bear, some of whom built traps to hunt the bears, affixing a rifle to a wooden frame baited with meat, so the woman has learned. When a bear, often a mother bear, approached, drawn by the scent, the frame collapsed on her, triggering the rifle, which shot her in the head, leaving her to bleed to death or the hunters to finish her off, hunters who might also capture her orphaned young. There is blood here, on the land, under the melting snow. The whale and walrus killers gathered elsewhere, on wider shores where they stripped the huge carcasses, rendered blubber to oil, discarded cascades of bones to be cleansed and whitened by time. She has no history in this landscape, other than that her skin binds her to the white-skinned hunters, Russians, Norwegians, English, Dutch, no ties to root her here, but she knows enough to know she isn't entirely alone. She stands in a land full of ghosts.

It takes four steps to cross the hut from the small bed built into the wall, its mattress little more than a husk covered in worn fabric, to the entryway, where there is a simple wooden bench and where, if one were a hunter, one might leave one's heavy boots and jacket and rifle, store whatever driftwood one has hauled in or dragged up from shore. Up here, logs float in from the Russian coast like exiles. Or refugees. Elsewhere, war is raging. It is summer, warm enough for the woman to unzip her parka. She doesn't need to light a fire in the tiny wood stove behind her, or attempt to light one and possibly fail. With every step she sways; after days at sea, her body carries the movement of water within it, deep in her inner ear, making the cabin around her sway along with her body. She reaches out an arm to steady herself.

Beside the wood stove, a cast-iron pan and an antique kettle sit on a shelf. On a shelf above the pan and kettle stands a row of bottles: whiskeys, tequila, even a bottle of Texas hot sauce. She eyes them: Jameson. Johnnie Walker. José Cuervo. Texas Pete! Interlopers all. There are, it seems, many ways to stay warm here. Swaying, she picks up one bottle after another, shakes them — empty, every one, save for the hot sauce, which she opens, taps a tiny amount of sauce onto her palm, licks it. The heat searing through her guts like a meteor makes her shout and toss the bottle back onto the shelf.

On the window ledge a stubby candle keeps company with the jawbone of some creature, teeth embedded in it, a relic that someone has gathered, abandoned, left for another to encounter. The woman touches the bone and moves the candle to the table, plucks a match from the matchbox also left on the ledge and lights the candle wick. Who has been here before her? What will she do with her time here? She will sit, she will listen, she will grieve, she will think.

Somewhere over the ocean, her lover has been following her journey by satellite link, charting the boat's coordinates up the island of Spitsbergen, but he doesn't know that she is in this cabin. No one knows exactly where she is other than the man in the red jacket. This pleases her, the beautiful disorientation of it. She has a phone in her knapsack but there is no reception given the remoteness of her location. The phone, a shell, is usable only to take a picture, which she does, aiming its camera into the bright glare of the outside world. Across the bay a glacier spills from the base of the low mountains into a wide, white mouth. Click. This time, when she glances away from the window, her vision, polarized, sears green, the contrast between the radiant outside and dim interior so great that, for a few seconds, everything inside, table, chair, her hand held out in front of her, are burned away.

Take off your coat, a voice says.

The woman recoils in shock.

Across the bay, the glacier moves. Because this is what glaciers do. It's what glacial means, the ice is always moving.

There is so much that is invisible in this landscape: mountains that descend underground as far as they table above; polar bears that roam out of sight; kittiwakes that wheel, tossing their high-pitched cries before diving into their cliff burrows along the walls of rock farther into the fjord; the ice that runs deep beneath the glacier's surface, channels of water tunnelling through it, the movement of ice and water carrying the upper ice with it towards the bay, towards the sea, where the ice will disappear into the dark blue Arctic waters. All this the woman knows as her gaze turns outwards, unsettled, eyes straining.

Again, a voice says, Take off your coat.

But she is alone, as alone as she has ever been. Unnerved, she looks about. Perhaps she has no business being here, despite her wonder and desire, yet this is where she is, breathing this air, asking the air, How am I to be in this landscape? What am I to be?

When the voice asks a third time, she struggles to shuck off her parka, to work her arms out of the sleeves and hook the coat's shoulders over the back of her chair, not cold but shivering a little, because who knows what will happen if she doesn't do as the voice commands, or what will happen if she does. She makes a choice.

There is no presence in her vision as powerful as the glacier, which seems to loom the longer she stares at it through the little window. The harder she stares at the mobile whiteness the more clearly she takes in its mouth, wide and white and scarred with crevasses. You? Is it you? Once more, she checks over her shoulder into the green, polarized air of the hut but sees no one, no glimpse of movement, not even of ghosts. She leans to peer out the window at the ground below, the space to either side of its frame. No one. Only the trickling sound of melting snow. Is she hallucinating? No sound of any person or creature stirring on the gritty roof.

How does one address a glacier, so ancient, such a miracle of compressed time, time turned to ice. Should she? Yet isn't this why she came? To open herself to some kind of encounter. Which may be hubris. And yet.

What she knows: On the surface of the glacier lies snow, beneath that, ice crystals, beneath that finer firn, which thaws and refreezes and slowly turns into the deep, compacted, deformed ice, that, stressed under its own weight, begins to move. Moves and turns to water. Time turns to water, the great mouth across from her cracking and breaking open into the bay. As the air warms, the water warms. Faster.

Days ago, she sped with others of the expedition in one of the Zodiacs through open water where their GPS said there should have been nothing but glacial ice.

Thou. The word comes to her. How art thou?

She speaks. In response, there is only silence. How dare she ask a glacier how it is and, ridiculous, expect a response? Yet the lack of response is, despite everything, a disappointment.

She sits, she waits, she listens, she breathes. Her skin crackles. Not silence: Water trickles over the ground outside. Everything feels still but isn't. She casts her mind outwards.

Take off your skin, the voice says, the voice that may or may not belong to the glacier.

The woman jumps, startled all over again. She stands stock still, listening, her ears abuzz.

You heard me, the voice says. Take off your skin.

I don't know how to do that, the woman says, still coursing with shock. Somehow, with something or someone, she is having a conversation.

Well, the voice says. Figure it out.

The woman's skin has always felt thin and porous to the world around her: to the cries of others, the way leaves grow flaccid in a drought or browned after spraying, the pores, the spores, the vines brought across the world from one continent to another that scramble and spread through their millions of seeds, metastasizing in the woodland park near her apartment. At night sometimes, as if in response, her body will twitch and vibrate.

The woman presses her face and chest to the window of the hut and as she stares down the slope to the water, the convexity of the slope seems to enter her, pulling her out through the window. Somehow, she's not exactly sure how, she is stumbling down the slope to the shore. Perhaps there was, indeed, some hallucinogen in the hot sauce. At the shore, the water laps against her bare feet, annihilatingly cold. Somehow, she does not know how, only that she feels compelled to do so and can do this, she finds herself wading into the water, an explosion against her, so cold on her skin it is like being irradiated, her blood vessels contracting until they are as thin as hair, her head throbbing so relentlessly it pushes out all thought. Somehow, she doesn't know how, she is in the water, swimming, hard and fast, trying to warm herself, limbs thrashing as they carry her across the bay.

She hears a sound, like a wire being unspooled, which, the first time she heard it, she was convinced was some peculiarity of the engine of the ship that brought her here, something mechanical coming terribly undone, but now knows to be the song of the bearded seal, thin, piercing, alive, coil after coil unwinding deeper and deeper into the water. She has seen the seals on shore, on ice floes, their dark heads surfacing in the water, staring at her. They are here, somewhere.

She finds herself close to the glacier, the wide spread of its mouth, a quiet one, this one, cracked ice trickling, not like some of the thunderous ones she has recently encountered, which crash and calve repeatedly, hurl ice into the water, blue floes that spin and disperse, still melting. There is the one blue iceberg slowly circling and dissolving in the water, becoming water, its colours a spectrum from near white to azure, light piercing the thickness of time as it disintegrates, the jostling of waves smoothing the ice into curves near the water's surface, granular, melting snow still coating the top of the iceberg. She finds herself touching the ice with her fingers, her lips, with as much tenderness as she can muster. Thou, she thinks again, oh, thou. This is the amount of sadness she can hold within her human body.

Elsewhere, not far off, a young polar bear ambles down from the hills and stops to sniff the air in the direction of the hut before setting off into the water, swimming across the bay to a small island where, shaking droplets from her yellowed pelt, she meanders among the seagull nests, beneath the screeching gulls, marauding and gulping down eggs full of unhatched young, swallowing the shells and warm yolks, until, sated, she sinks to the ground, among the flowering saxifrage, and, limbs out-stretched, pillows herself against the land's undulations as if they were her own.

In the still white light it is impossible to say how many hours have elapsed. Inside the hut, the woman finds herself seated on the floor, the small window above her. Her head throbs. She rubs her eyes. On the table the flame of the squat candle flickers. She pats her hand about until she finds her phone.

On its screen, only minutes have passed, it seems. Clambering to her feet, the woman returns to the chair at the table, facing the window. The same still light illu-minates the land outside. And yet it might have been a day. Two days? It strikes her that some time has passed and no one has returned to fetch her.

In a sudden panic, she fumbles for the walkie-talkie, switches it on, and out spills a nearly incomprehensible barrage of human voices. What are they saying? She struggles to decipher them. She clears her throat. She presses the *on* button. She attempts to speak. Hello, she says. Hello? The voices call to each other as if they haven't heard her.

She tries again. Hello? She turns the walkie-talkie off and once more flicks the *on* switch. Hello? She shakes the plastic. Hello? Hello? The voices give no sign that they can hear her.

Coatless, she stumbles to her feet, and there, in front of her eyes, through the window, a boat floats past, across the bay, a sailing ship with three tall masts, the boat that she travelled in on. There are tiny people on deck, including a man in a red jacket with his back to her. Another figure perches high in the rigging. No one looks in her direction. She waves her arms within the small cabin, but the gesture is useless. How can they see her, so far off and trapped within the hut? She shouts. Of course no one can hear her.

The woman doesn't feel fear exactly. Once more the light pries open her eyelids, the green world entering her, emptying her, until, slowly, she begins to see again.

Take off your skin, the glacier says. All of it. You haven't gone far enough.

What does that even mean? The woman takes off her boots. Her socks. Wriggles her bare feet.

The world is still cold, at least for now. Somehow, she doesn't know how, she is once more outside the cabin, her skin thin as a breeze. Out on the water, the boat of her little life floats past, unreachable, dwindling, small as a leaf.

The woman slides her legs under the snow, into the rocks, into the earth, her arms into the cool melt-water. This time, the shock of the water is much less.

There is no other way to move. She is moving, finding the depths of the rocks, the texture of water, the shifting border where water meets ice, salt water meets fresh, grief meets tenderness. She is taking off her skin, and it may be that, soon, there will be nothing left of her, but she is doing it, becoming skinless, expansive, she has no choice but to continue, no other way onward other than to abandon all that was for all that is.

Credit

Visions and Relations

Elsewise: Speculative Landscapes
in the Climate Pluriverse

Kathrin Eitel

Climate capitalism, technofixes, diffusion of responsibility: apocalyptic horsemen, etched into the foundations of hegemonic structures and inscribed in political dynamics. Often invisible, these forces permeate our everyday lives, our political decisions, our very existence. How we respond to the climate crisis–today and in the future–is therefore also a consequence of persistent habitats of political conduct in a perpetually unequal world. Or put differently: the 'climate subject', introduced in this book, is not a carefree fluttering butterfly that fulfills itself only through independent, reflective self-expression, as the humanist ideal suggests. Rather, it is also the result of its sociocultural and historical surroundings. The closer a subject resides on exploitable margins, the more likely it is not only to slip beyond the horizon, but also to bear the true costs of the crisis–often through creeping or acute violence (Parsons 2025). This is exactly where 'business as usual' pushes toward collapse–hidden in smog, toxic incineration fumes, and microplastics too small to see, it keeps grinding on.

By exploring more-than-human practices of repair, care, and collective response to climate-related crises in urban Southeast Asia–particularly in Ho Chi Minh City and Phnom Penh–this contribution seeks to reconfigure dominant approaches to resilience. It does so through a series of ethnographically speculative vignettes: some closely grounded in fieldwork, others more freely imagined. I call these vignettes 'speculative' because they navigate the tightrope between ethnographic data and storytelling, aiming to create and reconfigure reality–across histories, presents, and possible futures–in order to illuminate what remains unseen and untold. This feminist approach writes not only against 'a realistic real,' but inhabits the "interstices of what presents itself as reality," as Isabelle Stengers puts it (Stengers 2018, quoted in Jensen and Thorsen 2018: 4). Speculative fabulations are to be understood in this way as a mode of attention, a practice of worlding that materialize an elsewise that goes beyond the otherness (Haraway 2016; Gramlich 2020). While 'otherwise' casts the other as a distinct counterpart, set apart from the one who observes, elsewise gestures toward a more porous sense of otherness–one that is not only different, but also elsewhere, or otherwise still. This view provides possibilities to think in consequences, enabling ethnography to become an intervening and political endeavor (Eitel 2022a; Eitel et al. 2021).

The subject is always influenced by sociocultural conditions. The processes of subjectivation it undergoes–that is, the conditions under which it becomes a subject recognized as such by society–are dependent on historical, contemporary, and future factors, as well as on cultural and social ones. This list is, of course, not exhaustive. Subjectivations are thus produced not by individuals, but by conglomerates, networks, or assemblages that persist across extended times and spaces. One might recall Michel Foucault ([1981] 2017) here, who understands the subject not as self-evident, but as produced by force fields. Always embedded in forms of power/knowledge, the subject becomes habituated as a result of its environment, which is permeated by power structures. Subjectivation processes are socioculturally diverse and more-than-humanly situated, I argue in this contribution, and it not only considers humans as subjects, but also inquires into their manifold embeddings in–at times radically–different realities and how these affect the responses we give to climate change. From this perspective, subjectivations are more than processes determined solely by human interactions. Rather, the human is decentered and placed within a complex web of human and non-human actors and their interrelations (Braidotti 2013; 2019).

According to this logic, the conditions and obligating factors accompanying subjectivation processes are always more-than-human and diversely situated. They give rise to fluid and non-static subjects at different loci: "The posthuman nomadic subject is materialist and vitalist, embodied and embedded–it is firmly located *somewhere* (...)" emphasizes Braidotti (2013: 188; emphasis by author). This somewhere stems from what Braidotti defines as a "politics of location," underscoring that these conditions and factors–or, if one prefers: the extended environments of the subject–are never universal or neutral, but context-specific. Here, the locus is metaphysically lifted out of its geographic and terrestrial anchoring and becomes a site, or a landscape, as Anna L. Tsing (2019) would define it. A landscape that may be arranged vertically, horizontally, diagonally–entirely multi-layered. The politics of location then becomes a politics of landscapes, in which the subject is not extracted from its relations to its environments, but is seen as emerging from these landscapes.[1]

What follows turns toward landscapes that exist far from the desired materializations of hegemonic subjectivation. These intended materializations me-

---

1   This also resonates with Alfred N. Whitehead's (1929) notion of the "superject"—a subject always entangled with its surroundings and sustained by the multiple relations in which it is embedded. It is at once subject and many superjects, a subject-superject that shifts according to its environment and in doing so brings forth new entities of itself, which in turn imply new relationships to its environment.

diate concrete expressions of a particular socially sanctioned mode of being a subject–namely, as an environmentally conscious, responsible individual. These practices may appear, at first glance, to be morally or ecologically meaningful, yet they are simultaneously embedded in larger power structures that define what is considered 'good' or 'right' action. Instead, we turn our gaze to scenes that lie beyond those hegemonic processes of subjectivation and illuminate far-flung networks, companionship and collectiveness. This contribution, *first*, explores disaster ontologies that illuminate plural understandings of reality in relation to crises, as expressed through everyday encounters with floods, infrastructure failures, or urban improvisational practices. It becomes clear that crises are not defined universally, but experienced and addressed in situated ways – as dynamic relations between environment, technology, and social practice (Féaux de la Croix and Samalkov 2025; Barrios 2017; Faas 2016). *Second*, the part on subject formation in the ruins focuses on the conditions under which the climate subject – or more precisely, the shared climate subject–comes into being. Here, instead of individual autonomy, processes of collectivization, historical relations of violence, affective entanglements, and infrastructural embeddings take center stage. Subjectivation appears not as an isolated act, but as a relational, material practice–one that is always fragile, contradictory, and situated. *Third*, the section on the politics of possibility opens a window to speculative future scenarios in which non-human actors–such as water hyacinths–become co-shapers of urban ecologies. It is these quiet, often overlooked interventions that suggest new spaces of possibility and invite reflection on a different, non-anthropocentric becoming of the world. Together, these three sections map out landscapes of the elsewise: spaces in which climate change is understood not only as a technical or political problem, but as a collective experience and potential–one that takes shape through shared practices, relationships, and resistances.

Ultimately, however, these narratives also show how, in a changing world, a sense of collectiveness and companionship can emerge–not as a fixed we, but as a *shared elsewise* that is embedded in solidarity, respect, and reflexivity, and engaged in struggles with diverse relations of power and force. It sees itself as part of a different planetarism, refuses the maintenance and repair work of porous postcolonial and capitalist induced infrastructures and simultaneously reaches beyond the limits of the body, to where subject no longer means individual, but relation, movement, touch.

Disaster Ontologies in the Pluriverse

The sky had been leaden grey for days when Typhoon Yagi broke away from the Chinese mainland in 2024 and began moving with ominous slowness toward the western coast of Vietnam. In the streets of Ho Chi Minh City, a strange mix of calm and quiet tension prevailed. The air was oppressive, the light pale. And yet—life went on. I met Thảo in a small café at the edge of the neighborhood, where the trees were already bending under the first winds. She stirred her iced coffee. "Everyone is preparing for heavy rain, and also plan around it to avoid travelling during rain or flood," she said calmly, as if it were nothing new. "Some neighborhoods are preparing for it by cleaning their own sewage systems without help from local government too." I looked out onto the street, where two women were pulling trash out of a clogged storm drain. People here seemed firmly determined not to face the approaching catastrophe passively. Later, a few streets away, I came across an older street vendor offering steaming noodles from a rickety food stall by the sidewalk. I asked her whether she packed up her stand and went home when the rains got heavy. She just shook her head and laughed heartily. "Not at all!" I blinked in surprise. "Not at all? Even if the water rises and the floods take over the streets?" "Then I just move my stall further up, to the edge of the sidewalk," she replied, as if it were the most natural thing in the world. And as the typhoon crept ever closer, it dawned on me: these people did not feel uncertain. What was coming was not uncanny – it was a question of everyday pragmatics.

Imponderables are not crises everywhere and most importantly: their responses unfold differently. How imponderables are handled is deeply embedded in local logics of life, care, and infrastructure. Disasters and crisis do not act out in empty space; they encounter world-relations, historical lines of violence, lived routines. How we name, experience, and anticipate disasters—all of it is already an expression of a specific ontology, a specific understanding of the world we live in. Crises are relational.

As the fictive figure Thảo makes clear in the speculative vignette at the beginning of this chapter: crises are first approached pragmatically. For example, by helping each other clear out blocked drains that would otherwise prevent rainwater from flowing away. The first priority is to remain calm. This composure is part of everyday life, just as 'disruptions' or even crises are part of daily routines. Quyên, a young women in her thirties, tells me that she spent her entire childhood responsible for clearing floodwater from her parents' house. With a bucket and a mop, she says, she feels like she spent her entire youth keeping the ground-floor living room dry. Crises are generally part of the everyday. Sometimes the sewage system fails, at other times the electricity cuts out, or the street in front of the house becomes impassable due to flooding or indefinitely delayed construction work. Even when people gesticulate and discuss new situations with intensity, the approach remains pragmatic. If it can't be done one way, then it'll be done another.

This interplay between—in this case—flooding, local conditions, and people has taken shape over decades and can be aptly described as a practical disaster ontology, which shapes what is even understood as 'crisis' and how one deals with it—that is, how responses are formed. Especially within the research fields of interdisciplinary disaster studies and the anthropology of resilience, ethnographic studies have shown that both the definition of crises and the reactions or anticipatory stances toward them are relational and diverse (Eitel 2023, Voorst 2016; Bollig 2014; Hastrup 2009). In other words, what constitutes a crisis or a planetary disaster – as climate change promises to become—evokes different experiential contexts, rules, and normative practices by which people orient themselves. In Vietnam, as in many countries in Southeast Asia and the Global South, crises are not unusual precisely because they are everyday. At the very least, this is a point at which we can confidently let go of the Eurocentric perspective that stability and functionality frame the status quo—and this not only with regard to the example from Vietnam, but also in light of current political and economic developments in the northern hemisphere, where once-buried concepts such as trade war, despotism, and autonomy—albeit now tied to different understandings—are resurfacing.

The ideal of technological innovation, of the ever-new and ever-faster, is also reaching its limits in the Global North. While in Germany this results in panicked political alignments—as seen during the 2021 Ahrtal floods, where the disaster quickly became a battleground for political blame and bureaucratic dysfunction—citizens in Vietnam, as my research in Ho Chi Minh City illustrates, respond with far more complementary disaster ontologies.

The frequent non-functioning of infrastructure—or their outright absence—requires constant repair work and improvisation, which are neither random nor arbitrary but point to a reservoir of experience and knowledge that people have built up over time (Simone 2004). This includes the continual repair of essential infrastructure, particularly in the areas of sewage and flood protection. In doing so, people do not merely adapt to an environment in dynamic flux–the storm drain clogged with garbage, preventing water from draining, prompts individuals to take matters into their own hands through cleaning activities. More than that, this rebuilding, self-creating, and repairing produces knowledge that flows directly back into their living environments. It benefits not only the individual but also a collective, such as neighborhoods, colleagues, or those that exist beyond human and non-humans, such as animals. Shaped by communist economic and social systems–such as collective farming–or by Confucian philosophy, Thảo always finds herself embedded in a web of relationships that comes with responsibilities (Luong 2003).

Thus, repair and improvisation are not (only) for personal benefit, but necessary to maintain the environment of these companionship with other. Steven J. Jackson (2014: 221) identifies this way of being-in-the-world as "broken world thinking." He argues that societies do not function solely through innovation but through continuous maintenance and repair. This becomes particularly relevant in infrastructural contexts–like the example of the clogged storm drain, which provokes a collaborative action (cleaning). In short: cleaning the drains in this case benefits not only all those who are in some way entangled in the nexus of flooding–waste–neighborhood, but the act of repair is also part of collective knowledge forms. Or put differently: the ability to adapt, to respond to new or changing conditions, and to channel them into an order expresses the 'liveliness' of such communities.

But what this example also illustrates is that the practices of repair and maintenance have little to do with a world presumed to be broken–a world conceived from the assumption that progress and innovation always imply a sequential movement from a worse to a better state, a "modern infrastructural ideal" (Graham and Marvin 2001: 35; 2007), a technofix. No: here, people do not understand their world as broken and do not need to learn to cope with the collapse of infrastructures, or with systems that are spectacular but functionally deficient. From this perspective, the world does not need to be repaired, because it already functions (though from an ethnocentric viewpoint, it may appear deficient) in the way it always has. The repairs to materials, systems, and infrastructures serve instead as support for this world. Supportive–and thus enhancing. Enhancing world thinking can be understood as a cue for how to deal with climate change and its various consequences. Repairs do not only take place after a disaster – like a typhoon or the daily floods that cities contend with–but beforehand and continuously.

Within this web, however, care becomes a central practice–but not one that is distributed equally. As Quyên recounts, the burden of care within these various forms of companionship is often unevenly distributed, weighing more heavily on certain bodies than others. Over the years, she was the only one regularly taking responsibility for maintaining the house clean after floodings and high tides–a task that involved not only physical labor but also emotional strain. The accumulated weight of this solitary effort, marked by exhaustion and a deep sense of abandonment, has left lasting imprints on her. These accounts reveal that practices of solidarity and collective action are not free from conflict. On the contrary, they are frequently marked by violence and social toxicity. It reminds us that collectivity itself can both nurture and wound, depending on how care, responsibility, and power circulate within it. Resilience, then, always seems to be built upon power asymmetries as well as recurring practices of adaptation. It underscores the value of diverse disaster ontologies in times of climate change and intersecting crises (Eitel 2023). The importance of recognizing plural ways of being–that is, the multiple understandings of reality in relation to disasters and the ways they are navigated–has also been highlighted by anthropologist Arturo Escobar (2018). He argues that acknowledging plural ontologies not only offers alternative ways of perceiving the world and reality but also opens up new spaces for action: to respond locally and responsibly within the context of global emergencies.

Holding On in the Ruins

Sophea kneels in the dust beside a wasted TV casing. Around her:
the broken shells of old appliances, shattered plastic,
and tangled cords–the sharp-edged ruins of consumption.
Sometimes they cut her–literally.
Last week, a rice cooker's jagged rim split her hand.
"The world cuts back," she said dryly, binding the wound
with a scrap of cloth, before she continues
collecting valuable parts from leftovers.
But the edges are more than physical. They are the metaphors
of a culture that discards–goods, people, futures.
And yet, Sophea stays. Not to fix the world,
but to hold it together, piece by salvaged piece.
Sophea sorted copper from plastic, a boy from
the neighborhood arrived with a plate of leftovers.
"My mom said it's too much rice," he muttered.
They sat in the shade, sharing what was never meant to be shared.
The sharpness of the ruins didn't only wound–
it also outlined new forms. New solidarities.
New "we's" not defined by purchase, but by presence.
Here, in the ruins, a different kind of life flickers.
Not built on ownership, but on endurance.
Not progress, but presence.
And in this presence, sharp as it is, something else begins.

In light of pluriversal disaster ontologies the question arises of how it is not subject formation, but processes of companionship and collectiveness that shape entities in all their embeddedness. How, for instance, are social groups or collectives solidified–through specific discourses, narratives, or policies? Which collectives are invoked when we speak of 'the victims of climate change'? Who is being subjectivized here? Such formulations homogenize what is heterogeneous, dynamic, and relational. They lend certain groups of actors a presumed unity, historical innocence, or moral authority–and in doing so, obscure the unequal distribution of responsibility, agency, and visibility.

The (climate) subject emerges at the intersection of modes of governance, discourses, affects, and material realities. Technologies of the subject, as described by Aihwa Ong (2006), exemplify this: in the context of neoliberal governmentality, subjects are produced who self-regulate, self-optimize, self-responsibilize–under the banner of efficiency, market logic, and flexibility. Crucially, neoliberalism operates and is deployed differently in post-capitalist, extractivist industrial worlds where exploitation and colonial histories are part of the national repertoire, than it is in other regions. Neoliberalism with a lowercase "n," as Ong (2006: 3) defines it, is "a new mode of political optimization" applied in the Chinese context. Here, technologies of subjectivation, unlike in the West, do not primarily position individuals as entrepreneurial self-managers but are orchestrated by an active state that purposefully steers economic and social processes. While neoliberal mechanisms in Western contexts often go hand in hand with the withdrawal of the state and the promotion of individual market responsibility, a paradoxical development appears in China: the state actively intervenes in economic and social processes in order to selectively establish market principles–without relinquishing political control. Neoliberalism in China is thus understood as a codeword for America's presumptuous grasp for power–one that forces other markets into liberalization and privatization, subjugating and enslaving them. It is a mode of neoliberalism, which rescues capitalist structures in times of crisis, for example, by mobilizing subjects as entrepreneurial actors. This recalls Anna L. Tsing's concept of salvage accumulation (2015; 2007: 63), which identifies the unpaid exploitation of wage-dependent matsutake mushroom pickers. These laborers–similar to the many waste collectors around the world–contribute through their repair and recycling labor to the maintenance of the capitalist system, without directly benefiting from it themselves. In Cambodia's capital Phnom Penh, this salvage capitalism is linked to tropes of freedom and autonomy, which persist through solidarity with peers, 'rescuing' transnational value chains and their capitalist remains by feeding waste products back into them (Eitel 2022b).

In the ruins of capitalism, collectives emerge that become accomplices – not against something, but for a future we. The waste collector Sophea, for instance, works in these sharp-edged ruins to secure a livelihood for herself and her family. So that her children may have a better life. So that things might get better. She doesn't speak of competition with other waste pickers; instead, there's a shared understanding that everyone is in the same (miserable) situation—regarding poverty, societal status. 'Incidentally,' the waste collectors, through their solidaristically intertwined networks, also keep the city clean and drastically reduce harmful climate emissions—such as those produced by the burning of synthetic waste—by collecting, purchasing, and transferring these materials to recycling and reuse facilities (Eitel 2022b). In this sense, the practices of the waste pickers in Phnom Penh can be understood as a form of salvage solidarity—a solidaristic complicity that not only sustains the continuity of transnational value chains but also performs daily care work amidst systemic neglect. It is a practice that is neither purely subaltern nor oppositional, but relational, improvised, and carried by a shared hope that something might improve.

Because the causes and effects of climate change are never clearly identifiable as such—depending on which nexus, in which configuration, is being examined, the definition of what climate change is and what its effects are will narrow or widen. For example, the fine particulate known as black carbon is both a driver of air pollution and absorbs solar radiation, thus warming the atmosphere. In fact, black carbon has an impact on the climate 20 to 1500 times greater than CO_2, though it settles more quickly. When Bangkok declared a state of emergency in early 2025 due to excessive air pollution, it was not only state measures that offered protection, but also collective, informal networks: the distribution of masks, shared data, mutual aid.

These constellations show: the climate subject is not a fixed figure; nor is it endlessly open to potential connections. It is mobile, relational, always in the making—an effect of collectivization processes, not of autonomy. Rosi Braidotti's concept of "nomadic subjectivity" is useful here: a subject not defined by separation, but by convergence—by connectedness with other knowledge forms, other life forms, other entities (Braidotti 2019; 2011). Through care, through affect, through what is shared—even amidst destruction. In the light of pluriversal disaster ontologies, one might say: the climate subject is not made—it is brought forth collectively. In ruins, in residual waste, in fine dust, in the hands of those who have no lobby—but who have one another.

But these companionships are not exclusively human. They are also formed through non-human actors, who, in interaction with material, affective, and ecological dynamics, enable—or disrupt—new forms of living together. It is plants, infrastructures, weather patterns, and waterways that co-act in these processes—not as background noise, but as active agents in the becoming of the world. In the dense, fleeting texture of urban spaces, they appear as co-creators, inscribing themselves into collective politics, disturbing existing orders, challenging us to adopt new modes of engagement. One such example is the water hyacinth in Ho Chi Minh City—long misjudged, but never passive. What does it mean to think of a plant not only as an object of ecological control, but as an agent of collective transformation?

Politics of Possibility: Speculating the We in Crisis

At first, it was barely noticeable—a denser layer
on the water, a subtle shift in the currents.
The water hyacinths, long misjudged as an invasive nuisance,
began to take shape. Not chaotically, but with intention.
They grew where wastewater entered,
where the water was warmest, dirtiest.
"They're cleaning," said a farmer.
"They're blocking," said a technician.
"They're responding," thought an ecologist.
Because the hyacinths seemed to be doing more
than merely drifting. They spread like membranes
over the canals, gathering, filtering, slowing.
They disrupted the flow—in both senses of the word.
And they stayed. Not as passive plants, but as a response.
To heat. To waste. To time.
It was not the human who was the agent of change here.
It was nature itself.
Speculative, alive, defiant.

The climate collective, as sketched in my example from Vietnam, is bound to disaster ontologies—guiding constructs of social foundations that imply a more-than-individual and foreground processes of collectivization over processes of subjectivation. These elsewise worlds that emerge here are based on a reality that points toward an otherwise possible way of being—and with it, of acting—in the climate crisis. Technologies of the subject are adapted and deployed elsewise in order to shape the subject—or the collective—and at the same time: they can only persist because people, through their embeddedness in these processes, both sustain the system and identify new spaces of (sur)vivability. Reciprocal capture—as Isabelle Stengers calls it—is a mutual enclosing of different sociocultural systems or environments that are interdependent and, through this mutual "capturing," transform each other. "Whenever there is a reciprocal capture, value is created" (Stengers 2010: 36). Reciprocal capture of salvaging—a mutual saving—that, in the case of informal (recycling and collecting) economies, gives rise to new forms of capitalism. These go beyond what Ong (2006: 9) describes as "mutually constitutive relationships that are not reducible to one or another" by shifting the focus to the effects of those relationships. What counts and what "'could count' for that practice," Stengers asks (2010: 37).

If we no longer understand collectives as anthropocentric assemblages of human subjects, but instead as emergent configurations of human and non-human actors, then plants too come into view—not as silent backdrop, but as active co-shapers of ecological orders. Adopting non-human perspectives that decenter the Anthropos and bring other species into focus can help reveal political-ecological entanglements.

Water hyacinths, which flourish particularly during the rainy season (May–October) in the megacity of Ho Chi Minh City, both clog sewage canals–contributing, for example, to the city's flooding–and purify the water in which they float. Through their persistency, fish die due to missing sunlight, and mosquitos delivering dengue are increasing. Water hyacinths (*bèo tây* or *lục bình*) are part of a contested urban space: by intervening in socio-technical infrastructures, they alter how the city is perceived, how flood risks are negotiated, and what is understood as 'nature.' They disrupt the urban metabolism–and in doing so, are an active part of a world-in-the-making that is not–and never was–centered on the human. They generate orders, they draw boundaries, they shape ways of living together and apart. And they do so not in the abstract, but in practice–in water, in everyday life, in the flow of things. As symbols of love, desire, and destiny, water hyacinths speak through songs and literature. For example, in "Lục Bình Trên Sông[2]" ("Water Hyacinths on the River"), Nhật Kim Anh sings about her lost love that has, quite literally, drifted away.

Their underlying ontology is likewise practical–not something tied to metaphysical states of being, but brought forth through everyday practice (Jensen 2021; Blaser and Jensen 2021). They intervene not just visibly in the urban space, but in (disaster) ontologies–by, for instance, complicating the cleaning of storm drains, or by echoing the ethos of enhancing repair thinking. Water hyacinths have long been used as ingredients in soups or as animal feed. Basket weaving with their stalks has also become a popular activity, as the finished products are increasingly sold on tourist-trafficked markets and local online platforms alike.

Still, their growing presence in the city remains controversial. One article even claims that the water hyacinths are 'strangling' (*bức tử*) the Saigon River; another source refers to their never-ending story–how they populate bodies of water ceaselessly–as a trait that makes them resilient to external interventions, such as the city's numerous anti-flooding projects (Mai 2019).

> They remain resilient, clinging to the river of life, even when the waves bruise and batter them. The human condition may be small, but its vitality is never drained. On the contrary, adversity only deepens and intensifies that life force over time. (Nguyễn 2023)

In 2021, the city issued an emergency plan addressing the issue, seeking to confront the plant with new technological innovations that go beyond the mere collection of organic waste.

---

2   "Lục Bình Trên Sông", (https://www.nhaccuatui.com/song/yxTaCRBR5TC6).

This clearly illustrates how ecological challenges posed by invasive plant species become embedded in urban governance and infrastructural strategies (Minh 2021). The deployment of new technologies to 'clean up nature' is not merely an environmental initiative, but also an attempt to gain technical control over dynamic socio-ecological processes–whose origins often lie beyond the specific site being targeted. As the name suggests, the water hyacinth is a "western floating plant" –*tây* (western), distinguishing it from native aquatic vegetation like *bèo cái* or *bèo ong*. The plant was introduced during the period of French colonial rule.

The pluriverse offers us an understanding of many different worlds; it reveals that their realities are–and can become–radically different; it opens new possibilities for shared futures. Or, in the words of sociologist and philosopher Martin Savransky (2021:1): "Pluralizing the present, these other stories, these other worlds in this world, precipitate a pragmatics of collective imagination against ongoing desolation." Speculative narration brings worlds into being–those that are, and those that are still coming into being–entangled and interwoven, and radically different in their realities. They are neither parallel universes nor freestanding units, but "the wager on the possibility of rendering ourselves capable of thinking, against all odds, for other times to come, for worlds to be elsewise composed. To think, while we still can, in the hold of an improbable but insistent perhaps." (Savransky 2021: 2)

In light of pluriversal disaster ontologies, it can be said that it is not the subject that acts autonomously, but rather collective processes–as mobile, context-specific, and relational networks – that bring entities (including the climate subject) into being. These processes are shaped by their specific material-symbolic embeddings, by historical relations of violence, but also by present-day possibilities for action and forms of resistance. The climate subject is thus not predetermined, but shaped situationally in and through these collective processes–as a fluid, plural, and power-saturated figure.

The unknown that reveals itself in the pluriverse is not the alien–it is the not-yet, the becoming-possible. It demands not only recognition, but co-creation. In this sense, crisis is not failure, but a threshold moment: a site of refiguration, where political imaginations can reorient themselves. Where repair is not conceived as restoration of the old, but as the enabling of something else. The water hyacinth, the storm drain network, the typhoon, the repairing collective: all stand as exemplars of world-relational practices, in which new cosmopolitical orders begin to shimmer into view – not as grand designs, but in the concreteness of everyday life, in improvisation, in carrying on, in listening. These practices operate beyond state-sanctioned resilience programs, beyond techno-utopian smart-city fantasies. Their agency does not lie in scalability, but in situatedness. And they speculate–quietly, yet insistently–on a future that is neither universal nor plannable, but must be brought forth together. Perhaps, as Stengers and Savransky might suggest, it is precisely this improbable but insistent perhaps that points the way toward an elsewise tomorrow.

> *In this world, thought a cultural anthropologist later,*
> *crisis is not a disruption. It is the moment when*
> *the cosmos responds. In rhizomes, rhythms, and resonances.*
> *In mangroves that build while everything else falls apart.*
> *In water hyacinths that float in order to organize.*
> *Nature, once seen as a passive victim,*
> *reveals itself as an intelligent fabric.*
> *Not destroyed, but becoming. Not silent, but full of voice.*
> *And perhaps, she thought further, it was time to listen.*

Thinking in the Elsewise

Amidst a world permeated by multiple crises–ecological, epistemic, infrastructural–what is needed are new concepts of the political. Concepts that do not only address humans as agents, but that make visible the relational networks through which something like agency, resistance, or care can even come into being.

Ultimately, these narratives show how, in a changing world, shared climate subjects begin to emerge–as situated-practical constellations between humans, plants, infrastructures, memories, and hopes. 'Shared' here means several things at once: shared in the sense of collectively carried, jointly brought forth–but also divided, fragmented, traversed by difference and inequality. It points to connections as much as to ruptures. What emerges here is not the autonomous *I*, but a climate collectiveness in the making: relational, reparative, resistant. A form of subject-being that can only be thought in and through being-with–in the midst of a world that was never only human. Shared elsewises are enacted by many.

This contribution is an attempt not only to describe crisis, but to unveil it elsewise. To locate it elsewise. And perhaps: to feel it elsewise. The speculative landscape proposed here means more than a shift in perspective. It is a double undertaking: on the one hand, an effort to disrupt dominant narratives of climate change through theoretical displacements–along the lines of posthuman critique of the subject, plural disaster ontologies, and more-than-human materiality. On the other hand, it is also an attunement to those lived, situated, improvised more-than-human practices that are already now imagining, making, and living different futures. These landscapes are speculative because they evolve in unknowable, contingent ways, and they are themselves conjured through speculative modes of storytelling and ethnographic fabulation. They are not imagined instead of the real, but in order to deepen, stretch, and intervene in it—making visible that which is emergent, fragile, and not yet fully formed.

In this light, crisis does not appear as a temporary state of emergency, but as a productive in-between—a moment in which spaces of possibility begin to shimmer, if we are willing to listen differently.

The elsewise is not a utopian vanishing point.
It is a thinking in relations.
A practicing in the plural.
A politics of attentiveness.
In the city of the future,
there are no centers anymore—only relationships.
People live with water hyacinths, fungi, cats, and microbes—
not metaphorically, but practically.
Plants are no longer seen as 'invasive,' but as sensors
and signal-bearers. When they spread, everyone listens.
Children learn with plants, not about them.
At certain times, the streets belong only to the animals.
Light dims, data whispers. Once a week: co-maintenance.
Not a show, but a quiet exchange between species.
What have you noticed? What do you need?
No one asks whether the world is different anymore.
It is.
And being elsewise has become entirely normal.

Bibliography

Barrios, Roberto E. (2017): "What Does Catastrophe Reveal for Whom? The Anthropology of Crises and Disasters at the Onset of the Anthropocene." In: Annual Review of Anthropology 46/1, pp. 151–166. doi:10.1146/annurev-anthro-102116-041635.

Blaser, Mario and Jensen, Casper Bruun (2023): "Political Ontology and Practical Ontology. Continuing of a Debate." In: Berliner Blätter 84, Supplement S1–S18.

Bollig, Michael (2014): "Resilience – Analytical Tool, Bridging Concept or Development Goal? Anthropological Perspectives on the Use of a Border Object." In: Zeitschrift für Ethnologie 139, pp. 253–279.

Braidotti, Rosi (2011): Nomadic Subjects: Embodiment and Sexual Difference in Contemporary Feminist Theory. New York: Columbia University Press.

Braidotti, Rosi (2013): The Posthuman. Cambridge, UK, Malden, MA, USA: Polity Press.

Braidotti, Rosi (2019): Posthuman Knowledge. Cambridge: Polity Press.

Escobar, Arturo (2018). Designs for the Pluriverse: Radical Interdependence, Autonomy, and the Making of Worlds. Durham, London: Duke University Press.

Eitel, Kathrin (2022a): "In a Speculative Mood: Affective Waste-Knowledge and Sluggish Science Practices.", In: EASST Review, 41/3, pp. 11–20. (https://easst.n et/easst-review/41-3/in-a-speculative-mood-affective-waste-knowledge-and-s luggish-science-practices/).

Eitel, Kathrin (2022b): Recycling Infrastructures in Cambodia: Circularity, Waste, and Urban Life in Phnom Penh. London/New York: Routledge.

Eitel, Kathrin (2023): "Resilience." In: The Open Encyclopedia of Anthropology. http://doi.org/10.29164/23resilience.

Eitel, Kathrin, Laura Otto, Martina Klausner, and Gisela Welz (eds.) (2021): Interventions With/in Ethnography. Experiments, Collaborations, Epistemic Effects. Kulturanthropologie Notizen 83. https://doi.org/10.21248/ka-notizen.83.

Faas, A. J. (2016): "Disaster Vulnerability in Anthropological Perspective." Annals of Anthropological Practice 40/1, pp. 14–27. https://doi.org/10.1111/napa.12084.

Féaux de la Croix, Jeanne, and Aibek Samakov (2025): "Katastrophenforschung." In: Kathrin Eitel and Carsten Wergin (eds.): Handbuch Umweltethnologie, Wiesbaden: Springer VS, pp. 311–330.

Foucault, Michel ([1981] 2017): Subjectivity and Truth: Lectures at the Collège De France, 1980–1981. London: Palgrave Macmillan.

Graham, Stephen, and Simon Marvin (2001): Splintering Urbanism: Networked Infrastructures, Technological Mobilities and the Urban Condition. London: Routledge.

Graham, Stephen, and Nigel Thrift (2007): "Out of Order: Understanding Repair and Maintenance." Theory, Culture & Society 24/3, pp. 1–25. https://doi.org/10.1177/0263276407075954.

Gramlich, Naomie (2020): "Feministisches Spekulieren. Einigen Pfaden Folgen." In: Marie-Luise Angerer and Naomie Gramlich (eds.): Feministisches Spekulieren: Genealogien, Narrationen, Zeitlichkeiten, Berlin: Kulturverlag Kadmos, pp. 9–32.

Haraway, Donna J. (2016): Staying with the Trouble: Making Kin in the Chthulucene. Durham: Duke University Press.

Hastrup, Kirsten (ed.) (2009): The Question of Resilience. Social Responses to Climate Change. Copenhagen: The Royal Danish Academy of Sciences and Letters.

Jackson, Steven J. (2014): "Rethinking Repair." In: Kirsten A. Foot, Pablo J. Boczkowski, and Tarleton Gillespie (eds.): Media Technologies: Essays on Communication, Materiality, and Society, Cambridge (MA): The MIT Press, pp. 221–239.

Jensen, Casper B. (2021): "Practical Ontologies Redux." In: Michaela Meurer and Kathrin Eitel (eds.): Ecological Ontologies: Approaching Human-Environmental Engagements, Berliner Blätter 84, pp. 93–104:

Luong, Hy V. (ed.) (2003): Postwar Vietnam: Dynamics of a Transforming Society. Lanham (MD): Rowman & Littlefield.

Mai, Hà. (2019): "TP.HCM Làm Gì Để Thoát Ngập?", Thanh Niên, 6 November 2019 (https://thanhnien.vn).

Minh, Gia (2021): "Đề Xuất Chi 13 Tỷ Đồng Thuê Máy Vớt Rác Trên Kênh.", Báo VnExpress, 15 January 2021 (https://vnexpress.net/de-xuat-chi-13-ty-dong-thue-may -vot-rac-tren-kenh-4221252.html).

Nguyễn, Hiên (2023): "Lặng Ngắm Lục Bình Trôi." Thanh Niên, 2 December 2023. https://thanhnien.vn/lang-ngam-luc-binh-troi-185231130193054053.htm.

Ong, Aihwa (2006): Neoliberalism as Exception: Mutations in Citizenship and Sovereignty. Durham: Duke University Press.

Parsons, Laurie (2025): Carbon Colonialism: How Rich Countries Export Climate Breakdown. Manchester: Manchester University Press.

Savransky, Martin (2021): Around the Day in Eighty Worlds: Politics of the Pluriverse. Durham, London: Duke University Press.

Simone, AbdouMaliq (2004): "People as Infrastructure: Intersecting Fragments in Johannesburg." Public Culture 16/3, pp. 407–429.

Stengers, Isabelle (2010): Cosmopolitics I. transl. by Robert Bononno. Minneapolis, London: University of Minnesota Press.

Stengers, Isabelle (2018): "The Challenge of Ontological Politics." In: Mario Blaser and Marisol de la Cadena (eds.): A World of Many Worlds, Durham: Duke University Press, pp. 83–111.

Tsing, Anna L. (2015): The Mushroom at the End of the World: On the Possibility of Life in Capitalist Ruins. Princeton: Princeton University Press.

Voorst, Roanne v. (2016): Natural Hazards, Risk and Vulnerability: Floods and Slum Life in Indonesia. New York: Routledge.

Whitehead, Alfred N. (1985): Process and Reality: An Essay in Cosmology: Gifford Lectures Delivered in the University of Edinburgh During the Session 1927–28. New York: Free Press.

Acknowledgments

I would like to sincerely thank Matthias Grotkopp, Martin Zähringer and Simon Probst–the editors of this book–, as well as my colleagues around Prof. Dr. Annuska Derks at the Institute for Social Anthropology (ISEK), University of Zurich, for their careful reviewing of this contribution and for their inspiring thoughts and ideas. This research is part of the research project "Radical Resilience" funded by the Deutsche Forschungsgemeinschaft (DFG, German Research Foundation) – 511266686.

Climate Justice Activism in the Global South
A Conversation

Evelyn Acham, Aidah Nakku and Nicholas Omonuk Okoit

In late autumn 2024, a group of activists from Uganda and Botswana, representing different movements and initiatives united under the Agape Earth Coalition hub, travelled through Europe to gather support for climate finance negotiations that were scheduled for COP29. Apart from talking to NGOs and politicians, they also addressed academics and young people in different countries. On 29 and 30 November they visited Freie Universität Berlin. The following is a transcript of a conversation with film and media scholar Matthias Grotkopp as a part of a lecture series on film and the ecological crisis.

Matthias Grotkopp: You have traveled several European cities, London, Strasbourg and Berlin. Bonn is next. And you will go to Baku, Azerbaijan, where this year's conference of the parties to the United Nations Convention on Climate Change, COP29, is taking place. And you do this as the Agape Earth Coalition, which is an umbrella organization for several youth climate initiatives.[1] You three all are from Uganda, but you also represent people from Botswana, Kenya and other African countries. For most people in Europe, including myself, climate justice activism comes from a place of abstract, mediated knowledge and anticipation of possible futures. But how is it for you, who are much closer to the frontline communities that have experienced the effect of the climate emergency for years already. What made you decide to engage actively in this way that you are doing, both engaging in local communities and in global policy negotiations?

Evelyn Acham: We come from a country that is being impacted most by climate change. But there is a big knowledge gap and a lot of misinformation. Some communities in our country are connecting climate change to the gods being angry. And yet the climate crisis is costing people's lives. It's costing lives for children, for women. It's worsening food insecurity. For us, climate change is beyond the

---

1   "Agape Earth Coalition", (https://www.linkedin.com/company/agape-earth-coalition/).

statistics or coming up with solutions like electric cars and renewable energy. Climate change is about the food systems, the education system, gender equality. It connects to everything. We do not have any other choice but to talk about it because it's affecting us now. It's not some far off problem. We wake up to the effects of climate change every day, and they are affecting the community. Even the people who are misinformed about climate change testify that they're experiencing the changes in the weather patterns, but they can't connect it. They can't explain it. They don't understand which solutions to take.

Because of the big knowledge gap, we are very much compelled to talk about this and not stay silent. Because if we stay silent, then what? What will the next generation have? We are not just fighting for ourselves, but we are fighting for our communities to have a future, to have a life. We are fighting for the animals to have a life. We are fighting for the young people to have a life. That's why we reach out to organizations, universities, academia and come and share our stories because we require that international solidarity. It's a global crisis where we need to share knowledge, to talk to each other and come up with solutions together. We are moving around different European countries to share our stories. We are meeting up with universities and with politicians to understand how to support each other and our struggles.

Nicholas Omonuk Okoit: I think my stepping point came from a personal perspective. I come from Pallisa, a region in eastern Uganda that doesn't have access to electricity or water. I grew up in a small village, coming from the Iteso tribe. This is a tribe that is mostly relying on farming and pastoralism. When I was still young, my brothers and I had to look after our livestock. You have to walk with them to get water, to get grass. Initially we would take very short distances to get water from around a borehole. But as time passed by, it became very difficult. We had to walk longer distances. We had to leave very early in the morning and came back late in the evening. And then you find whole villages relying on this water source and not all the livestock would get enough food and water. For most of the families, it was difficult to look after a large number of livestock. We had to sell them off. My dad resorted to looking after chickens and started selling eggs to help us go to school.

When I reached university, I saw that most of the students were not coming from rural communities. Over 70% of the population in Uganda are coming from rural areas and these are marginalized communities. I came to think about other young people who have been denied the right to education because they were denied the right to their culture, the right to their source of income because of the climate crisis. That was a huge stepping point for me to keep fighting so that I can be a voice for them and for others who might not understand what they are facing.

Aida Nakku: I don't come from a rural community, but I'm grateful to have a platform like this because different perspectives are important. I was always passionate about issues around women and gender. And then, as I grew up, during the COVID-lockdown, there was a young girl called Vanessa.[2] I think some of you know her story. Vanessa was always talking about climate and about viewing climate from an intersectional point of view. I understood that gender and climate are intersected in many ways. So that's what drew me into becoming a climate and gender advocate.

We are not Coming as Victims

MG: The last stop of your journey is Baku, the COP29. Having been to previous conferences, what are your experiences with talking to politicians and people from powerful organizations? How do you experience their reaction to your words? Why do you think it is important to go to these conferences, even though they have been so disappointing for years and decades now?

AN: On this tour we've met several Members of the European Parliament, mostly allies, the ones that are trying to push the agenda of climate finance and not so much from other parties. But even if you meet a politician from another party, they'll make it seem like 'yeah, we're trying, but it looks like we can't do much if the other people are not pushing too.' But even if COP29 has its downside – being in an oil country, even the venue is next to an oil field – this is the COP where the focus really is on climate finance as the top tier thing on the agenda. It's important that voices like ours find ways to influence. There are decisions being made and at the end of the day, these decisions affect communities like ours. It's important for us to be there even if we disagree with the venue.

NO: I always feel like if I don't go there, then I'm failing a lot of people, especially in my community. The event is structured in such a way that people who have observer badges, especially youth, cannot access every room. The only way for you to speak up is from outside the rooms. And what happens at COP is that there are always a lot of media looking at what the youth are saying. And whenever you get a chance, you can raise your voice through the press and try to put pressure on these leaders. There's this saying that it is not your fault that the world is this way, but it's your fault to leave the world the way it is. We try to be heard there and we have to keep going until everyone realizes how important it is for us to fight for justice, for equity, for everyone.

---

2   AN refers to the influential Ugandan activist Vanessa Nakate, who was at the center of a media scandal when she – as the only person of color – was cropped out of a photo showing young climate activists at the World Economic Forum in 2020.

EA: We are all in the same storm, but some boats are already sinking. Some people are drowning in the storm. What do you do if you're among the people that are drowning? You hold on to that one little thing that gives you hope. We are looking for hope in the people that have the privilege to understand the technologies better, to share their knowledge with us. When we come to countries like Germany, we are not coming to beg for climate finance. We are coming to make them accountable for a crisis that they caused. We are not coming as victims. No, we are coming to raise our voices. We keep going to these Cops to continue pushing for accountability. Because when we stay silent, it will seem like we don't care what they're doing. We have to keep putting the pressure on them to make the right decision to pay up for the loss and damage finance.

A phase out of fossil fuels matters a lot because we must keep temperatures below 1.5 degrees. But we need the resources as well for our communities to adapt to climate change, to pay for the loss and damages. We are not just travelling through Europe. It's very uncomfortable. Most of us don't get much sleep, we don't even have time to speak to our families. But we have a mission, and we want to see that mission accomplished. During COP27, we were among the group of activists that campaigned on loss and damage, and we had a win.

MG: You mentioned two very important ways to change the conversation. One is to change the conversation concerning finances. To step away from this idea that it is about aid that can be given out of the kindness of our hearts. It is about repairing the damage that has been done and that continues to be done. But you also change the conversation about how people in the Global South are perceived: not as dependents who are asking for something, but active agents demanding justice and fighting as the avantgarde of sustainability and the future. The solutions that are developed in local communities have to be funded, because they are the laboratories of our global future. What are the examples that you give or images that you try to use and the kinds of language that you want to change?

NO: One of the things that we have tried to change this narrative has been making films. And of course, when most people think about Africa, they think of a poor continent. Most of the things that we try to bring out is the potential that we have in Africa and the injustices. Because since the Industrial Revolution most of the resources were going from Africa to develop other countries. You find some countries, like the Democratic Republic of Congo, where they have a lot of resources with an estimate of $21 trillion in terms of wealth. But the DRC is the fourth poorest country in the world. And why is it this way? It's because of different political dynamics that are interrupted by Western countries to get these minerals at a low cost and keep these countries poor.

For example, we say we are in a just transition. But do you see electric cars? Do you see solar panels in Africa? In Africa we have two seasons. We have a dry, sunny season which happens almost the whole year, and we have a rainy season. So why is it that such a continent with enough sunlight does not have access to solar panels? We are talking of leapfrogging, Africa developing without oil but in the form of renewables. But the injustice is that the resources for renewable technologies are going from Africa to the developed countries. At the same time, we also have to address other connected crises like the debt crisis, because climate change is accelerating a debt crisis with the increased climate events that happen. Germany, after World War Two, was going through an economic crisis and it had some debts. But the Allies signed the London Agreement and they cancelled their debts. Why is it that our debts are not canceled? There is a lot of proof that they can be canceled. And instead of Africa getting more debt, they will use the money to finance a just transition.

EA: The relevant topic that is being talked about is 'just transition.' When you ask yourself our question: What is Africa transitioning from? Africa, a whole continent with over 54 countries, is only responsible for less than 4% of global fossil fuel emissions. How do we talk about a just transition to benefit Africa as well? For me, it goes back to the loss and damage fund being filled up. These are the ways that Africa will be part of the just and equitable transition. But without that, it will be impossible. It's going to be the same old thing of extracting minerals from Africa and leaving Africa and the Global South behind. We cannot have a just transition without an equitable distribution of climate finance, without empowering people to adapt to climate change, without bridging the knowledge gap.

People are being exploited in Africa because of the knowledge gap. People are not speaking up for vulnerable communities because of misinformation. I know very many people also in the university are misinformed about climate change or some of them are just denying. But if you accept and acknowledge that climate change is happening and it's disproportionately affecting certain people, and there is an injustice when it comes to the solutions, then I don't think you can stay silent because there are many human beings out there who deserve a good life, access to clean water, access to food. I want to change your perspective today, for those who are willing to listen and to stand in solidarity. And when you speak for the people from vulnerable communities, you're speaking for yourself as well, because this is a crisis that might be affecting Africa so much right now, but tomorrow it might affect some communities in Germany hard as well. If you speak up for us, if you fight for us, we fight together. Because African activists are always amplifying campaigns from the Global North. When we get campaigns from different organizations here, we speak about it, we put ourselves on the front line. We need you to stand with us. We need you to amplify our stories. We need you to have that solidarity with us. That's the only way we are going to build power and pressure on the leaders to be accountable for a crisis that they have caused and that they should pay for.

Educate Yourself on How Best to Support the Activists from the Global South

MG: What is the situation of climate activists in Uganda? For example, here in Germany, we have a right-wing media campaign criminalizing activism, people are preventively put in jail even before they could do activism. But still, we have the privilege to go to the streets and to do disruptive actions. Please tell us about how it is like in Uganda, what kind of repressions are there and what you do to fight this.

NO: I have been part of the Stop EACOP campaign. EACOP is the East African Crude Oil Pipeline, one of the longest heated pipelines in the world that is to be constructed in Uganda.[3] We started this campaign about four years ago, we got support from an NGO in France that realized that this project is a disaster because of the way it was affecting communities and how we were silenced. They decided to make sure that they can amplify our voices. EACOP has two subprojects. One, called Tilenga, is in the middle of a national park, which is home to lions, elephants, giraffes, different animals that are very beautiful and a source of our culture. The other subproject is called Kingfisher and is close to Lake Albert, which has been a source of income to Indigenous people who live around there and who were denied the right to fish. Ever since this project started, over 10,000 people lost their land, with very unfair compensation.

And at the same time people who have been trying to speak against this project, including me, have been blackmailed, have been kidnapped. There is a case where seven comrades from another movement group, Students against EACOP, were arrested and detained for two months. And when they were arrested, no one was ready to speak up for them. Last year the CEO of TotalEnergies attended COP, and we confronted him about these students and that's how they were released. But when they were released, two of them were seriously injured. They were tortured. Another incident that happened was a climate activist who was kidnapped for about a week. Then they left him about 400km away from his home, in a very critical condition and he was rushed to hospital.

What big oil corporations do is that they look for small gaps within the government. One of the loopholes are dictatorships. They reach out to the leader, and then it seems like the leader is the one putting pressure on the people, yet it's coming from the corporation. When we started this campaign, a few activists came to France and

---

3   "#StopEACOP", (https://www.stopeacop.net/home).

spread the knowledge of what TotalEnergies is doing. Many people in France did not know what was happening because of their own company. We exposed a lot of banks that were involved, including Deutsche Bank. We started putting pressure on different stakeholders and many financial institutions stepped out of this project.[4] This happened because of different movement groups coming together. It was not just activists. It was researchers, lawyers taking legal action to hold TotalEnergies accountable.

Our activism is heavily oppressed, very risky. But if we have a lot of solidarity, then we can achieve something. I don't think that you have to be an activist to create change. But you have to use what you can. Lawyers supported us, different universities and NGOs like Human Rights Watch, Amnesty International were talking about this project. We need to expose how these big corporations do it. Because these corporations are the ones funding the misinformation. We need everyone to pick out the truth and expose all the dodgy business that they do.

AN: As white people in this country, it's important to educate yourselves, especially on issues like my position as a Black person from Africa in your country. We were organizing this whole thing with a team of 17 people, but only eight people made it to come on this tour. And among those eight are the people supporting us from Austria. So, six African activists made it. And one of the major challenges was the issue of visas, that took like a month, which is unusual. "We need you to have insurance. We need you to have accommodation booked. We need you to have our flight booked." Every day it was a different issue.

Last year in June we were in Bonn and these activists came to us: "We're going to have a campaign where we're going to glue our hands on the road. Please come and join us." And the first thing that came to my mind was: Do they see my skin color before they ask me to join such a campaign? In my own country we are already at risk with many people being kidnapped. Now what about a country where I can't even speak the language? Who am I supposed to call if I get arrested? It's important that you educate yourself on how to support and how to avoid putting us in risky situations.

In our own country, when we speak about issues like EACOP we are at risk. But even when we travel here and just attend a conference and give interviews talking about EACOP, the moment you land in Uganda, security forces are already there: "Who sent you? Why did you go? Why did you talk about it?" If you're saying: "Come and speak about EACOP or any other pressing issue", it is important to consider how

---

4   "East Africa: Five banks incl. Deutsche Bank, Citi, JPMorgan Chase opt out of financing EACOP due to human rights concerns", 29 May, 2022 (https://www.business-humanrights.or g/en/latest-news/east-africa-five-banks-say-they-will-not-finance-eacop-due-to-human-ri ghts-concerns/).

to make sure that there is some form of protection for these activists, to make sure they get home, they are okay, they are safe. The activism here is so different. In my country, personally, I don't even have a contact for a lawyer. But you hear people from XR: "Our lawyers will bail us out." I'm going to get kidnapped, and no one is going to know where I am for a month, you know? It's important that you educate yourself on how best to support the activists from the Global South.

MG: Just considering oneself an ally is not enough to really enlarge your own perspective and to know the context and the dangers in which the other person is moving. What you told us about the EACOP campaign shows the need to share different kinds of tasks and that to support each other in the best way means to think about what you can do that the other one can't do. But you also mentioned a topic that is shared all over the world, which is the way powerful companies are using their financial resources to pay PR firms, but also individual influencers. For example, there is this campaign supporting the EACOP pipeline using the hashtag #ActionForSustainability. And if you don't know what's behind this, you might think, it's a good thing. How do you fight these kinds of powers to get your knowledge across to the people on the ground and online?

EA: Activism in Uganda has a lot of security risks. In 2022, I got arrested while protesting in front of the Ugandan parliament, and the police told me that they would make me disappear and no one will ever know where I am. I got so scared. We pleaded with them to forgive us for doing the right thing. They told us: "We're going to let you go, but you need to give us all your banners and you need to take down the posts that you put on social media." They took our phones, accessed our Twitter accounts, Instagram accounts and we forcefully had to delete our posts. Then they told me and these other activists never to stand in any public place again. Since that time, I don't go to any public place to stand with my placard. I just do it online. But I came up with a strategy where I go with other activists to schools because there is a big knowledge gap, and climate education is not included on our school curriculum. We go to schools and universities to educate young people about climate change in a simple way. And afterwards, we plant trees. Because in our communities you can't just go and talk to people. You have to give something, for them to listen to you. And then we use online platforms to amplify this. But a very big number of people don't even have smartphones.

We use climate education in schools to do our activism and also platforms like COP29. Every time we go to these conferences, there's a tension that we build in our countries. The number of people understanding that there is a climate emergency has increased since 2021. These conferences are working for us because local media start following them and try to understand why we are at this conference. We recently also started doing conferences within our countries. We organized a conference called African Climate Change Adaptation Conference where we invited politicians, faith leaders, people from the private sector, students, Indigenous communities to share knowledge and explore possible solutions.

NO: The different strategies that we used, were giving workshops together with different NGOs based on research they got from us and from local NGOs and making short documentary videos on social media. At the same time, we try to expose financial institutions, like banks and insurance companies, who are very afraid for their reputation. We give information to media and press to publish. And you don't need to be an activist to just say: "This bank is financing this disastrous project." There's a lot of information, different websites on banks funding fossil fuels, like banktrack.org or Urgewald.[5] You can look at the different projects that are run in Africa and the Global South and how they are impacting people. There's a lot of information around; it just has to come from your interest to make an impact. Some people are using art to expose what's happening. Yesterday we were in London at one of the campaigns called "Insure our Survival" with Extinction Rebellion and there were people using art and music to share the message. It doesn't have to be through blockades and civil disobedience. It can also be a poem. It can also be a message that you give on a bank or an insurance company. Everyone within their capacity, joining together to fight a system that is causing harm.

AN: The face of activism in our country completely changed. If you're holding placards, the message is not reaching and you're getting arrested. We have more effective ways in collaboration with the different Fridays For Future groups. And we had to go through social media trainings to know how to utilize social media. Because if you're making a video talking about EACOP, you're going to get 20 views. But if you look at a platform like TikTok and you're using a trending video, portraying a different message, using certain hashtags, it's more likely that people will view your video. It's like clickbait.

If We Want to Save Our Planet, You Cannot Be the Only Savior

MG: It's important to think how it's not just a technical, financial and social issue, but also a cultural issue. It is about the way we relate to each other, to the earth, the air and the water, about these kinds of relationships that we build on different levels, locally but also globally. How do you think about your own cultural context that is changing through the emergency?

---

5   "Banktrack", (https://www.banktrack.org); "Urgewald", (https://www.urgewald.org); "Banking on Climate Chaos", (https://www.bankingonclimatechaos.org/).

AN: I come from the Baganda tribe. And one of the things that have really helped in the preservation of biodiversity, without even people knowing it, is that we have a surname which belongs to a particular clan and that clan is an animal or a plant. From a young age, we are taught to have an attachment to our clan. If I'm from the N'jobu clan, I'm told to love the elephant, to protect the elephant, to educate people about the elephant. It's like my spirit animal. I have to defend it with my life. And the same goes for plants. That's one way where culture blends with conservation and helping it in climate change.

NO: For me, it's about us sharing resources and knowledge. There are many Indigenous communities, not just from Africa, but also from South America, who are fighting against corporations and sometimes win cases against them. When you are coming from an Indigenous community, you have your own culture and a very strong connection with nature, with every living being around you. This is something that we have to share with people in other countries that have gone beyond it. If we want to save our planet, you cannot be the only savior. It's not that the Western countries are the ones saving the planet. It's about how each of us can contribute to saving one another, to saving our home.

When you go to COP, you don't find so many Indigenous communities occupying the spaces. You're going to find people coming from privileged positions. And there are a lot of things that limit Indigenous knowledge in terms of creating solutions, including language barriers in that some communities cannot even speak English or any of the international languages. If we start to include different perspectives, we can achieve something. It's very difficult for an Indigenous person to even travel because they cannot get a visa. If you want to think about how change can happen, you have to imagine a world before borders were created. Because it was not always like this. It was only just territories. And we cannot have a sustainable future if the people in other areas, the people of different cultures, are not included.

EA: Earlier this year I was doing a survey in northeastern Uganda, in a region called Karamoja, with a group of Indigenous people called Karamojong, who are mostly cattle keepers, pastoralists. This region has about 1.4 million people and is one of the regions that are affected by most of the challenges, if you look at all the 17 SDGs[6]: there is poverty, hunger, no education, gender-based violence. These people have experienced climate change, they've experienced droughts. But they are using a lot of Indigenous knowledge to try and be resilient to the impacts of climate change. One of them told us, how they know that the rainy season is coming. They slaughter some animals and check the blood of the animal. If the blood is red and very thick, then

---

6   The Sustainable Development Goals adopted by the UN in 2015: "The 17 Goals" (https://sdgs
     .un.org/goals).

they know that the rain is coming. And when you think about this, it is connected to science, because that means the animals have started feeding. Climate change is so much connected to cultures, to indigenous knowledge and the solutions are also connected to the spirit world. We need to bring in the perspectives of the Indigenous people into these climate spaces, because when we come up with solutions without including these people, then they will not be able to adopt to the solutions.

About three years back, we installed an eco-friendly cookstove in a school. And then two years later, when we went to do the monitoring and evaluation, the cook-stove was as new as we installed it, like they have never used it. Because we didn't first ask them, what solution works for them? We imagined that this is what the schools needs and just brought solar and eco-friendly cookstoves. When we went back, they were still using firewood and there was too much smoke. If we are going to talk about supporting communities to adapt, we have to understand what are the solutions that work for them. Otherwise, communities will not be able to adopt to the solutions that you're bringing in.

Question from the audience: Thanks a lot for your engagement and the information you gave to us. A lot of young people in Europe or Germany feel really strange when they see that they're protesting on the streets and basically it gets worse. How do you manage to not be feeling strange and to still remain nonviolent, facing so much violence yourselves?

AN: You can't do advocacy alone. You need to have something where you draw your strength from. For me personally, every time I feel discouraged and that the leaders, the policies and the system are failing us, I go back to where I draw my strength, and I draw my strength from a place of love for the people and the planet. And I draw my strength from what I believe in: the saving power of God, the saving power of Jesus. And that's why I also say that climate activism is very spiritual. You can't do it, if you think you're going to do it just from your own strength. Because the leaders are so powerful, they have the money, they have the resources. How can you even fight them just using your own body? You need a certain supernatural strength. And I think it's always important to take breaks and take care of your mental health. We had a session one year back where we all sat and everyone kind of aired out what is hurting them. Sometimes it's not even the political leaders, sometimes there's other issues within the movement that certain people feel oppressed. Even some of the people from Europe, who are allies, are racist and just want your face for diversity and after that they are done with you. It's just important to have a community.

NO: We need to build a bond beyond just going on the street together but also get-ting to know each other. And that's why you also have to understand the different cultural beliefs. Being open minded, looking at someone's strengths instead of their weaknesses and seeing how you can help them. A lot of activists that I've talked to, especially in Europe, have been depressed by how things are not moving on. Activism takes so much work, sleepless nights and all this. But in the end, I always reflect upon the achievements that we have accomplished with activism and how these achievements can be our standing points to push forward. Because you might be going on the street, but someone else might speak to the decision makers. You find that these leaders don't know what we go through. We recently met MEPs and some of them had met activists from the Global South, especially from Africa, for the first time. They were very surprised listening to us. We have to find ways of an intergenerational connection with the people who are ruling us now asking the younger generation and seeing how we can address this crisis.

Us Are Them
Interview with Angelina Davydova

Vera Shchelkina

Angelina Davydova: How do you as a choreographer work with the ideas of the non-human actors and agents?

Vera Shchelkina: Partly because of me being on the autism spectrum, I always had a better connection to the non-human parts of the world. In dancing and choreography, I was always fascinated by pieces or research that give back the agency to the body but not the personality – to the cells, the tissues, the flow of breath or the always transforming liquids inside of us. This somatic approach allows me to relate not to the stories and narrations, but to the matter itself. We are the matter in a direct sense, and in a sense that connects us to the rest of the world with its non-human agents.

In short, choreography consists of two processes: movement research and composition of found material.

In the stage of movement research, I work a lot by witnessing and looking at non-human processes and patterns – on video, in real life. I read about biological processes. In a way, non-human thinking brings everything back to the question of living matter being held by some sort of holding principle. Different cells, liquids, and tissues, millions of particles are thinking of themselves as some unit, organism, as a whole, having some kind of agency. This is every living thing. This is also us: a bunch of cells, thinking of themselves as a whole. We started from one cell growing, dividing, multiplying, and mutating into a multicellular organism. This type of thinking embryologically allows me to attend to the human body as living matter, a sort of non-human agent.

As a choreographer, I have been working with different types of non-human contexts:

- behaviour of animals (quite recently in a dance piece "Everyone here is a bit of a horse" about the hidden violence of civilisation towards animals and children);
- swarm consciousness – behaviour of bird flocks or bee swarms, trying to recreate the algorithms, within human crowds;

- vibrating qualities of different types of matter – in a piece "Vibrant Matter" (un-hand of Jane Bennett's "Vibrant Matter" theory[1]);
- different processes of biological death and decomposition – in a dance piece "SMRTъ"[2] (meaning death) and many laboratories about death in performing practices.

Also, I have been working on a series of online classes during the pandemic called "Human spaces" with a focus on perception of different timespaces, combined to a human.

AD: Can we really abandon our anthropocentric approach in body-based practices, dance, movement? How can we go beyond the human/non-human divide?

VS: I doubt we can really abandon anthropocentric approaches, hence we are living through the human body and human experience. Current eco-practices that have been a trend in contemporary dance for a while have been trying to rethink our positioning towards animals and living nature in general as not hierarchical but symbiotic relationships. There have been many attempts for this symbiosis, from dancing for plants or animals to Judith Butler's idea of animal kinship[3] and different methods developed out of it. I have also been practicing, for example, a "Body weather"[4] approach, which took a form of embedding into nature through direct touch with it, underlining the permeability of the body.

My critique towards this variety of methods lies exactly in this point: I doubt we can just stop being, thinking, behaving, attending, and relating like humans, being conditioned into human civilization from early on. However, I believe in broadening or expanding our experience. Through imitating, understanding, trying out non-human behaviour we can get a glimpse of understanding how to be someone else.

For the last piece, I have been researching perceptual time, or temporal resolution of pets – cats and dogs. It can also be perceived as a sort of biological frame rate, allowing different animals to hear and see the world slower or faster than we are used to as people. Using video-simulations of animal perception as inspiration, I have been working on the speed of movement of the dancers.

Also, because of the difference in the retinas (two cone cells instead of three), dogs, for example, see the world in blue-yellow tones. So, there is much research out

---

1   Bennett, Jane (2010): Vibrant Matter. A Political Ecology of Things, Durham and London: Duke University Press.
2   "SMRTъ", (https://movingtouch.site/smrt).
3   "Feminist theorist Judith Butler rethinks kinship", 19 April, 2012 (https://www.columbiaspect ator.com/2012/04/19/feminist-theorist-judith-butler-rethinks-kinship/).
4   "Body Weather Laboratory", (https://www.bodyweather.org/).

there allowing us to have animal experience. Maybe, there is hope for forgetting our anthropocentrism eventually.

AD: The new climate era brings to light the existence and importance of the new climate subjects, including non-human actors, and animals among them. What stages do you think are important for their further integration into our existence?

VS: As I understand the development of human-non-human relations, we started off fighting anything that would pose a danger to our species, thus creating the 'us versus them' paradigm. Then it became clear in the 20th century that with this approach, we almost eliminated a lot of other species. Then the whole paradigm of 'us for them appeared, and then 'us and them.'

From my somatic point of view, I would choose the "us are them" approach. 'Us are them' in a sense of the human body being just a form of living matter consisting of the same molecules and minerals on a microlevel and having the same evolutionary developed social behaviours on a societal level. This might lead to different consequences, from giving rights of a non-human person to a whale or a river, which is basically an inclusion program, to leaving society to live in the woods, to dedicating one's life to creating climate simulations that can help us stop rising temperatures. I do not have the answer what would help bring us back to the ecosystems we left – but I have an example of teenagers from a specific subculture of quadrobics[5] . Teenagers playing animals in the woods and learning how to move on four legs are for me an example of a first teenage step of our reintegration – and refusal to be a human. Other steps might follow: understanding what exactly I refuse, changing in a small and detailed way – and thus proceeding with reintegration.

AD: Have you worked with other non-human actors apart from the animals?

VS: I think the way we speak about such things is highly important. I have worked not with, but in touch with. Like any living body, I have worked in symbiosis with my microbiota on the inside. Also, in direct touch with everything that I am embedded in in the form of dust on the outside, the rest of the dead cells of humans and other animals. Quite literally, one of my performances was called "Skin to dust"[6] and it was a solo piece about living and non-living organisms becoming dust. For the piece "Vibrant matter"[7] we have been working with human collaborators as well as the sound waves that pierced our body, making it tremble and vibrate – and with light that changed our hormonal state and excitement of the nervous system. I have also been

---

5   "Quadrobics", (https://therian.fandom.com/wiki/Quadrobics).
6   "Skin to dust", (https://movingtouch.site/skin2dust).
7   "Vibrant Matter", (https://movingtouch.site/vibrant_matter).

working with algorithms of bird flocks usually known as 'murmurations' – creating scores for masses of people during big dance festivals.

AD: How do you think artistic and speculative methods help dealing with global crises?

VS: In general, my artistic approach is about using speculation, or imaginary body maps, that change or alter our internal image of our body. Our nervous system is ready to imagine parts of our bodies or change our posture according to the way we move. I am using that adaptability to imagine something new:

- to rethink ourselves as an animal with the longest tail possible, sticking out of the window;
- to grow not into a human embryo, but into the embryo of a cat;
- to separate our clavicles from our sternum to become a body with different qualities.

Dance involves using images in order to widen the variety of movement, to let go of some usual muscular tension, and so on. I believe that speculation and imagination are tools that can change not only our body, but also our cognition in a broader sense – as the embodied, the embedded, the enacted, and the extended cognition.[8] Those mind-games are clearly just games, yet they help us not take ourselves as humans and as agents too seriously. Making us subject to change, allowing us to consciously play with this change. And if we think about the many global crises we live through now, including the climate crisis, that is ultimately also a change.

AD: When do you think choreography becomes a political act?

VS: There is a quote from the famous essay of Carol Hanish that everyone is fond of: "Personal is political"[9]. Well, it is. You first take your personal dream or feeling that haunts you. Then you research about the others who are also affected by it. Then, you begin to work with, in, together, as your body – the most personal process possible. And then, you create a situation where this bodily personal process touches the body of each audience member. Where they touch each other, change happens. It can be just an exhale, a down-regulation of the nervous system, or, on the contrary, in-

---

8   Albert Newen, Leon De Bruin, and Shaun Gallagher (eds) (2018): The Oxford Handbook of 4E Cognition, Oxford: Oxord University Press.

9   Hanish, Carol (2006/1969): "The Personal is Political", (https://www.carolhanisch.org/CHwritings/PIP.html).

creasing anxiety. This first communication is already political, because it will spread further – through the bodies directly into changes in the whole system.

AD: You also explore various aspects of human cognition and intelligence. With the climate crisis and polycrisis we often speak about the need to change human values, attitudes and shift perspectives. Can body-based practices help us with that?

VS: First of all, I think that the ambition to change human values or shift perspectives comes from the same hierarchy as 'us versus them.' 'Us' as in 'We know better what the world needs.' In a way, this paradigm deprives 'them' of agency, and it basically can be applied to animals, to climate, or to humans. All of them are all of us – parts of an interconnected tissue. So, the body practices that I practice cannot change the world, no. They can make you curious: you can ask yourself, for example, how does this ant perceive its time? Why did polar bears start attacking people? What if I move the way oil moves coming up to the surface? Does the food I take in influence the process of decomposition of my body after death? This curiosity is infectious, some of the answers are increasing the connectivity to the world we are embedded in – and some not. This curiosity falls out and steps out of the whole process of living things becoming objects, becoming a commodity. For me, it brings back the world from the times I was a child – where I did not know the value of a fallen tree.

My second way is re-humanising everything back. And I speak about that in an ancient sense, before being human became horrible so to say (in the sense of humans being violent, hierarchical creatures trying to own things). These body, dance, and performance practices are playing a lot with being witnessed and being present as you are: awkward, shy, strange, queer in all senses. And this state of being witnessed in all your feelings, states, and behaviours – makes you breathe out, makes your nervous system jump out of the stress mode where everything becomes either an aggressor or an object for your aggression – and then the whole situation gets much more nuanced. Looking at things in this soft and tender state makes you acknowledge that they are not things. They are living (even if they are described as non-living from the point of view of biology) agencies that you are in communication with. And this communication can sometimes be different from just a state of owning or destroying. In a way, body practices take away the arrogance of having control of the whole world. Because you cannot even control your own sweating. Then why do you need control over the whole world?

AD: New emerging climate subjects speak a lot to us about inequality, suppression and discrimination. How do you work with these ideas in your performances?

VS: As I said, I think there are many more ways of relating to others than just being hierarchical in any way, suppressing, knowing, paternalising, or controlling. Hierarchy in living organisms and systems is sometimes really different from what we think we know. In nature, being eaten can become an act of survival and symbiotic strategy (this is actually one of the theories explaining to us how multicellular organisms appeared).

So, in my pieces I often give this control away – to other agents: to our cells that are either dividing or dying out. To the cascades of death (yes, they are actually called like that), to the sound that vibrates my body whether I want that or not, and stays for hours. To the insects that perceive my body as just another space to walk, eat, and have sex. I am sure that giving away control over my own body or its behaviour is a first step to feel other, more complex relations. I also sometimes over-amplify hierarchical relations, putting the audience above the dancers, playing with levels of power and authority and theatre rules, making it so obvious that it becomes kitsch. Say, in my last piece, "Everyone here is a bit of a horse", which I showed in June in Berlin, we just put all audience on a higher level than the dancers, so they can witness their behaviour in a pit. This shifts a usual frontal focus and underlines hierarchies that are always there, but we are so used to them that we do not perceive them anymore.

AD: In the new climate reality there's a lot of discussion about loss (ecosystems/species, etc) and also the need to accept it (psychology of loss etc). You explored the topic of death, mortality, dissolution in your earlier work, how do you see it from the current, also climate, perspective?

VS: Therapy (and embryology) says we start our lives from the largest loss we can imagine – with being born. We lose 40 thousand cells a minute from the surface of our skin, dying out constantly. We have lost so much human touch in the process of cultural isolation. Half of all people in the world have lost psoas minor – a muscle in the body that slightly flexes the lumbar spine. There are thousands of losses we just do not notice.

That is why there is a whole movement in performing practices of mourning. To get back the feelings of loss, to make things matter again, to slow down and try to have less forgotten – even with the high speed of life we have. But also, personally I am not a great fan of mourning of everything – I feel that mourning is often misused in order to hinder or prevent constant change which is happening anyway, and that excessive mourning can just lead to eternal reflection on the states and experiences which are no longer with us.

In my practices of death, I want the people to experience this state of permanent change, that is ongoing within and outside us, as with every other living thing. We are constantly losing dying cells, and constantly growing at the same time. Without this loss, we would have died of malignant tumours. I perceive holding on to the bodily states and memories that have been before the present moment as this inability to deal with loss and constant change. Mourning is a process that comes to an end. Being human is a process that comes to an end. Every living thing is a process that comes to an end but then gets continued in a form of another life, for example, in its molecular form. When I observe the climate crisis from the perspective of a human, it looks like a giant loss – of a habitat, of a safe haven, of the ground that holds me. When I see the climate crisis from a perspective of constant change, I know: maybe it is just a loss for (and of) human species, but the whole world will proceed further, and will forever create other species from the remnants of people.

AD: What gives you hope and strength at the times of climate crisis?

VS: There is no hope. There is just living your life every day, every day as the last one, being humane to others – in a long-forgotten sense of being soft, understanding, respectful, and loving – to all and to everyone that is out there. Because we are exactly the same lost ones as those around us, we will be dead soon, reborn as something totally different.

Living Climates: Subjectivity beyond the Human

Blanche Verlie

Introduction

In contemporary dominant (Euro-Western-Modern-Industrial) cultures, climate has been figured as largely separate from human societies and systems, with recent fossil-fueled climate change and its subsequent impacts on humans understood as a transgression of the previously clean distinction between the human world and the atmosphere (Verlie 2017). More recently, as this book exemplifies, we are acknowledging that climate change affects people and can influence individual subjectivities and identities; in a way that echoes and extends pre-scientific Western philosophies regarding how climate, air and weather shape culture (Horn 2018). This recognition of the ways that humans and climates are entangled draws on and moves towards Indigenous and First Nations cosmologies, which have for a long time emphasised that both humans and weathers are part and parcel of Country/land (Bawaka Country et al. 2022; Todd 2016). Nevertheless, these recent moves within Western culture and philosophy retain a rational/positivist materialism (Schaeffer 2018) that positions climate/weather/air as agential, but not necessarily – indeed, rarely – animate. By contrast, First Nations cultures, and indeed older and less dominant Western cultures such as the Ancient Greeks and the Vikings, have long understood atmospheric phenomena not simply as materially enmeshed with humans, but as sentient entities with desires and agencies – that is, as subjects (Bawaka Country et al. 2022; Todd 2016; Burman 2017; Leduc 2011). Weather personified as judgemental and often vengeful deities has arisen in many cultures the world over. Perhaps most famously, Zeus and Thor, the Greek and Norse Gods of Weather, personified the moody atmosphere.

In this chapter, I work with multispecies, more-than-human, feminist materialist and, to the extent I am able to,[1] Indigenous philosophies to expand conceptuali-

---

sations of climatic subjects. Such cosmo-ontologies, while diverse in detail, share a broadly animate worldview, understanding the non-human world as inherently teeming with liveliness. I begin by outlining the notion of *living climates*, and how this conceptual framework can clarify how human worlds and subjectivities have always been entangled with the climatic, and thus how the subjectivities that compose our worlds are changing in line with our changing climates. I begin by unpacking four inter-related articulations of the phrase *living climates*, and then outline six distinct but connected forms of climatic subjectivity that this approach identifies, ranging from individual humans who engage consciously with climate change, to the bio-regional assemblages that compose hemisphere-wide weather patterns such as the El Niño Southern Oscillation and the Indian Ocean Dipole. I conclude with an example of the diverse climatic subjectivities that emerged during Australia's 2022 floods crises, including the Tinnie Heroes who rescued human and non-human people from rooftops, the out-of-place animals, and the trauma-monger itself, the Triple La Niña.

Living Climates

The dominant way of understanding climate in Western-modern cultures – as the average weather of a defined place – has been as an external system with which humans occasionally interact (Verlie 2017; 2022). In contrast to this approach, *living climates* describes the ways that climates live and are lived. Building upon approaches which understand that atmospheric phenomena participate in the formation of human subjectivities (Shacke 2024; Singh 2013), *living climates* recognises that subjectivity is not solely the purview of humans (albeit climatically-influenced ones), but rather, that subjectivity is a condition enacted by enmeshments of biological-atmospheric becomings (Verlie 2022; Verlie and CCR15 2020). Climatic subjects are thus not just climate-impacted individual animals, but emergent collective subjects composed of climate-life entanglements where self-knowledge-agency are distributed, circulating, collectively-produced and dissipating. *Living climates* offers four inter-related ways of understanding the entanglements between life and climate.

i.

Firstly, with 'living' as an (ontological) adjective, *living climates* informs us that climates are alive: they are active, sentient, biological, animate. Earthly climates are not 'things' or even 'systems' but a "set of relations" (Knox 2015), a "sentient commons" (Todd 2016), composed by the births, lives and deaths of literally every species that has ever existed. But it is not only the biosphere, but also the rocks and waters – whether glaciers reflecting solar radiation while watering carbon-sequestering lichens, or mountains creating updrafts upon which eagles soar – that contribute, every day and all-millennium, to creating and re-creating local and planetary climatic conditions. In one day's weather in one specific place, temperatures, atmospheric pressure and humidity are shaped by the ecological actions of ancient species there and globally, as well as currently-alive beings literally exhaling and excreting the airs that we inhale in the next breath. From such a perspective of climate as a set of living planetary relations, climate pollution becomes not just 'environmental degradation' but rather, industrialised murder on a planetary scale: "omnicide" as Celermajer refers to it (2021).

ii.

Secondly, with 'living' as a (normative) adjective, *living climates* means that we want climates that are living and liveable, not dead or deadly. Yes, Mars has a climate, and Jupiter's moons have climates, and the Earth's core has a climate: but they are not living climates, they are not liveable, at least not without extreme prostheses that intergalactically translocate small, totally enclosed and insulated, and tightly regulated pockets of Earth's Holocene climatic conditions. Yes, life in a 6-degree hotter world might be survivable for some, but it is unlikely to be liveable (joyful, nourishing, vibrant) for many beings at all.

iii.

Thirdly, with 'living' as a verb, *living climates* means we live (in, as and with) climates. That means that climates are experienced, which is also to say, they are subjective. Living climates refers to how we (humans and non-humans) are made and shaped by climates, even as we ourselves make and shape climates in return. Climates are felt; they are lived day-by-day, moment-by-moment; climates change our worlds, and structure our lives, in mundane and extraordinary ways. Climates influence the foods we eat and the internet on which we share photos of food. Climates influence the ways we dress, the sports we play, the restaurants we patron, the jokes we laugh at, the friends we make, the homes we build, the holidays we aspire to, the pets we keep, the jobs we have. And climates affect us even more intimately too: how much we sweat and how much our local community judges us for that; how easily we breathe and whether our joints ache, meaning: how old we feel; how frequent our headaches are, meaning: how tired, grumpy and frustrated we get at our families. Climates are *lived*, and they are lived by (human and non-human) people, that is, by subjects.

iv.

Fourthly, following Haraway's contention that "worldly embodiment is always a verb, or at least a gerund" (Haraway 2008: 249), *living climates* posits 'living' as a gerund (i.e. a noun) and "climates" as a verb (conjugated in third person singular). Understood this way *living climates* articulates that to live is to engage in climating. We make climates, we do climates, we climate in our everyday practices of living and making a living. Working, shopping, eating, breathing, pooping, cycling, campaigning, complaining, laughing, partying: all our practices of living participate in and co-create climates. Through our practices of climating, we participate in the ongoing reiterative co-production of atmospheric matters and patterns. Climate is something we all do, all the time, and we are always doing it together, even if we are not doing it in coordinated, similar or equal ways.

Living climates as an onto-ethico-epistemology (Barad 2007) is informed by multispecies (Haraway 2008), posthuman (Alaimo 2008; Haraway 2016), Indigenous (Bawaka Country et al. 2022; Wright 2008; Todd 2016), and feminist philosophies (Neimanis and Walker 2014; Neimanis and Hamilton 2018; Tuana 2008). These approaches share a number of interdependent principles. The first is about interconnection, entanglement or *relationality*: that to exist is to be composed, and continually re-composed, through relationships with others, and that climate is not an object so much as a patterned "set of relations" (Knox 2015). These relationships are always *more-than-human*: we cannot escape our entanglement with climate and the wider ecological world. Relatedly, it is not just humans that change climate; nonhumans also participate in creating, stabilising and changing climate, although this does not discount the significance of the changes being wrought by some human systems in this geological moment. In addition, climate is *embodied*, and all earthly beings are viscerally enmeshed with climate; indeed, we become (with) climate. Building on this embodied approach, climatic phenomena are inherently *affective*: they are energies, forces, intensities, feelings. Collectively, these principles articulate climate as "a living phenomenon" (Sasser 2016) that emerges from the interactions and relationships between all bodies: human, non-human and "inanimate"; living, dead, ancient and yet to come. *Living climates* thus focuses on the intimate and multi-scaled ways that living and once-living bodies are entangled with the gaseous world, and how the patterns of these relationships generate the atmospheric conditions in which we live. It therefore attunes to how the planetary and epochal phenomenon of climate change is metabolically and experientially enmeshed within our everyday, mundane, inter/personal lives. Through doing so, *living climates* helps unpack how climatic subjectivities are formed, what is at stake in them, how they might operate, and thus provides a more materially-informed analysis of climate politics.

Climatic Subjects

Living climates as a framework helps identify at least six ways of thinking about 'climatic subjects.' Here I develop a typology, loosely organised according to those I think might be the easiest subjectivities to identify from our current standpoint within modern-capitalist-anthropocentric society, through to those that might be less frequently imagined and identified. In brief this is 1) individual human subjects who consciously engage with climate change, 2) all human subjects, as all humans are only able to exist within certain climatic conditions, 3) more-than-human individuals who also live within and are dependent on climatic conditions, 4) more-than-human collective subjects in which climate and/or climate change is unavoidably a participant, 5) atmospheric phenomena (i.e. weather events and regional weather patterns) and 6) Planet Earth's global climate. Of course, any attempt to delineate one type from another is somewhat troubled, as the key point is that they each participate in creating the conditions for the others; nevertheless, hopefully this typology helps expand the kinds of climatic subjects we might recognise, rather than result in hardline categorical boundary-policing.

1.

Perhaps the go-to interpretation of 'climatic subjects' would be the individual human subjectivities that develop through explicit engagement with climate and climate change. From the climate activist to the climate denier, these are ways of being and identifying as an individual human oriented explicitly in relation to climate change (even if, for climate deniers, the explicit articulation is that climate change does not exist). The climate warrior, the climate striker, the carbon accountant, the climate educator, the climate scientist, the renewable technology engineer, the climate influencer, the climate fiction writer, the pro-climate action politician: these are all ways of responding to climate change that involve occupying a particular role in society, and either require or encourage a wholesale changing (or intensifying) of one's identity, affective disposition, social relationships and socio-economic position.

2.

A second way to understand climatic subjectivity is to understand all human subjectivity as climatic. Every human that has ever lived has existed within, and depended upon, a safe global climate, and has lived within a particular local climate which influenced who they could be, whether that be the wide grasslands of the African Savannahs, the damp valleys of Aotearoa, or the icy peaks of Patagonia. From this perspective, global and local climates shape – but never determine – the diverse human subjectivities that have emerged throughout history and are yet to come. The invest-ment banker, the Olympic athlete, the blacksmith, the philosopher, the shaman, the private school kid, the subsistence farmer, the skiing instructor, the tuk tuk driver: climates shape their lives, their ways of being, relating, doing and knowing, and thus how they become and perform being human – whether they know it or not, whether they care about it or not. And as with our first category of climatic subject, this cli-mate-subject relationship goes both ways: climatic subjects are shaped by climate, just as they shape climate in turn.

3.

Figure 1: Solar doggie soaking up the winter rays.

Author provided.

Thirdly, *living climates* helps us move beyond the human, and attend to non-human climatic subjects, beginning with a focus on individualised organisms. I think firstly, as perhaps many of us would, to my pets: I recall my fifteen-year-old terrier-cross who would track the sun's annual movements throughout our apartment, to catch her morning sunbake time (see Figure 1). Never did she look as content as when soaking up her daily dose of Vitamin D. Yet at the same time, on warmer mornings she was lethargic on our walks, getting the zoomies only on the fresher, cooler days. Her mood, and how people (both human, dog and otherwise) encountered and perceived her depended significantly on the weather of the day. Jessie-dog also suffered from thunderstorm anxiety, demonstrating the ability of non-humans to attach feelings to the atmosphere's grand workings. But science also tells us of storm birds, and other animals, whose unique sensory capacities can 'predict' the weather; and of species who have developed unique cultures according to their local climatic conditions, such as the Japanese macaques who bathe in the hot springs in their snowy climes.

4.

Fourthly though, *living climates* helps us move beyond individual subjects to think more collectively. Climatic subjects might include human collectives, as well as more-than-human collectives. As climate disasters increase, 'resilient communities' are becoming a frequently heralded collective subject; and this example demonstrates that climatic subjectivities might differ in practice from how they are narrated in theory. 'Resilient communities' are often made up of many people who do not feel resilient, and/or are traumatised, and/or who don't want to be resilient as they would prefer to not have to suffer through climate disasters. We also have collective climatic subjects who work tirelessly to protect the climate, such as school strikers (see e.g. Figure 2), and those whose livelihoods also impact the climate, albeit in different ways, such as mining unions. Moving beyond the human again though, collective climate subjects might include entities such as coral reefs or the Amazon rainforest. Ecosystems and human-and-more-than-human assemblages such as these play fundamental roles in creating climates (in 'climating'), and at the same time, they are also subject to the changing climates, as coral bleaching and the burning of the Amazon both demonstrate.

Figure 2: School strike amid-and-because-of-and-despite the rain: A collective climatic subject coalescing at Sydney Town Hall (Gadigal Country) to protest the government's climate inaction in the wake of catastrophic flooding in 2021 and 2022.

Author provided.

5.

Moving further beyond the human again, *living climates* can help us recognise atmospheric phenomena as climatic subjects. Cyclone Tracey, Hurricane Katrina and Typhoon Haiyan are just some of the protagonists who have redefined human lives across the last half-century. Perhaps not always understood as subjects (as sentient, agential, conscious living beings) in modern-Western philosophies, many cultures have or continue to recognise weather systems as subjects capable of feeling, responding, making decisions, and having influence. For example, the Aymara people of the Andes understand mountains to be the embodiment of *ajayu*, which may be loosely translated as spirit, which constitutes subjectivity and bestows agency (Burman 2017: 926). "Ajayu is what makes all beings persons. Ajayus are all around; they permeate landscapes, territories and places; they infuse being and existence, body and mind." Greater Ajayus are known as "achachilas (grandfathers or male ancestors) and awichas (grandmothers or female ancestors)" and these ajayus control the weather (Burman 2017: 927). As such, the Aymara people "have to live what is understood to be morally sound social lives in community if the achachilas are to establish the conditions for the crops and pasture to grow and the animals to produce off-spring [rather than cause] extreme weather events or [alter] the yearly cycle" (Bur-man 2017: 927). Similarly, *Sila* for the Inuit is an "ever-moving and immanent force that surrounds and permeates Inuit life, with it most often being experienced in the weather" (Jaypeetee Arnakak cited in Leduc 2011: 19). Métis scholar Zoe Todd, ex-plains that Sila "is bound with life," citing Inuk author Rachel Qitsualik:

> 'Inuit noticed that the breath, a force seemingly no different from wind and be-ing drawn from the air itself, appeared to be the animating principle of life. They logically concluded that life itself was in fact the breath, the sila, and that when the Sila was drawn into a body, it was alive and animate... Eventually, Sila became associated with incorporeal power, quite understandable, since not only does Sila — through breath — convey the energy that drives life, but sila also manifests it-self as tangible weather phenomena, such as the slightest touch of breeze, or as the flesh-stripping power of a storm. Sila, for Inuit, became a raw life force that lay over the entire Land; that could be felt as air, seen as the sky, and lived as breath.' (Qitsualik cited in Todd 2016: 5).

Even in the Anglophone world, echoes of Sila can be found in the term *respiration*'s etymology, which stems from *spirit*. And despite our intensively colonial-rational history, given heatwaves are the deadliest climate disasters, there is now a push to give them names, as we do with cyclones, in recognition of the cultural responsivity that arises when something so powerful is identified as a named, and thus discrete, identifiable, and agential being. Similarly, in Australia we have named days that had extremely bad bushfires (Black Saturday, Ash Wednesday), and even seasons (Black Summer), albeit not with anthropomorphised names. Extending in scale again, El Niño de Navidad – the Christ Child – was the name given by Peruvian fishers as early as the 1600s to refer to the warm atmospheric conditions that typically arrived in December, just before Christmas. This anthropomorphic phenomenon is comple-mented by his opposite, La Niña, and collectively they now make up what is called the El Niño Southern Oscillation (ENSO), one of Planet Earth's most significant weather patterns. ENSO bring hot and dry weather (El Niño) and cooler, wetter weather (La Niña) to the place I call home, southeastern Australia.

6.

Finally, we have the global climate as subject, known variously as Gaia, Pacha Mama, Mother Nature. Recognised at the Os Mil Nomes de Gaia (The Thousand Names of Gaia) conference[2], personifying the whole environment as living subject is a

---

2   https://osmilnomesdegaia.eco.br/

cultural practice that has arisen many times in human societies. In many Australian Aboriginal dreamings, the Rainbow Serpent is the creator spirit who birthed the world and who can create weather events (Wright 2008). In Ancient Greek philosophy, Gaia is the personification of nature writ large. James Lovelock and Lyn Margulis brought Gaia into the modern-ecological world, hypothesising that all of Earth's ecology, both living and non-living, interact holistically as if as one being to create and maintain our 'Goldilocks' atmosphere which in turn enables life on Earth to keep living, and to keep maintaining our planetary homeostasis (Lovelock and Margulis 1974). Bruno Latour contended that in our current times of mass-scale ecological devastation, the extreme weathers we are experiencing are evidence of Gaia's vengeful nature (2013), bringing together Lovelock and Margulis' ecological philosophy with ancient narratives of weather beings as almighty, if short-tempered gods. Such accounts, both scientific and spiritual, recognise that global climates are composed by all living and non-living earth beings, and exert agency planet-wide.

The Torrential Times

In this section, I identify an example of each of the six types of climatic subjects outlined above. I do this through the example of the repeated catastrophic floods that affected eastern Australia – from Queensland to Tasmania – in the early 2020s, with particular reference to the town of Lismore and the region of the Northern Rivers of New South Wales, which was the worst affected and thus, the most documented. In doing so, I weave together the four meanings of *living climates* to show that local and global climates are living subjects that are experientially lived.

On 28 February 2022, after months of unprecedented rain, a particularly heavy downfall along wide stretches of Australia's east coast met already sodden soils and overflowing rivers, and the land had no more capacity to absorb the excess water. In Lismore, on the country of the Wijabal-Wia-bal people of the Bundjalung Nation, the flood waters measured 14.4m. Given the waters rose rapidly overnight, they caught many residents by surprise and many had to climb into their ceiling cavities and then cut holes in their roofs in order to be rescued by neighbours. Many people's experiences of survival were incredibly traumatic. Twenty-two people died in the floods in Queensland and New South Wales (O'Dell, Clancy, Eagland, Iellamo and Anicich 2022), and in New South Wales over 14,000 homes were damaged or destroyed (O'Kane and Fuller 2022), with an estimated 70,000 tonnes of flood waste created (Lismore City Council 2022). This was the most expensive disaster in Australian history (Chenery 2023). These floods in Lismore arrived just five years after a previously catastrophic flood which had reached 11.6m. Yet just a month later in 2022, on March 30, another major flood occurred in Lismore, reaching 11.4m and forcing many residents to evacuate yet again, and clean debris and mud from their homes yet again, and try to rebuild and recover, yet again.

1.

Figure 3: Flooded shed: My family home's shed floods for the third, and worst, time in a year. Note location is in central Victoria, a long way from Lismore, but we too were very flood weary.

Author provided.

In this context, one of the climatic subjects that arose was the flood-weary subject; this is a climate change-responsive individual human subjectivity. These were people who had survived previous floods, and in the wake of the most recent catastrophic flood, voiced frustration at local, state and federal policies that had left them

254 Visions and Relations

in the path of disaster. Some decided cleaning up – again – was not worth it (see e.g. Figure 3), given the likelihood of future floods. Within this context, some sought to leave the area, although moving households, families and livelihoods is not easy.

2.

The flood-weary subject brings attention to another human subjectivity pre-dating the floods: the Lismore locals. The Lismore locals are an example of how individual human subjectivity has always already been shaped by climate. The Northern Rivers region is widely noted for its (usually) agreeable subtropical climate and beautiful landscapes of lush forests, vibrant rivers, rolling hills and stunning beaches. Amid this setting, post-colonisation settlements have drawn various anti-establishment, hippy types, often with a love of nature. Post-flood, many Lismore locals defied assertions from those further afield that they should move out of the region, attesting to their deep (albeit settler-colonial) sense of connection to place (and thus, to local climatic regimes) and well-established community relations. In doing so, the Lismore locals demonstrated that human subjectivities are always already climatic, and that despite catastrophic floods, their lives and liveability were tied to this particular climatic region.

3.

At the same time as some humans sought to affirm the viability of this subtropical riverplain, news reports were flooded with images of animals out-of-place, demonstrating the third kind of climatic subjectivity: individual non-humans whose lives are shaped, and shape, climate. Whether cows on beaches, goats on roofs, or frogs and mice clinging for dear life to swimming snakes, these uncanny multispecies assemblages epitomised the ways that climates are lived by other-than-humans (see Figure 4), and how well-established identities such as snakes as predators of mice were washed away, if only temporarily, by the floods.

Figure 4: Snail mail: a local neighbourhood letterbox becomes a snail metropolis as the damp intrudes into spaces humans tried to insulate from the weather.

Author provided.

4.

In the context of these catastrophic emergencies, one of the collective climatic subjects that emerged was the Tinny Heroes. These were people, often but not exclusively white middle-aged and older men, who used their tinnies – small open aluminium boats – to rescue human and non-human people who were stranded by the floods. In frequently horrendous circumstances, these people were converted overnight from recreational fishing enthusiasts to the emergency service personnel that help when the official emergency personnel do not. As posthuman materialist theory would attest, these subjectivities are evidently more-than-human, with the affordances of the tinny very evident: small and cheap enough to be owned by many working-middle class families, yet sturdy and powerful enough to navigate rising flood waters and carry multiple (human and non-human) bodies, the tinny's aluminium body, the local place-climate (perfect for fishing) and the human bodies experienced at driving them came together to form this collective climatic subjectivity.

5. and 6.

All of these subjects emerged and/or were transformed due to the agency of the floods themselves (our fifth kind of climatic subject, an atmospheric phenomenon), and the floods in turn due to the global climatic conditions (the sixth type of climatic subject). Just a few years prior, Eastern Australia had suffered through its worst ever bushfire season (the Black Summer noted earlier), thanks to many years of drought and increasingly hotter summers, capped off with an especially hot and dry El Niño season. Those fires generated such high quantities of carbon emissions from the combustion of the living forests, that the smoke circumnavigated the globe, and, as scientists have found, this smoke may have catalysed the rare triple La Niña period that followed and produced the chronic torrents of rain, and thus, the coastal, flash and riverine flooding (Fasullo, Rosenbloom and Buchholz 2023).

In this situation, a deteriorating Gaia (our global climatic subject, i.e. type 6) interacting with Eastern Australia's bio-socio-geography produced localised extreme climates characterised first by fires and then by floods (each an example of type 5). While the nation named the 2019–2020 bushfires the Black Summer, no equivalent name was forthcoming for the floods. Nevertheless, whether known as the Triple La Niña, the years of floods, the Torrential Times (my suggestion), or whatever else we each might call it, this period of mass moisture made itself felt on many Australians up and down the east coast. One morning, I was so tired of the months of deluge and the corresponding drudgery of walking Jessie dog in the rain, cycling to work in the rain, trying to dry washing in the rain – trying to live in the never-ending rain – and I noticed myself urging the weather to "JUST STOP" in my mind, pressing it to "*be reasonable*," and then I caught myself: was I really trying to speak to the weather? An atheist with a science degree, I had never before conversed with the clouds, but the affective desperation of those times pressed my subconscious self to interpellate this climatic assemblage as a subject, one that was being preposterous. How could it *still* be raining?

We have told ourselves that modern rationality was the inevitable evolution of human culture away from animist cosmologies. But perhaps what has really happened is that the short period in time when some humans were able to control and mobilise fossil fueled energies to insulate them from the worst of the weather, while not yet experiencing the delayed-onset climatic implications of the planetary heating of those technologies, meant that for a short period, we were able to believe that the weather was just brute matter, airs that moved but did not think or act or feel, an object we could control or at least keep at a distance from us. Perhaps as we live with the reverberations of that fossil fuel combustion and we again realise that the weather will always escape our control, more of us, more often, will again, consciously or subconsciously, find ourselves heralding the climate as subject in and of itself, not just a force that constitutes our own subjectivity.

These six manifestations of climatic subjects epitomise the four notions of *living climates*. Firstly, climates are alive, composed through the interactions of myriad living and non-living beings, and acting, changing and affecting change. Secondly, as the Tinny Heroes and flood-weary citizens show, we all desperately want liveable climates; 14m of floodwater is not liveable even if the pre-industrialised climate of this region was delightful. Thirdly, climates are lived: from the animals out-of-place to the Lismore locals, subjectivities live in and as part of climates. These climates shape their subjects' affects, life histories, comings and goings, preferences, relations and aspirations. Finally, to live – to inhabit, to survive, to make a living, to have a family – is to participate in making climates, in 'climating.'

Conclusion

Post-structuralism worked hard to prevent the worst forms of dogmatism and authoritarianism that believed subjectivities and identities were God-given according to biological sex, race or other physical characteristic. Through emphasising the social construction, political coercion and performative nature of human subjectivity, post-structuralism sought to decouple human lives from biological essentialism. Understanding all subjectivity as inherently climatic is not in opposition to this. Rather than figuring climate as raw nature that forms a static and therefore unchangeable basis for subjectivity, *living climates* recognises that climates are dynamic phenomena which are never determinate, but nevertheless, are always influential. Indeed, the contemporary climate crisis serves to illustrate just how intermeshed human and atmosphere are, and that these entanglements contribute to our mutual ongoing processes of becoming. As such, living climates, and its attention to six types of climatic subjects, serves not to reaffirm a teleological belief in climatic determinism (where human destinies are determined by the climate) or misanthropic despair (where climate futures are determined by an inherently destructive humanity). Rather, living climates helps us ask: In what climates do we want to live? And thus, how do we need to live – *who do we need to be* – in order to help create and live-with those climates?

References

Alaimo, Stacy (2008): "Trans-Corporeal Feminisms and the Ethical Space of Nature." In: Stacy Alaimo/Susan Hekman (eds.), Material Feminisms, Bloomington: Indiana University Press, pp. 237–264.

Barad, Karen (2007): Meeting the Universe Halfway: Quantum Physics and the Entanglement of Matter and Meaning, Durham and London: Duke University Press.

Bawaka Country/Wright, Sarah/Suchet-Pearson, Sandie/Lloyd, Kate/Burarrwanga, Laklak/ Ganambarr, Ritjilili/Ganambarr-Stubbs, Merrkiyawuy/Ganambarr, Banbapuy/Maymuru, Djawundil. (2020): "Gathering of the Clouds: Attending to Indigenous understandings of time and climate through songspirals." In: Geoforum 108, pp. 295–304.

Burman, Anders, (2017): "The Political Ontology of Climate Change: Moral Meteorology, Climate Justice, and the Coloniality of Reality in the Bolivian Andes." In: Journal of Political Ecology 24/1, 921–30.

Celermajer, Danielle (2021): Summertime: Reflections on a Vanishing Future, Penguin Random House Australia.

Chenery, Susan (2023): "The never-ending fallout of the northern rivers floods: 'People are just worn down'." In: The Guardian, February 20 (https://www.theguardian.com/australia-news/2023/feb/20/the-never-ending-fallout-of-the-lismore-floods-people-are-just-worn-down).

Fasullo, John T./Rosenbloom, Nan/Buchholz Rebecca (2023): "A Multiyear Tropical Pacific Cooling Response to Recent Australian Wildfires in Cesm2." In: Science Advances 9/19, article no. eadg1213.

Fuller, Michael/O'Kane, Mary (2022): 2022 Flood Inquiry Volume One: Summary report, State of New South Wales (https://www.nsw.gov.au/nsw-government/engage-us/floodinquiry).

Haraway, Donna (2016): Staying with the Trouble: Making Kin in the Chthulucene, Durham and London: Duke University Press.

Haraway, Donna (2008): When Species Meet, Minneapolis: University of Minnesota Press.

Horn, Eva (2018): "Air as Medium." In: Grey Room 73, pp. 6–25. https://www.greyroom.org/issues/73/96/air-as-medium/

Knox, Hannah (2015): "Thinking Like a Climate." In: Distinktion: Journal of Social Theory 16/1, pp. 91–103.

Latour, Bruno (2017): Facing Gaia: Eight Lectures on the Political Theology of Nature, Cambridge (UK) and Medford, MA: Polity.

Leduc, Timothy (2011): Climate, Culture, Change: Inuit and Western Dialogues with a Warming North, Ottawa: University of Ottawa Press.

Lismore City Council (2022): Flood Response June 2022, Lismore City Council (https://www.lismore.nsw.gov.au/Community/Natural-hazards-and-emergencies/Floods/Past-floods).

Lovelock, James E./Margulis, Lynn (1974): "Atmospheric Homeostasis by and for the Biosphere: The Gaia Hypothesis." In: Tellus 26/1–2, pp. 2–10.

Neimanis, Astrida/Hamilton, Jennifer Mae (2018): "Weathering." In: Feminist Review 118/1, pp. 80–84.

Neimanis, Astrida/Walker, Rachel Loewen (2014): "Weathering: Climate Change and the 'Thick Time' of Transcorporeality." In: Hypatia 29/3, pp. 558–574.

O'Dell, Adrienne/Clancy, Victoria/Eagland, Sarah/Iellamo, Tayla/Anicich, Felicity (2022): 2022 Flood Response and Recovery: Children's Needs Assessment, Royal Far West And UNICEF.

Sasser, Jade (2016): "Population, Climate Change, and the Embodiment of Environmental Crisis." In: Phoebe Godfrey/Denise Torres (eds.), Systemic Crises of Global Climate Change: Intersections of Race, Class and Gender, Milton Park and New York: Taylor and Francis, pp. 57–70.

Schack, Lotte (2024): "Climate Subjectivity: Youth, Innocence and Willfulness in the Swedish Climate Movement." In: Mobilization: An International Quarterly 29/2, pp. 229–244.

Schaeffer, Felicity Amaya (2018): "Spirit Matters: Gloria Anzaldúa's Cosmic Becoming across Human/Nonhuman Borderlands." In: Signs: Journal of Women in Culture and Society, 43/4, pp. 1005–1029.

Singh, Neera M (2013): "The Affective Labor of Growing Forests and the Becoming of Environmental Subjects: Rethinking Environmentality in Odisha, India." In: Geoforum 47, pp. 189 – 198.

Todd, Zoe, (2016): "An Indigenous Feminist's Take on the Ontological Turn: 'Ontology' Is Just Another Word for Colonialism." In: Journal of Historical Sociology 29/1, pp. 4–22.

Tuana, Nancy, (2008): "Viscous Porosity: Witnessing Katrina." In: Stacy Alaimo/Susan Hekman (eds.), Material Feminisms, Bloomington: Indiana University Press, pp. 188–213.

Verlie, Blanche (2017): "Rethinking Climate Education: Climate as Entanglement." In: Educational Studies 53/6, 560–72.

Verlie, Blanche (2022): Learning to Live with Climate Change: From Anxiety to Transformation, London: Routledge.

Verlie, Blanche, and CCR15 (2020): "From Action to Intra-Action? Agency, Identity and 'Goals' in a Relational Approach to Climate Change Education." In: Environmental Education Research, 26/9–10, pp. 1266–80.

Wright, Alexis (2011): "Deep Weather." Meanjin Autumn 2011 (https://meanjin.com.au/essays/deep-weather/).

Aktru glacier ablation area, Altai, Russia

© Alexander Nikolsky

Authors

Evelyn Acham is a climate activist from Uganda and was the Rise Up Movement national coordinator from 2019 to 2022 where she successfully organized four Global Climate Strikes. She has participated in the Vash Green Schools projects that involves installation of solar and eco-friendly cookstoves in rural schools. She founded the Plus One Tree project whose target is to plant and distribute 9 million trees. Evelyn Acham co-founded Agape Earth Coalition which was created to advocate for African led climate solutions with an African perspective and is currently focusing on climate finance for the African continent in order to fund a just transition.

Catherine Bush is the author of five novels, including the widely acclaimed *Blaze Island* and *The Rules of Engagement*, a *New York Times* Notable Book. Her books have been shortlisted for the Trillium Prize, City of Toronto Book Award, and Books in Canada First Novel Award. The recipient of numerous fellowships, she was the 2024 Writer-in-Residence/Landhaus Fellow at the Rachel Carson Centre for Environment and Society in Munich. An Associate Professor of Creative Writing at the University of Guelph, she lives in Toronto. *Skin* (2025) is her first collection of stories.

Angelina Davydova is an environmental and climate journalist and essayist, based in Berlin. She is a fellow at the Institute for Global Reconstitution, climate projects expert at Dialogue for Understanding e. V, co-host of the podcast The Eurasian Climate Brief. She has been an observer of the UN climate negotiations (UNFCCC) since 2008. She is a councillor with the World Future Council.

Kathrin Eitel is a postdoctoral researcher at the Department of Social Anthropology and Cultural Studies at the University of Zurich. As a cultural anthropologist and feminist STS scholar, her work focuses on urban resilience, technological megaprojects, and environmental issues related to water, waste and the underground. Moreover, Kathrin is particularly interested in how other forms of ethnographic knowledge can be creatively shaped to provide alternative responses to climate change. She is author of *Recycling Infrastructures in Cambodia* (Routledge, 2022) as well as editor of *Klimageschichten* (edition assemblage, 2024) and the Handbook *Environmental Anthropology* (Springer, 2025). More information on her website: www.kathrineitel. com.

Matthias Grotkopp is Assistant Professor for Digital Film Studies at the Seminar for Film Studies at Freie Universität Berlin. He is the author of *Cinematic Poetics of Guilt. Audiovisual Accusation as a Mode of Commonality* (Berlin/Boston: De Gruyter 2021). His research interests include the audiovisuality of the climate crisis and ecological disaster, genre theory and the relation of politics and poetics, the films of the so-called Berlin School as well as digital methods of film analysis.

Mike Hulme is professor of human geography at the University of Cambridge. His work illuminates the numerous ways in which the idea of climate change is deployed in public, political, religious and scientific discourse. He is the author of 12 books on climate change including, most recently, *Climate Change Isn't Everything* (Polity 2023). He is the author of the widely acclaimed *Why We Disagree About Climate Change* (Cambridge University Press 2009) and from 2000 to 2007 was the Founding Director of the Tyndall Centre for Climate Change Research.

Ilya Kalinin is Einstein Visiting Researcher at Humboldt-Universität zu Berlin and a Fellow at the Institute for Global Reconstitution (Berlin). His recent researches focus on the field of Energy Humanities as well as on Russian literature, early Soviet intellectual and cultural history, and the historical and cultural politics of post-Soviet Russia. He is an author of the book (in collaboration with G. Orlova and N. Nikiforova) *Soviet Energy Imagination: Electricity, Atom, Oil* (Saint-Petersburg, 2022, in Russian) and more than 200 academic articles and public essays which have been translated into 15 languages.

Aidah Nakku studied Business Administration and is a climate and gender Justice advocate from Kampala, also working with Fridays For Future MAPA (Most Affected People and Areas), Rise Up Movement and Agape Earth coalition and taking part in different platforms for education and advocacy. She founded the "Hold Her Hand Initiative" to address the challenges of women in local communities, providing activities like climate education, mental health sessions, restoration of nature through tree planting and community outreach and delivering better climate resistant seeds and creating opportunities for income.

Lebogang Neidhardt-Mokoena is an emerging researcher in media and journalism studies with an interest in visual environmental communication. Lebogang is a trained journalist. Their contribution to this book emerged from a project they stated within the frame of the Alexander von Humboldt's German Chancellor Fellowship for Prospective Leaders (2022–2023). Lebogang holds a Master of Arts in Journalism from the University of Johannesburg, South Africa.

Alexander Nikolsky is an artist and assistant professor in the Department of Visual Arts at Kemerovo State Institute of Culture and the Department of Film and Television at the Russian State Institute of Performing Arts. He is a participant and curator of several exhibition projects related to the ecological crisis and the interaction between humans and space. His artistic interests include the study of the interaction between humans and non-human actors, extractivism, the planet's systemic feedback loops, and the representation of the climate crisis in art and science.

Nicholas Omonuk Okoit is a climate activist from Uganda with a degree in Land Economics. He is a grassroots organizer as well as assistant administrator at Agape Earth Coalition. He is part of Fridays For Future MAPA (Most Affected People and Areas), Global Youth Biodiversity Network, and Rise Up Movement. He represented the Most Affected People and Areas (MAPA) at COP27, COP28 and COP29 together with other young climate activists. He organized protests both online and physically in Uganda and Europe demanding organizations help stop the East African Crude Oil Pipeline (EACOP) including advocating for the EU's Supply Chain Law.

Simon Probst works as a postdoctoral scholar in the DFG-project "Natural-cultural Memory in the Anthropocene. Archives, Media, and Literatures of Earth History" (2024–2026), which addresses cultural dimensions of planetary crises such as climate change or the sixth mass extinction from the perspective of interdisciplinary memory studies. At the intersection of literature and knowledge, his work brings together cultural and literary theory with different fields of scientific knowledge such as climatology, earth system science, or ecosemiotics, developing planetary and ecological perspectives on German literature from the 18th to the 21st century.

Juliane Miriam Schumacher is a researcher, journalist and author working on the political ecology and economy of climate change. She is a post-doctoral researcher in the project BioMaterialities at Humboldt-Universität zu Berlin, and author of *Die Regierung des Waldes. Klimawandel, Kohlenstoffmärkte und neoliberale Naturen in Marokko* (Bielefeld: Transcript 2022).

Vera Shchelkina is a dance artist, somatic movement educator, graduate from Somatic Academy Berlin, Master of Arts in Choreography (graduated from HZT, Hochschule für Schauspielkunst "Ernst Busch"), facilitator and curator for professional and non-professional dance and performance programs i.e. Contemporary Dance for Deaf Community at GES-2 (Moscow), Summer School for Performance at HFBK (Hamburg), and Here + Now + Everyone at Kampnagel Sommerfestival (Hamburg). Vera's artistic research investigates the body as a political and transpersonal agent, where touch, perception, and form reveal states of rebellion and intimacy. They research and teach perception as a form of action in different contexts.

Mark Simpson is a professor in English and Film Studies at the University of Alberta who investigates energy cultures and the politics of mobility, especially in the US American context. A co-founder of the After Oil Collective and a core member of the Petrocultures Research Group, he has authored many works on energy impasse and energy futurity, including most recently the collaborative theor-poetical book project *Energy Emergency Repair Kit* (Fordham University Press 2024).

Imre Szeman is Director of the Institute for Environment, Conservation and Sustainability and Professor of Human Geography at the University of Toronto Scarborough. His current research focuses on the socio-cultural dimensions of energy use and its implications for energy transition and climate change. He is the author or editor of more than thirty books, including *Futures of the Sun: The Struggle over Renewable Life* (University of Minnesota Press 2024). Szeman is a fellow of the Royal Society of Canada.

Jane Tversted, born and grown up in Copenhagen, is a freelance journalist in Berlin and cofounder of the Climate Cultures network berlin e.V. Her curatorial and journalistic interests lead to a broader knowledge about cultural awareness of climate change and the polycrisis at all. Her current working fields are energy cultures with special interest in right wing manipulations and strategies against climate action and energy transformation. She studied Philosophy and German Literature and her works contain literary translation, investigative documentaries and political as well as ecological and cultural orientated radiofeatures. She is specialist for creating and running websites, multimedia and audio productions.

Blanche Verlie is a Research Fellow in Gender and Cultural Studies at the University of Sydney, living on unceded Gadigal Country. Blanche is the author of *Learning to Live with Climate Change: From Anxiety to Transformation*. Blanche is interested in the complex ways that humans and climates are entangled, and what attention to these entanglements might offer us as we work towards climate justice.

Michaela Vieser is a Berlin-based award-winning and best-selling nature writer of eleven books, radio features and TV documentaries. In her work, Vieser seeks to explore liminal spaces through science, sensing, and sense-making, playing with narrative, language, and research. She has a degree in Japanese Studies and East Asian History of Art and Archaeology from SOAS, London and a research scholarship at

Tohoku Daigaku, Japan, immersing into Japanese Buddhist Mountain Art. Her writing has earned her the Rachel Carson Center Environmental Writing Competition in creative non-fiction, the German Prize for Nature Writing Fellowship, the Wave Writer Fellowship Okeanos Foundation for the Sea, with two of her books shortlisted for best German Science Writing.

Miriam Ysa Calista is a poet, artist, philosopher & sociologist (PhD) from Heidelberg, Germany. In her work, she explores diverse forms of attraction, attention, sensuality, reciprocity & responsibility between bodies of different sizes (flames, swirls, streams, minerals, plants, animals, humans, planets, stars), with a focus on remembering planetary sensibilities, creating new imaginations, and slowing down & deepening relations.

Isaac Yuen, a first-generation Hong Kong-Canadian, pens essays and short fiction exploring the intersection of nature, culture, and identity. He is the author of the essay collection *Utter, Earth: Advice on Living in a More-than-Human World* and the co-author of *The Sound Atlas: A Guide to Strange Sounds Across Landscape and Imagination* with Michaela Vieser. Recipient of a Pushcart Prize in literature with a Master's in environmental education and communication, Isaac has been awarded residencies and fellowships in Switzerland, Germany, and France.

Martin Zähringer is a literary critic and climate cultures journalist based in Berlin. He writes documentaries and radio features with an international approach often on climate crisis relations. He is one of the founders and art director of the Climate Cultures network berlin e.V., which connects people from different professional branches and with interests in science, arts, journalism, literature, politics and activism. The main idea is to gather global impressions of climate cultures bottom up and Connecting Climate Cultures.

Zara Zerbe is a fiction writer based in Kiel. In her literary works, she explores the intersections between ecological topics, social justice, utopian/dystopian futures and magic realism. She studied literature and media studies and has been active in Kiel's literary scene since 2012—as co-editor of the magazine Der Schnipsel and host of the reading stage Lesebühne FederKiel. Her short story *Limbus* (SuKuLTuR 2020) won the "Neue Prosa Schleswig-Holstein" award in 2018. In 2021, she published the novella *Das Orakel von Bad Meisenfeld* (Stirnholz Verlag), followed in 2024 by her debut novel *Phytopia Plus* (Verbrecher Verlag), which received the "Phantastikpreis der Stadt Wetzlar" and was also nominated for the Kurd Laßwitz Award. In 2022, she was honoured with the Art Promotion Award of Schleswig-Holstein.

GPSR Authorized Representative: Easy Access System Europe, Mustamäe tee
50, 10621 Tallinn, Estonia, gpsr.requests@easproject.com

www.ingramcontent.com/pod-product-compliance
Lightning Source LLC
Chambersburg PA
CBHW061609120626
46550CB00004B/1660